Huntington Library Publications

David S. Terry of California

DUELING JUDGE

by A. RUSSELL BUCHANAN

The Huntington Library
SAN MARINO, CALIFORNIA

1956

B
Terry

LIBRARY OF CONGRESS CATALOG CARD

NUMBER 56-10065

Terry, David Smith

PRINTED IN U.S.A. BY

ANDERSON, RITCHIE & SIMON : LOS ANGELES

DESIGN BY JOSEPH SIMON

To Ethel

Acknowledgments

THIS BIOGRAPHY had its beginning and much of its preparation in the Henry E. Huntington Library, and I am grateful to the Board of Trustees for including it in the library's publications. I am especially indebted to Dr. Robert G. Cleland for his early and continued encouragement. He and Dr. John E. Pomfret have been generous with their friendly and wise counsel. Mrs. Winifred Gregory of the research staff read the manuscript and made numerous valuable suggestions.

Staff members of the following libraries have been unfailingly helpful in making available research materials: the Huntington Library, the Bancroft Library, the California State Library, the Stanford University Library, the public libraries of Stockton and Fresno, the Santa Barbara County Law Library, and, for microfilm, the University of Texas Library and the Library of Congress.

I cannot express adequately my debt to my wife, Ethel Buchanan, for her inspiration and aid both in research and writing. She and our daughters, Barbara and Joanne, made the research outside libraries an enjoyable family project which took us to valley cities, Sierra foothills, and Nevada ghost towns.

The University of California's policy of sabbatical leaves of absence increased time for research. University research funds and a Huntington Library-Rockefeller Foundation grant-in-aid facilitated materially the preparation of the manuscript.

A. RUSSELL BUCHANAN

NOTE ON NEWSPAPERS

Since many of the newspapers underwent several changes of name during the period covered by this volume, the following list has been compiled to help the reader check sources. In the left-hand column are the names of the newspapers as cited in the text and footnotes. In the right-hand column are the names of the newspapers as they appear in the *Union List of Newspapers*.

Bulletin	*San Francisco Bulletin*
Daily Evening Bulletin . .	*San Francisco Bulletin*
Daily Evening Herald . .	*Stockton Daily Evening Herald*
Daily Examiner	*San Francisco Examiner*
Mail	*The Evening Mail* (Stockton)
Morning Call	*Call-Bulletin* (San Francisco)
Stockton Daily Evening Mail	*The Evening Mail* (Stockton)
Stockton Daily Herald . .	*Stockton Daily Evening Herald*
Stockton Daily Independent	*Stockton Morning Independent*
Stockton Mail	*The Evening Mail* (Stockton)

Contents

David S. Terry of California: DUELING JUDGE

Chapter I

From Texas to California

THE LIFE OF David S. Terry constitutes a significant, spectacular, and tragic chapter in California history. While a justice of the state supreme court, he became the most celebrated and troublesome prisoner of the San Francisco Vigilance committee of 1856. In 1859, while serving as chief justice of the same court, he mortally wounded Senator David C. Broderick in California's most famous duel. At the outbreak of the Civil War Terry aroused grave concern among Union sympathizers as a potential leader of secession in the West, but in 1863 he secretly left California by way of Mexico to serve as an officer in the Confederate army in various Southern states.

Returning to Stockton after the war, Terry in time regained both professional and political prominence and played an important part in the second California constitutional convention. Thereafter he became involved in a notorious and bitterly contested lawsuit that ultimately brought a tragic end to his tempestuous life and added still further to the controversial nature of his career.

Terry was born in Kentucky, March 8, 1823. The intense Southern sympathies that he manifested throughout his life came to him from his background, birthplace, and early training. His ancestors migrated to America prior to the Revolution, and for the most part became prosperous Virginia or Carolina planters.[1] Both grandfathers were patriot officers in the Revolutionary War and subsequently moved across the Appalachians.[2] Little is known of Joseph R. Terry, who married Sarah Smith in Christian County, Kentucky, in April, 1816.[3] David Smith Terry was the second of four children born to this couple. The eldest, Benjamin Franklin Terry, gained prominence during the American Civil War as head of "Terry's Texas Rangers." Aurelius Terry secured neither fame nor notoriety, and was the only brother to die a natural death. The youngest son, Clinton, became a respected attorney in Texas.

Joseph and Sarah Terry moved with their sons to the rich delta lands of Mississippi, but soon afterward the couple separated. Mrs. Terry took the boys and joined her mother, who had gone to Texas. Joseph Terry remained in Mississippi and after his wife's death remarried and raised another family. There is no evidence that he maintained any contact with the children of the first marriage.[4]

The Texas to which the Terry family went in 1833 or early 1834 was hardly more than primitive. Politically it was a distant outpost of Mexico, and the land itself was little developed. Much of the city of Houston was to grow on lands earlier acquired by David Terry's grandmother, Obedience Fort Smith. Although Terry later wrote that he "played a mans part" in the Texan war for independence, he was

[1]Information on the early Terrys is scattered. E.g., "Virginia Council Journals, 1726-1753," *Virginia Historical Magazine*, XXXVII (1929), 24n, 25n, 26n; Maud Carter Clement, *The History of Pittsylvania County Virginia* (Lynchburg, Va., 1929), pp. 34, 36.

[2]E.g., W. R. Jillson, "Old Kentucky Entries and Deeds," *Filson Club Publication*, No. 34 (Louisville, 1926), p. 365; John Haywood, *The Civil and Political History of the State of Tennessee, from Its Earliest Settlement up to the Year 1796* (Knoxville, Tenn., 1823), pp. 435-36.

[3]"Christian County—Index to Marriages—1795 to 1825," *The Register of the Kentucky State Historical Society*, XXV (1927), 166.

[4]A. E. Wagstaff, *Life of David S. Terry* (San Francisco, 1892), p. 35. Wagstaff is valuable for parts of Terry's life but is subject to inaccuracies. Charles S. Potts, "David S. Terry. The Romantic Story of a Great Texan," *Southwest Review*, XIX (1934), 296; J. W. Terry notes to Klette, MS in the Bancroft Library, p. 1.

too young to have had an actual military role. The greatest effect of the war was on his state of mind. Finding it difficult to "sink from the *Soldier* to the Schoolboy," he terminated his formal education at the age of thirteen.[5] His mother had died, and young Frank Terry, as head of the family, could hardly be blamed for laxity in this matter, especially since schools in the region were relatively casual institutions.

During the Mexican War David S. Terry joined the Texas Rangers, already famous as a fighting unit. The records of his war service are few and not especially illuminating, for he was a private. Virtually the only way for a common soldier to gain notice in accounts of the Mexican War was to be killed or wounded, and since Terry was unscathed he was also unsung.

It is known at least that he was in Captain Samuel L. S. Ballowe's company in the First Regiment of Texas Mounted Volunteers and that he participated in the Battle of Monterrey.[6] During the actual attack on the city the regiment dismounted and engaged in street fighting from door to door—"pick them from housetop to housetop and such fun you never did see."[7]

It is impossible to understand Terry without considering his Texan background, of which his experience as a Ranger was an important part. Terry was an indirect or direct participant in two wars and a member of a frontier society. He became accustomed to the companionship of vigorous and at times rough men. The planters along the river bottoms of South Texas were often a heavy-drinking, bellicose group, and the Rangers were to an even greater degree hard-living men. From his associations Terry developed characteristics that had come down to him from his ancestors. The frontier

[5]D. S. Terry to Cornelia Terry, June 30, 1856, Terry MSS, Huntington Library; J. W. Terry notes to Klette, 29-30.

[6]Testimony of R. P. Ashe, in *Trial of David S. Terry* (hereafter cited as *Trial*) (San Francisco, 1856), p. 35.

[7]James K. Holland, "Diary of a Texan Volunteer in the Mexican War," *The Southwestern Historical Quarterly*, XXX (1926), 26.

was no place for weaklings, and that Terry lacked courage was never claimed even by his enemies.

Another trait of the Rangers was their fellowship. They passionately admired their leaders, and when Lieutenant Colonel Samuel Walker fell at Huamantla, "His own men wept like children, and their stout hearts were melted."[8] Many of the friendships made by Rangers were kept for life. When Terry was on trial in 1856, among those testifying to his character were men with whom he had served in the Mexican War.

Not all the frontier and Ranger experience can be placed on the credit side. Texas was a brawling frontier. The gamut was run from "free fights," in which anyone and everyone could and often did participate, to duels. Violence of reaction was the order of the day. The ingredients were all there— bitter invective to stir men to anger, an overweening sense of personal justice, the tradition of dueling and fighting passed down by generations of frontiersmen, and weapons at hand. Little wonder it was that from leaders of the state to boys on the plantation personal encounters were the rule.

As young Terry learned the code of personal honor and violence he became accustomed to the usual weapons of the day, and especially attached to one. The bowie knife in Texas during the 1830's and 1840's was as respected a weapon as the revolver, and had certain advantages. The real bowie knife was an instrument of the finest steel, so strong that it could disjoint a bear without turning, and so sharp that after being used to whittle a hickory ax handle it could still split hairs. Some men preferred it to the revolver since it never misfired or "snapped," and it was reported that the knife always appeared larger when it was in someone else's hand.[9] While Terry was involved in no difficulties in Texas, he became fond of the knife and throughout his life

[8]Albert G. Brackett, *General Lane's Brigade in Central Mexico* (Cincinnati, 1854), p. 92.

[9]J. Frank Dobie, "Bowie and the Bowie Knife," *Southwest Review*, XVI (1931), 351-68; R. W. Thorp, *Bowie Knife* ([Albuquerque], 1948), passim.

6

preferred it to the revolver, which by the 1840's was becoming definitely superior as a weapon. To a certain extent, this preference was typical. Terry clung to an antiquated weapon as he adhered to outmoded customs of satisfying insults to personal honor.

The rectitude of slavery was another belief which became deeply ingrained in Terry, and he came to look almost with scorn on those with opposing views. He did not hate the Negro but he felt that he belonged in the institution of slavery.

Rough though society was in frontier Texas, Terry could see changes made while he was growing to manhood. A member of the wealthier class, he witnessed the development of a social life modeled on the older plantation regions of the South. Throughout his life Terry maintained a courtesy toward women that sometimes stood in marked contrast to his actions in the company of men.

Terry studied law in the office of his uncle, T. B. J. Hadley, and in 1845 took the bar examinations, which were most perfunctory.[10] His legal experience in Texas was valuable, for on the frontier, whether in Texas or in California, knowledge of the law was secondary to ability to deal with the rough court procedure.

Early in 1849 David S. Terry took one of the most decisive steps of his life. He joined the gold rush to California. Although he loved Texas, several factors prompted him to leave the state. A romantic affair with a distant "cousin" seemed to have ended unsatisfactorily, and although he had strong friends and close relatives, he disliked some of his associates. Furthermore, if Terry had political ambitions, he was not realizing them in Texas. In 1847, for example, he had sought unsuccessfully the position of district attorney of Galveston.[11]

[10]Wagstaff, p. 42.

[11]See letter of recommendation, W. G. [probably H. G.] Runnels to M. B. Lamar, Dec. 11, 1847. *The Papers of Mirabeau Buonaparte Lamar*, IV, Pt. 1 (Austin, 1924), 188. Runnels wrote of Terry, "If high-toned chivalry and unquestionable integrity serve as a recommendation, he has them."

The chance to leave came opportunely. Frank Terry was planning to go with a party to the California gold fields; David Terry persuaded his elder brother to let him take his place. When the coming of spring made an overland trip feasible, David Terry terminated his affairs and headed for California. The known details of the trip are meager. The expedition was well outfitted, and included in the group of twenty or thirty men were prominent Texans and a few slaves. The party passed through Austin about the middle of April, 1849, and by the time it reached El Paso late in June, Terry had become its leader. The expedition continued on its way and Terry was in California September 3, 1849.[12]

He engaged briefly in mining in Calaveras County, but soon he was down in the valley where people and law courts could be found. The young lawyer began his practice in rapidly growing Stockton, the principal distributing center for the southern mines. Mining disputes and frequent acts of violence offered him a chance for livelihood that seemed more attractive than the dry diggings in the Sierra foothills to the east.

James R. Reynolds, the alcalde of Stockton, had accepted the offer of Bob Collins, proprietor of the Central Exchange Saloon, to move his office to the saloon, rent free, with a place in the attic for his bed. For a time both judge and saloon-keeper profited by the arrangement. The judge usually had a full court, but such a situation could not continue indefinitely. Terry and his partner, D. W. Perley, introduced a case that led to a change. Their client asserted that he had left some money for safekeeping with Collins, but the saloon-keeper denied that any funds had been deposited with him. The judge leaned back in an old armchair which had been placed on a dry-goods box and listened to the arguments. The money in question was on a nearby table. Since the case

---

[12]*Texas Democrat* (Austin), Apr. 21, 1849, quoted in *The Southwestern Historical Quarterly*, XLVIII (1944), 92. The date of arrival is that supplied by Cornelia Terry McClure for the California State Library Pioneer Record (MS).

involved one man's word against another, it was suggested that defendant and plaintiff divide the money equally. The attorneys, however, objected. Terry said, "But I want my fee out of this," and Perley reached toward his pocket as if to draw a weapon. Perley's action precipitated an already tense court into action and, according to one report, over fifty revolvers or bowie knives flashed in the hands of partisan spectators and participants.

Judge Reynolds dealt quickly with the situation. He moved to the table on which lay the money and saying, "The court must take care of itself," swept the entire sum into his hat. So unexpected was this action that it brought the case to a close without bloodshed. Shortly thereafter Collins extracted the money from the judge in a poker game and then called upon the prefect of the town to evict the loser from the saloon.[13]

Terry was involved in an attack on Reynolds' successor, Benjamin Williams, described as "the most corrupt official who ever sat on the bench of San Joaquin County." Williams' actions produced increasing resentment, and the firm of Terry and Perley at last brought charges. The district attorney, however, refused to press the allegations.[14]

Even when the judges were honest, court procedure in early Stockton was rough. It was customary for attorneys, principals, and audience to attend court well armed. Captain Terry, as he was then called, not only carried a bowie knife but on occasions used it. His enemies later made an issue of some of the incidents arising from his early legal practice in Stockton. Terry and his friends on the other hand were inclined to view these episodes as a normal part of a vigorous frontier society.

One such incident was the Roadhouse affair. Terry was attorney for the plaintiff against Roadhouse, a large man,

[13]George H. Tinkham, "History of San Joaquin County," in *History of the State of California and Biographical Record of San Joaquin County* (Los Angeles, 1909), I, 271-72.
[14]Ibid., 272.

9

crude in manner, and intolerant of court procedure. When Judge George W. Wood fined him for contempt of court, the defendant threw the ten dollars on the table and stated with an oath that he had money to pay all his fines. When, however, the judge added twenty dollars to the fine for swearing and continued insolence, Roadhouse picked up the money he had deposited and swore that he would pay nothing. Roadhouse then turned on Terry, who had begun to address the jury, accused him of falsehood, and moved toward him in what Judge Wood later called a "boxing attitude." Terry raised his hands and Roadhouse shouted, "Come on, G—d d——n you, I am ready for all your sort." Declining to meet the challenger with his choice of weapons, bare fists, Terry resorted to his own favorite. Drawing his bowie knife as the two men came together, he inflicted a slight wound in Roadhouse's shoulder.

The story has two endings. Both agree that Roadhouse left the courthouse in haste. Judge Wood later stated that Terry sent Dr. O'Neill after the man with orders to dress the cut if necessary; and he said, "I fined Terry for this assault fifty dollars, which he paid. I fined Roadhouse fifty dollars, which he never did pay." Terry on the other hand said that he was brought up for jury trial for the attack, found guilty, and fined one dollar, a sentence that could be construed as a moral victory for the defendant.[15]

Terry made no apology for stabbing Roadhouse and described his action in going armed into court as standard practice. In fact he said, "I have, on more than one occasion, been compelled not only to go armed into a Court House, but to have a man stand behind me, whilst arguing a case, to prevent an attack in the *rear*." He had to take such precautions because often in the course of his practice he was "compelled to speak plainly of desperate characters" and "liable to be called to account by them at any moment."[16]

[15]For various affidavits and sworn testimony, see *Trial*, pp. 26-27, and passim.
[16]Ibid., p. 27.

Another episode, to be publicized later, was the Purdy affair. John H. Purdy was the editor of an obscure San Francisco paper, the *Pacific Statesman*, which printed an anonymous attack on Terry. The lawyer, accompanied by two friends, went to the editor's office in San Francisco and demanded the name of the individual who had written the article. When Purdy refused the request, the attorney struck him with a cane that broke at the first blow. Thoroughly angered, Terry pulled out his bowie knife. The story from this point becomes somewhat confused. According to Purdy, the tall Texan raised his knife and said, "Now, d——n you, give me that name or I'll take your life." The other witnesses, all partial to Terry, denied that he made such a threat.

Terry's explanation of the affair was that he struck the first blow at Purdy with a "small rattan, intending not to hurt him, but merely to inflict upon him an indignity." Regarding the use of the knife, he said, "As I never learned the art of using my hands, I struck him twice, I think, on the head with the handle of the knife." Terry was brought to court for this assault and paid a fine of $300.[17]

Undeniably Terry lost his temper on occasions during the early fifties. Two corollary observations should be made. One is that his anger usually arose from what he considered an affront to his reputation. The second is that the outbursts were by no means as numerous as claimed by his enemies, and in some cases Terry was blamed for the acts of others.[18] The picture of David S. Terry as a rowdy, bloodthirsty, and quarrelsome villain is a distorted one, drawn by personal or political enemies. Normally he was reticent and self-contained, rather than noisy and blustering. When, however, he became angered at an insult, real or fancied, he was inclined to strike with any weapon at hand. Usually it was a bowie

[17]Ibid., pp. 21-22, 27, 43-46.

[18]S. H. Brooks and R. Porter Ashe statements, in *Daily Evening Bulletin* (San Francisco), July 22, 1856. (The name of this newspaper was later changed to the *Bulletin* and *San Francisco Bulletin*.)

knife, but it might be an inkstand or even a hatchet.[19] His temper was quick and in most cases short-lived. The intervention of friends generally brought any demonstration to a rapid close.

Actually Terry himself made a good analysis of his own acts of violence when in 1856 he said:

This is the end of the specifications, as to my violent and turbulent habits; and what do they prove? That I will promptly resent a personal affront. One of the first lessons I learned was to avoid giving insults, and to allow none to be given to me. I have acted, and expect to continue to act, on this principle. I believe no man has the right to outrage the feelings of another, or to attempt to blast his good name, without being responsible for his actions. I believe, if a gentleman should wound the feelings of any one, he should at once make suitable reparation, either by an ample apology, or, if he feels that circumstances prevent this—that is, if he makes charges which he still thinks true—should afford him the satisfaction he desires. I know that a great many men differ with me, and look with a degree of horror on anyone entertaining such sentiments. My own experience has taught me, that when the doctrine of personal responsibility obtains, men are seldom insulted without good cause, and private character is safer from attack; that much quarrelling and bad blood, and revengeful feeling is avoided.[20]

The picture of Terry that emerges from the contemporary newspapers is of a promising young attorney rapidly rising in ability and prestige rather than of a man of violence. Terry had become acquainted with Duncan W. Perley in Houston and the two men formed a partnership that lasted until 1855. Their cases varied widely in nature and in importance. In the spring of 1851 they lost a murder case. Before his public execution, George (alias Mickey) Baker was permitted to make an address. Exhibiting rare courtesy, he thanked the sheriff and the members of the prison staff for their kindness,

---

[19] G. W. Wood statement, *Trial*, p. 69. In an altercation with a Mr. Jackson in Judge Wood's court, Terry threw an inkstand at Jackson, picked up a hatchet that happened to be on the table, but permitted Wood to take it from his hand. Judge Wood stated that he fined Terry $50 for his actions.

[20] *Trial*, pp. 27-28.

and he continued, "I also thank my lawyers, Messrs. Terry & Perley—it is little else they have received—for all they have done for me."[21]

Terry also assumed civic responsibilities, and in May, 1852, accepted appointment as one of three trustees for the state hospital for the insane, located in Stockton. A few months later, when Terry returned to Texas for a visit, a Stockton paper paid him the following tribute:

David S. Terry, Esq., one of our most prominent citizens, is about to leave this city on a short visit to the Atlantic States. Mr. Terry came with the first settlers to Stockton, and by his integrity of conduct in business, his abilities as a lawyer, and his attention to his duties, has succeeded in laying the foundation of a fortune.[22]

This fortune was wrecked more than once in the years that followed, but in 1852 the newspaper's comment did not seem extreme. In addition to his practice Terry had begun to acquire property, a joint interest with John Hodges in a ranch on the Mokelumne River about twenty miles from Stockton.

Terry had the ability to make and hold strong friends. Dr. R. Porter Ashe and John McMullin had been Texas Rangers with him. Ashe was sheriff of Stockton from 1850 until he went to San Francisco in 1853 as naval attaché for that port. McMullin bought a ranch near Stockton, and his friendship with Terry continued until he died and was buried across the road from the Terry plot in the Rural Cemetery in Stockton. Dr. Samuel Langdon and Samuel H. Brooks were also very close friends of Terry from his first days in California. In the early fifties these young men could not only depend on each other for enjoyable company but for assistance in time of trouble. On several occasions Terry and others helped Sheriff Ashe quell local disturbances.

It was natural for these men to move into politics. The occasion arose when a new city government was proposed in the summer of 1850. One group nominated David S. Terry

<hr />

[21]*San Joaquin Republican* (Stockton), May 31.   [22]Ibid., Sept. 11.

for mayor, in opposition to the other candidate, Samuel Purdy. The election ended with what a local paper termed "excitement of feeling." A few persons who arrived after the polls were closed resented being unable to vote. In the ensuing altercation someone suggested, "Let's take the ballot box." Either thinking that they had won the election or desiring merely to guarantee an honest vote, Terry, Frank Cheatham, Ashe, Langdon, and others pressed around the ballot box to protect it. Although Terry really acted somewhat as a peacemaker, he was later charged with instigating the affair.[23]

If the Terry party thought it had won the election it was mistaken, for when the votes were counted Purdy emerged victorious with a vote of 481 to 288. The city election was hardly a party struggle. Instead the issue appeared to be "New York or Texas." The defeat was but a minor disappointment for Terry, and soon he, like Purdy, who was elected lieutenant governor of the state in 1851, moved into the larger field of state politics.

The political situation which he entered was confused if not chaotic. The major parties of the nation had expanded to the new state, but only one was destined to be important, for the Whig party was already on the decline. Its disintegration left the field fairly open for the Democratic party, which dominated California politics throughout much of the fifties. There was one exception. Briefly, around 1855, the Know-Nothing party rose rapidly to power and as quickly declined.[24]

Terry entered politics in California as a Democrat. By the summer of 1851 both he and his friend Sheriff Ashe were members of the Democratic county committee. Always

<hr>

[23]*Stockton Times*, Aug. 3. James E. Nuttman and James Lynch, politically opposed to Terry, denied that he had tried to interfere with the election. *Trial*, pp. 67, 68.

[24]Peyton Hurt, "The Rise and Fall of the 'Know Nothings' in California," *California Historical Society Quarterly*, IX (1930), 16-49, 99-128.

strongly pro-Southern, Terry was interested in a possible division of the state, in the hope that slavery might be introduced in the southern part.[25] By 1852, while still a member of the Democratic committee, Terry was beginning to acquire some prominence as a public speaker and he presided over a number of party gatherings. After one of these the *San Joaquin Republican*, which was strongly Democratic, enthusiastically reported, "Captain David S. Terry, by invitation, addressed the meeting in an eloquent and logical speech for about an hour, tracing the history of the principles of the two parties and proving the superiority of democratic over whig measures."[26]

In 1853 Terry demonstrated that sectional interest was stronger than party ties. He had strongly supported the Chivalry candidate, Richard Roman, in the race for Democratic nominee for governor against the incumbent, John Bigler, who had formed a political alliance with David Broderick. When the Democratic state convention nominated Bigler, Terry bolted the party and in August publicly renounced his allegiance to what he termed "California democracy."

Toward the end of the month Governor Bigler went to Stockton. The city always took its political gatherings seriously, and about 2,000 persons met to hear the governor. They demonstrated their endurance by cheering the speaker loudly as he harangued them for three hours. It is a sign of Terry's courage that he followed this address with a brief one of his own in which, according to the press, he sought "to justify himself in the charges he had made against Gov. Bigler." The comments of the Democratic paper on the man who was bolting the party are of interest:

We were pleased to listen to this gentleman's speech as there was an absence of all rhodomontade. His remarks were conceived in a moderate spirit and for this reason did him credit.[27]

[25]Terry to Cornelia Terry, June 29, 1852, Terry MSS. Terry was chosen as a delegate to a convention on state separation in Santa Barbara in 1851 but did not attend.

[26]Sept. 4. [27]Ibid., Aug. 27.

Terry had joined a losing cause. William Waldo, the Whig candidate, was not strong enough to offset the weakness of his own party nor the power of the Bigler-Broderick faction. Governor Bigler was re-elected to his post.

The Stockton attorney did not find it difficult to return to his party, and by the end of March, 1854, he was engaging once more in the local operations of the Democratic party. If he had been making his moves purely for personal advancement, he accomplished little. When he left the Democrats in 1853 they won, and when he rejoined them they lost, at least in the local elections of May, 1854.

Political morality was at a low ebb in California. One editor wrote, "The body politic stinks with corruption. The atmosphere appears to be infected with malaria." He recommended that if anyone doubted his appraisal he should visit Sacramento, "and if, after twenty-four hours of observation, he hold not up his arms in astonishment and utter horror, we will confess ourselves in error."[28]

A climax in the factionalism within the Democratic party was reached in the state convention in June, 1854. Terry was an active but minor participant when he and other Chivalry men pushed their way to the front of the room and placed on the platform one of two rival presidents who vainly attempted to direct the meeting. An accidental pistol shot produced a state of near riot and caused numbers of people to jump from the windows to the ground fifteen feet below. There were about six hundred people crammed into the Baptist church of Sacramento which the trustees, to their rapidly increasing regret, had rented for the occasion. The pastor, fearing for the edifice, entered and begged the men to leave "and never enter it again as politicians."[29] His plea was ignored and only nightfall ended the bickering. Finally the two presidents locked arms, to avoid leaving anyone in possession, and led

[28]Ibid., Mar. 13.

[29]James O'Meara, *Broderick and Gwin* (San Francisco, 1881), p. 95.

16

their flocks from the battered building. On the following day the rival forces met separately.

The situation was favorable for the rise of the Know-Nothing party. Just when Terry joined the movement is not certain. General David F. Douglass, who was to be one of his closest friends, was an early convert, but it is not clear whether the friendship of the two antedated 1855. Douglass, one of the first leaders of the state militia, had been a prominent figure in the Whig party, but by 1854 was rumored to have joined the secret political organization.

Whatever time Terry may have joined the Know-Nothings secretly, he was out in the open on the matter by June, 1855. On the twenty-sixth of the month he declared in an address in Sacramento that the new party constituted the real "national" party.[30] When the state convention met, Terry emerged as one of its candidates. By this time he had built a solid reputation as a lawyer, and it was no surprise that he received the nomination for justice of the supreme court. The party supported the incumbent chief justice, Hugh C. Murray, for re-election and nominated Terry for the short term.

Naturally Terry received criticism for bolting his party. The *San Joaquin Republican*, although it represented a pro-Southern point of view similar to that of Terry, chose to remain Democratic. It implied that Terry had deserted his party to gain an office and predicted that he would fail. The prophecy was incorrect, for in the election the Know-Nothings were voted into office.[31]

Terry had won his race for the supreme court post. Unquestionably one of the reasons for his shift in party allegiance was the desire for office, but there were stronger forces that prompted his action. Uppermost was his intense interest in furthering the cause of states' rights and of Southern sectionalism. The Democratic party had become deadlocked in the

[30]*San Joaquin Republican*, June 26.

[31]Winfield J. Davis, *Political Conventions in California* (Sacramento, 1893), p. 50. Terry won by a vote of 49,677 to 46,892 for his opponent, Charles H. Bryan.

struggle between Broderick and Gwin, and if either side was gaining it was that of the former Tammany politician. On the other hand the Know-Nothing party was sweeping large sections of the country. After all, a prime requisite for advancing one's policies was to get into office. Terry like others, therefore, felt that the new party would be a convenient vehicle in which to ride into power. Once before, when not seeking office, he had deserted his party when he felt that its leaders were not working for the political goals he sought. Terry had numerous faults, but they did not include exorbitant self-interest or ambition.

A study of Terry's career shows clearly that the major constructive influence on his life was that exerted by his wife, Cornelia Runnels Terry. Yet this marriage, which was so important to Terry, for a time seemed destined not to take place. A descendant of the same sort of fighting stock that had produced Terry,[32] Cornelia Runnels met the young lawyer in Texas. Terry fell in love with her and for a time the romance prospered. Then for reasons that are not clear, "Cousin" Cornelia turned against him. As we have seen, convinced that the breach was permanent, Terry left Texas, as he later stated, "with feelings very nearly akin to entire indifference to the future." The rigors of the trip to California made him lose this "indifference." He worked hard at his practice, took part in politics, and had a warm group of masculine friends. Hearing that Cornelia Runnels "did not cherish kindly feelings" toward him and that she was engaged to another man, he made no effort to correspond with her.[33]

This state of affairs continued until October 7, 1851. On that date Terry received a letter with an enclosure. The letter was incidental, but the note changed the course of his personal life, for it was a message from Cornelia Runnels indi-

[32]Cornelia Runnels' father was an officer in the War of 1812. Dunbar Rowland, "Mississippi Territory in the War of 1812," *Publications of the Mississippi Historical Society*, IV (1921), 200.

[33]Terry to Cornelia Runnels, Nov. 7, 1851, Terry MSS.

cating that he was "still regarded" by her "as a Friend." Terry resumed his courtship by mail. This time he was successful, and the couple made plans for marriage. The attorney's increasing business delayed his departure until September, 1852. Arriving in Galveston, he married Cornelia Runnels, probably November 25, 1852.[34] The couple did not leave Texas until January, 1853, and were in California toward the end of February. Mrs. Terry must have realized that she was entering a man's country when she read the following notice in a Stockton paper:

David S. Terry, Esq., one of our first, most able, and useful citizens, returned by the Golden Gate, from a visit to the Atlantic States. He brings with him a wife—a valuable acquisition to society in San Joaquin County[35]

Fortune was favoring young David S. Terry. His practice was flourishing, he had a fine ranch, a house in town, and in October 1853, his wife gave birth to a son, Frank Davis.[36] The parents had the baby's daguerreotype taken and sent it to Texas for relatives to admire. Then on May 6, 1854, came the first of a series of tragic blows that were to strike Terry throughout the rest of his life. The infant, around whom the aspirations of the couple were centered, became ill and died.[37] Fortunately a second son, Samuel Langdon, was born to the Terrys, February 1, 1855,[38] and a third son, David Smith, arrived probably in December, 1856.[39]

[34]Ophelia Runnels Hardesty to Cornelia Terry, Nov. 25, 1853, Terry MSS.

[35]*San Joaquin Republican*, Feb. 23.

[36]Terry to Cornelia Terry, Jan. 31, 1854, Terry MSS.

[37]*San Joaquin Republican*, May 8.

[38]From headstone of Samuel L. Terry in Rural Cemetery, Stockton; see also *The Mail* (Stockton), Apr. 1, 1885.

[39]Ophelia Hardesty to Cornelia Terry, Nov. 15, 1856.

Chapter II

The Champion of Law and Order

IN THE SUMMER of 1856 David S. Terry became involved in the first of a series of episodes that made him one of the most controversial figures in California history. To that date his life had been merely one of a number of modest success stories. Born of good stock, he had grown to manhood on the Texas frontier, participated in the Mexican War, led a small party to the California gold fields, failed as a prospector, prospered as a lawyer, and had been elected a member of the California supreme court at the age of thirty-three. This was a good record, but it was not outstanding. It is probable that outside political and legal circles not many persons had heard of the young associate justice. By the end of the summer few people had not heard of the judge, and few did not have a strong feeling one way or the other toward him.

The episode was Terry's connection with the Vigilance committee of 1856. Violence and corruption had risen again in the mushrooming city of San Francisco.[1] Sentiment became aroused when the Italian gambler, Charles Cora, shot General William H. Richardson after a quarrel, and feelings went even higher when it seemed that the assassin might

[1]Extended treatments of the second Vigilance committee are in Josiah Royce, *California from the Conquest in 1846 to the Second Vigilance Committee in San Francisco* (Boston and New York, 1886), pp. 440-465; William H. Ellison, *A Self Governing Dominion* (Berkeley, California, 1950), pp. 232-67; H. H. Bancroft, *Popular Tribunals* (San Francisco, 1887), II; Theodore H. Hittell, *History of California* (San Francisco, 1898), III, 460-649. Bancroft and Hittell are strongly pro-Vigilante, as are most treatments of the subject. For a critical view, see *Judges and Criminals: Shadows of the Past. History of the Vigilance Committee of San Francisco, Cal.* (San Francisco, 1858), passim.

20

escape punishment, for lawyers appeared to be able to make a mockery of the law. Cora retained a group of able attorneys, including two who later became United States senators,[2] and they persuaded the jury to hang itself and not the defendant.

Newspapers built up the tension. Leading them was the *Daily Evening Bulletin*, edited by James King of William, variously described as a high-minded champion of justice or as a virtual blackmailer who used the power of the press to squeeze contributions from politicians afraid of their past. King courted assassination by lashing furiously at those whom he hated, and the list was not small. One day in June, the editor divulged to the public the fact that James Casey, a local politician, had served a term in Sing Sing. The politician intercepted King on the street and fired a bullet into his chest.

Shortly thereafter, repeating their performance of 1851, a group of San Francisco businessmen engineered what has been called a "businessman's revolution." William T. Coleman, who had headed the committee in 1851, became the leader of the new organization.

The situation was a little different from what it had been in 1851. In contrast to the earlier ineffectiveness of state officials, the governor in 1856 was not disposed to stand idly by and see the laws set aside in the largest city of the state and replaced by a "popular tribunal." Surrounding the executive were David S. Terry and others who were even more strongly opposed than he to the Vigilance committee.

Like Terry, J. Neely Johnson had taken advantage of the rising Know-Nothing party and he had won the governorship in the triumph of that party in 1855. California society in the fifties was characterized by the youthfulness of its residents. To this extent Johnson was a true representative of the people, for when he was elected governor he was not over twenty-seven or twenty-eight years of age. Some of Johnson's diffi-

[2]E. D. Baker, senator from Oregon, and James A. McDougall, senator from California.

culties in office may have stemmed from his inexperience and youthfulness.

Disturbed by Vigilante developments, Governor Johnson left Sacramento and traveled to San Francisco. Accompanied by his brother, William Johnson, he met William Tecumseh Sherman, whom he had appointed major general of militia for the area a few days before the assassination of King. To date Sherman's military career had been unspectacular. A graduate of West Point, he had been sent to California during the Mexican War. Remaining on active duty after the war, Sherman witnessed the gold rush, visited the mining regions, and even engaged in some moderately successful business transactions. Then after further military duty in St. Louis and New Orleans, Sherman left the army to accept an offer to return to San Francisco as head of the branch bank of a well-known St. Louis concern. His bank weathered the financial crisis of 1855, and by the time of the Vigilance committee's organization in 1856, Sherman was recognized as a prominent businessman in the city.

Although he had accepted the post as major general of militia, Sherman as yet had done nothing about the position. Governor Johnson was a personal friend of William T. Coleman, the president of the Vigilance committee. The governor, his brother, and Sherman consequently went to Turnverein Hall, where it was said that the committee was to be found. The resultant meeting with Coleman is one of the most controversial incidents in the Vigilante affair. The Coleman version differs sharply from that of Johnson and Sherman. Perhaps the most nearly disinterested person present was Sherman. According to his account, after shaking hands with various members of the committee, Johnson asked, "Coleman, what the devil is the matter here?"

Coleman replied, "Governor, it is time this shooting on our streets should stop."

Governor Johnson agreed, but the question was how the matter should be stopped. Coleman insisted that the people had lost faith in the representatives of the law and that the people themselves would settle the affair. Johnson on the other hand argued that the time for mobs and vigilance committees had passed in the state.

Finally, after considerable discussion, Johnson offered to assume personal responsibility that Casey would be guarded and forthcoming for trial and executed at the proper time. Coleman had already expressed the committee's lack of trust in Sheriff Scannell, and made a countersuggestion that the governor's plan be accepted, but that a posse of eight or ten Vigilante police be authorized to assist the sheriff's men in guarding Casey.

Johnson agreed to the proposal and he and Sherman left with the belief that the difficulty successfully and rather easily had been brought to an end.[3] By the following noon they found that their optimism had been mistaken. The Vigilante military forces continued to grow, and the leaders determined to seize Casey and Cora. Unless someone was lying, a possibility that cannot thoroughly be discounted, Coleman and the members of the Vigilance committee had a different interpretation of the agreement with the governor than did that official and Sherman. Coleman asserted later that the agreement was merely a truce and implied that it could be terminated simply by one party giving notice.[4] In the opinion of Johnson and Sherman, the pledge was much stronger than that and promised that the law was to take its normal course, with the exception that a Vigilante posse was to aid the sheriff.

Believing, or at least assuming, that the agreement could

[3]William T. Sherman, *Memoirs of Gen. W. T. Sherman*, 4th ed. (New York, 1892), I, 149-51. The agreement to permit Vigilance men to join the sheriff pleased neither extremes. *Judges and Criminals*, p. 26.

[4]"San Francisco Vigilance Committees," *The Century Illustrated Monthly Magazine*, XLIII (1891), 140-141. Hereafter referred to as Coleman, *Century statement*. Coleman wrote, "We proposed that a small force of our men be placed in the prison as an additional guard, and we pledged ourselves not to take the prison or make any movement against it without giving the Governor notice, all of which was agreed to and complied with."

23

be terminated by either party, the Vigilance committee on the following morning wrote the governor a letter indicating clearly that it was reversing itself. The note stated, "We beg to advise you that we have withdrawn our guard from the County Jail."[5]

Johnson received this letter sometime before eleven o'clock in the morning. At noon a Vigilance force in excess of 1,500 men marched on the city hall. Sheriff Scannell was in no position to dispute the matter, and Casey was taken by force to Vigilante headquarters. Shortly thereafter similar treatment was accorded Cora.

By their action the members of the Vigilance committee had taken the law into their own hands. In so doing they had alienated the governor of the state, who was under the distinct impression that he had exacted from the leaders of the movement a pledge to keep the peace and observe the law. Johnson was, to quote Sherman, "with reason furious." The two men sought Coleman at Truett's store, in which the executive committee of the Vigilance committee was reported to be in session. As Sherman expressed it, Coleman was "not forthcoming" and Johnson had to content himself with vigorous criticism of the committee's actions to another member.

The committee went ahead undisturbed with the dispensation of its own brand of justice. It gave Cora and Casey what were generally agreed to have been fair trials. Casey's fate was sealed during the trial by the death of James King of William, who had lingered after the shooting.[6] Both defendants were found guilty and were hanged May 22, 1856.

[5]Quoted in "The Law and Order View of the San Francisco Vigilance Committee of 1856. Taken from the Correspondence of Governor J. Neely Johnson," ed. H. G. Florcken, *California Historical Society Quarterly*, XIV (1935), 354. Hereafter cited as "Law and Order View." Although based primarily on Johnson's papers, this source is also a convenient reference for other letters and documents of the Vigilante period.

[6]One physician charged that King's death was the result of bungling by attending doctors rather than of Casey's bullet. George D. Lyman, "The Sponge. Its Effect on the Martyrdom of James King of William . . . ," reprint from *Annals of Medical History*, X (c. 1928), 460-479.

Johnson, Sherman, and others who came to be known as the Law-and-Order group were disgusted with the actions of the Vigilance committee, but the governor and Sherman were prepared to drop the matter. There had been no time to raise a militia, and, after all, Casey and Cora were murderers who had met their just punishment, although at the wrong hands. Further it was expected that the committee, having performed its self-appointed task, would disband.

It soon became apparent, however, that the Vigilance committee did not plan an immediate dissolution. It continued in being and in action. Its leaders took a building on Clay Street as headquarters, employed guards and armed sentinels, made arrests, and issued writs of banishment.

Although the majority of San Franciscans probably supported the Vigilance committee in its actions, conditions in the city were abnormal. Undesirable residents were being ejected by the committee or leaving in fear, but business was unsettled. Some men were neglecting their affairs to attend to Vigilance matters. Others were nervous in a situation in which established law had been supplanted by the less predictable will of the people. Tom King had picked up the vitriolic pen of his dead brother and in the *Bulletin* was angrily denouncing all who dared oppose the Vigilance committee.

Some San Franciscans, hostile toward the committee, decided to appeal for outside aid. A meeting of Law-and-Order men on May 27 selected a three-man committee to request the governor to call out the militia "to suppress the said insurrection and to restore the supremacy of law and order."[7] Two of the members of the committee, Volney E. Howard and Calhoun Benham, were close friends of David S. Terry. The third member was former Governor John McDougal.

The letter written by this committee moved Johnson to action. Since a militia needed arms and ammunition to be

[7]"Law and Order View," pp. 354-55.

effective, the first task was to consult army and navy officials. Consequently Johnson, Sherman, and Secretary of State D. F. Douglass went to Benicia and conferred with General John E. Wool, commandant of the army on the Pacific Coast and in charge of the arsenal at Benicia. After discussion it was decided that Wool was to make arms and ammunition available for the militia, and the navy would be called upon to provide transportation. Assured of this support the governor could then declare San Francisco in a state of insurrection, and General Sherman would have a militia armed to restore law in the city.[8]

These plans were shaken somewhat when the senior naval officer declined to co-operate. Captain David Glasgow Farragut, commandant of the Mare Island Navy Yard, had a dislike for involvement in civil strife, and stated that he would act only on orders from the navy department. He further declared that he had no vessel to use except the sloop *John Adams*, which needed repair. Finally he agreed that after repairs were made the vessel could lie off San Francisco "for moral effect."[9] Later the *John Adams* was placed in this position, but it seems clear that the person responsible for the move was not Farragut but the vessel's commanding officer, Captain E. B. Boutwell.

Farragut's attitude made Sherman want a firmer pledge from General Wool, and as the men walked toward the wharf at Benicia, Johnson made Wool reiterate his promise that when the governor called out the militia he would "order the issue of the necessary arms and ammunition."

Judge Terry may well have been working behind the scenes with Governor Johnson prior to this time. The men were good friends and fellow politicians and viewed with

[8]Sherman, I, 152. Johnson's version of the meeting is substantially the same. "Report of the Secretary of War . . . Correspondence in Relation to the Proceedings of the Vigilance Committee in San Francisco, California," Ex. Doc. No. 43, 34th Cong., 3rd. Sess. (Washington, 1857), pp. 22-26.

[9]Sherman, I, 154; Loyall Farragut, *The Life of David Glasgow Farragut* (New York, 1882), pp. 172-73.

distaste the developments in San Francisco. Terry now entered the picture directly. According to the plan agreed upon in Benicia a writ of habeas corpus was to be issued commanding the Vigilance committee to produce one of the men arrested by them. Judge Terry issued such a writ for William Mulligan, in the custody of the Vigilance committee, to be brought before him.

The Vigilance authorities, as anticipated, rejected the writ. The governor then telegraphed the sheriff of San Francisco County asking him if he "required a military force" to aid him "in executing any process, civil or criminal."[10] Sheriff Scannell's reply was in the affirmative. He explained that he had attempted to execute the writ "but was resisted in doing so by a body of armed men and that the power of the County is inadequate to resist the armed force." Scannell further asserted that "there is a combination here to resist the law, which cannot be put down without exercising the Military power of the State."

The plan was proceeding according to schedule. On June 2, 1856, the governor ordered General Sherman to call upon "such numbers" of the militia as he considered necessary "to report, organize, etc., and act with you in the enforcement of the law."[11]

Two days later the governor issued a proclamation declaring the city and county of San Francisco to be in a state of insurrection.[12] Rough drafts of the proclamation indicate that Johnson worked carefully over the document, and it is possible that men like Terry and Douglass advised him in its preparation. The document further directed members of voluntary military companies of the county and "also all persons subject to Military duty within said County to report themselves for duty, immediately" to General Sherman.

The proclamation was not received without protest. It was

[10]"Law and Order View," p. 357.   [11]Ibid., pp. 357-58.
[12]"Message of the President . . . in Relation to the Self-styled Vigilance Committee in California," Ex. Doc. No. 101, 34th Cong., 1st Sess. (Washington, 1856), p. 6. The proclamation appeared in the press of the day.

denounced by those in sympathy with the Vigilance committee. The editor of the *Daily Evening Bulletin* wrote, "The Executive has at last lent himself to the thieves and bullies of San Francisco against the honest citizens."[13] More important was the passive resistance. The men of the city did not respond in numbers to the call to military duty. Many able-bodied men who were indifferent to the issues had no wish to become involved.[14] At first Sherman was not particularly concerned, for he counted on General Wool's promise to supply weapons. Some of the leaders of the Vigilance committee went to Sherman and told him that his course of action would lead to bloodshed, since a collision would certainly result from the formation of the militia. Sherman, taking a position that seems not illogical, cast the burden of responsibility upon the Vigilantes, saying, "Remove your fort; cease your midnight councils; and prevent your armed bodies from patrolling the streets."[15] The Vigilantes of course rejected the suggestions, and ever after they or their protagonists have damned Sherman with a bitterness nearly equal to that engendered in the souls of Southerners as the general later marched through Georgia. One committee member subsequently stated that if Sherman had done anything to check the Vigilantes they "would have strung him up as we would a dog."[16] Bancroft in his lengthy discussion of "Popular Tribunals" has a page headed with the caption "Sherman's diabolism."[17]

Sherman was not disturbed by the Vigilance committee's protests, but shortly thereafter he received news that did cause him deep concern. When Governor Johnson sent his aide-de-camp, Colonel E. A. Rowe, to General Wool with a

[13]June 4.

[14]A pro-Vigilance writer stated that about 75 men were enrolled during the first day or two. *San Francisco Vigilance Committee of '56*, ed. Frank M. Smith (San Francisco, 1883), pp. 57-58. Two of the companies were headed by friends of Terry, R. P. Ashe and Jack Hays, his old Texas Ranger colonel.

[15]Vol. I, 155.

[16]James Dows, quoted in Bancroft, *Popular Tribunals*, II, 316.

[17]P. 317.

request for the release of arms, Wool refused the request. Making no reference to previous understandings, the general stated that on examination of the laws of Congress he had found "that no person has authority to grant the request herein presented but the President of the United States."[18]

Rowe reported the matter to Sherman. Explaining his reactions in a letter to his father-in-law, Sherman wrote, "I was thunderstruck, as I could look nowhere else for arms, and the idea of enrolling the militia without arms was an absurdity."[19] The general then wrote to Wool, asking for clarification. Equally perturbed, Johnson requested Sherman to meet him in Benicia.

Meanwhile a new element was entering the picture. Politically this group consisted of middle-of-the-roaders. On the one extreme were the Vigilantes who thought that by a temporary overriding of law and established government they could suppress crime and corruption. Opposing them were men who insisted that law and order should be maintained even at the risk of bloodshed between the militia and the Vigilante forces. The middle group was composed for the most part of respectable businessmen who could not accept either position. They disliked the lawless actions of the Vigilantes, but at the same time they feared the results should an armed militia be raised in a city policed by Vigilante forces.

Actually, although Sherman was head of the militia, he was in sympathy with the middle group, and when he took the boat for Benicia a delegation of these men went with him in hope of reaching a compromise. Arriving ahead of the governor, Sherman met Wool who attempted "to explain away the effect of our misunderstanding, taking good pains not to deny his promise made to me personally *on the wharf*."[20]

[18]U. S. War Dept., *Report of the Secretary of War . . .*, op. cit. (above, note 8), pp. 3-5.
[19]Sherman to T. Ewing, June 16, 1856, *The Century Illustrated Monthly Magazine*, XLIII (1891), 303.
[20]Sherman, I, 157.

Governor Johnson arrived in Benicia surrounded by Law-and-Order men, including David S. Terry. Among the others in the party were Volney E. Howard and E. D. Baker. In view of later developments it seems odd that Baker and Terry should have been working together, but in 1856 Baker was not the Republican senator from Oregon; he was simply a San Francisco lawyer attempting to advance himself. The fact that he had been an attorney for Charles Cora helped explain his critical view of the Vigilance committee.

Unfortunately the delegation of middle-of-the-roaders was not accorded the reception it felt it merited. The men with the governor regarded the group with suspicion. They were in an angry mood. As Sherman expressed it, "All were talking furiously against Wool, denouncing him as a d——d liar, and not sparing the severest terms." The discussion broadened to include the Vigilance committee. David Terry took part in the discussion and was vehement in his utterances. Reportedly, he termed the members of the Vigilance committee a "set of d——d pork-merchants" who were becoming frightened and who were in collusion with General Wool to bring the state into contempt.

The introduction of a moderate group into such a heated atmosphere was psychologically unfortunate. When they sent their cards to the room, Terry and some of the others denounced the group as no better than Vigilantes and argued that they should not be received. When Johnson decided to meet the men, Terry sat with his hat pulled down over his eyes and with his feet on the table, as did some of the other members of the party.

J. B. Crockett, one of the leaders, stated the case of his group and expressed the hope that the Vigilance committee could be persuaded to adjourn in the near future and submit to trial. The governor heard him, dismissed the delegation, and prepared a written answer. He had more than enough assistance from those who were with him. After numerous corrections and changes had been made, a final reply was agreed upon. In view of the state of mind of those who wrote it, the document was a fairly moderate response, but it did assert that if any violence occurred "the responsibility must rest upon those who shall choose to continue to disregard the authority of the state."[21]

Instead of being won, as Sherman hoped, to the governor's side, the conciliation group had been alienated. The Benicia meeting also ended Sherman's active support of the governor. The general had failed to bring the moderates and Johnson together, and, as a practical man, he realized that a militia without arms was useless. Though he was irritated with Wool's reversal, he was sufficiently realistic to appreciate its results. He did not like the men with Johnson at Benicia and they did not like him. He felt that Terry and the others were not only extremists but that they had judged the situation incorrectly. They believed that the Vigilance committee was faltering and that bold action was needed to force its quick dissolution. Also Sherman was a businessman first and general of militia second. His bank was beginning to feel the effects of adverse public opinion, and if he became further involved in the quarrel between the governor and the Vigilantes his business might be seriously hurt.

Even as the discussion continued at Benicia, Sherman came to his decision. He stated in his memoirs, "Seeing that we were powerless for good, and that violent counsels would prevail under the influence of Terry and others, I sat down and wrote my resignation, which Johnson accepted in a complimentary note on the spot."[22]

[21]Ibid., 157-58.

[22]Vol. I, 158. In his letter to Ewing, June 16, 1856, Sherman comments on the pressure exerted on businessmen by the Vigilantes: "Had I been otherwise situated, I might from sympathy have continued to aid him, but by so doing I would have driven off our business, for so high has this feeling run that all business men have yielded to it, and have regarded those who favored the cause of Law and Order as enemies of the people, and withdrawn their patronage from newspapers and all other interests controlled by Law and Order men." "Sherman and the San Francisco Vigilantes," *The Century Illustrated Monthly Magazine*, XLIII (1891), 305. Sherman's resignation created a sensation. For letters between Sherman and the governor, see "Law and Order View," pp. 367-68, 372-73.

With Sherman out of the picture, Terry assumed a more important role in the move against the Vigilance committee. Sherman's successor as head of the militia was Volney E. Howard. A close friend of Terry, Howard had been a politician in Mississippi and Texas before moving to California. His task as commanding officer of the militia was a hopeless one. Sherman in a letter to the newspapers made it clear that arms were not to be available to the forces of the state, and enlistments, which had been modest, now became meager.

Encouraged by the news of Wool's stand, the Vigilance committee issued a lengthy statement defending its existence and actions[23] and on June 14 held a mass meeting in front of the Oriental Hotel. The pro-Vigilante press continued its extreme utterances. The *Bulletin* published a series of bitter attacks on Chief Justice Hugh C. Murray, accusing him of personal and political wrongdoings. Then on June 11 the *Bulletin* attacked Judge David S. Terry. Even this paper admitted that all crimes could not be charged to the judge and wrote, "justice compels us to say, what even his enemies admit, that he could not be approached with a bribe, and that while on the bench he will act impartially, so far as he is able, between man and man." Despite this grudging compliment, the *Bulletin* considered Terry unfit for office and charged "his mind is so warped with false notions of chivalry, and his tendency to mobocracy is so great as to render him unfit for the high position he holds." The *Bulletin* then charged Terry with acts of violence while resident in Stockton, thereby giving the public a slight foretaste of accusations to come in a week or so.

Although enrollments in the militia were slow and General Wool had failed to provide the expected arms, Governor Johnson and his new major general of the militia went ahead with their plans. Working closely with them were General William C. Kibbe, quartermaster in San Francisco, who con-

---

[23]*San Francisco Vigilance Committee of '56*, pp. 59-61.

tinued in charge of enlistments, and David S. Terry.[24] There is strong doubt as to the wisdom of Terry's direct participation in the actions against the Vigilance committee. There is no doubt, however, that he was working in full co-operation with the chief executive of the state and in fact under his orders. A letter from Johnson to Terry, dated June 10, 1856, although it urged the judge to be cautious, clearly authorized him to attempt to procure arms for the militia:

Yours of yesterday is at hand. I have this day forwarded to Gen. Howard orders in connection with Gen. Kibbe to make arrangements for the various matters you speak of; in the meantime you must exercise caution in provoking a conflict at this juncture of affairs when we are not ready for action. The result would be suicidal in the extreme and defeat all hopes or expectations of success. Proceed in organizing and arming such forces as can be relied on for the emergency. Can't we buy any muskets in San Francisco for the use of the State, can't they be procured from the same sources as the V.C.'s procure? No answer from Gen. Wool yet in reply to my communication of last Saturday.

Write me daily.[25]

Terry was not only involved in the military planning of the state government, he was also drawn into the financial side of the matter. Realizing that funds would be needed, the governor appointed Terry as a member of a loan committee whose duty was to raise $25,000. Johnson frankly admitted that he did not know "what evidence of indebtedness" would be required by those making the loan. The money was to be used for the militia and to send a two-man commission to Washington to request federal aid against the Vigilance committee.[26]

The governor and his associates continued their efforts to procure arms. They recalled that the war department normally made an annual distribution of arms to the state government and they promptly requested the remainder of the

[24]"Law and Order View," XV, Pt. II (1936), 70.
[25]Ibid.   [26]Ibid., pp. 78-79.

allotment. After some delay, General Wool agreed to furnish the allotment indicated by the ordnance department at Washington, 113 muskets, one horse saber, and two bullet molds.

It was planned to ship the arms to San Francisco. General Howard's hope was to place the militia in barracks or a camp "to avoid the danger of an accidental conflict." At the same time the men needed to have arms and to be in camp before the steamer left for the East, "that we may make a showing to the President of being in an actual State of War." Howard felt, as no doubt did Terry, that a continued demonstration of strength by the militia would gradually wear the Vigilantes down. Time would be on the side of the militia, for the people supporting the committee would tire of the heavy expense it entailed.

Howard was so intent upon achieving the ultimate goal that he warned the governor not to weaken in the face of such popular pressure as a massive petition presented by citizens of Sacramento. Signed by over 2,000 persons, the petition requested Johnson to recall his proclamation and "to forbear for the present the contemplated organization of the Militia." Even Hittell, generally hostile to the governor's actions, conceded that there was some merit to Johnson's reply to the committee bearing the petition:

Gentlemen, which do you think the more proper—for you to come here and ask me, the governor of the State, to yield to a set of men who openly defy the constitution and laws which I am sworn to defend, or for you to go to San Francisco and ask those men to give up their illegal and dangerous association?[27]

General Howard clearly expressed the aim of Johnson and the men around him in a letter to the governor. This objective involved the risk but not the desire for armed conflict. The "ringleaders" of the Vigilance committee "must be arrested, indicted and punished." If the affair were permitted to pass without an "example," Howard predicted that a "Vigilance

[27]*History of California*, III, 563.

Committee will become an ordinary remedy." In other words the right to set aside the law might become a part of the "common law" of California. "The dignity of the State and the laws," wrote Howard, "must be vindicated as soon as possible, but we must not move until we can command the result."[28]

Unfortunately for the governor, a series of unforeseen incidents disrupted the program. As already noted, a small number of arms procured from the arsenal at Benicia was to be sent to San Francisco for the use of the militia. Three members of Dr. R. P. Ashe's company of militia were detailed to effect the transfer in a small schooner, the *Julia*, chartered for the purpose. Vigilante officials, however, heard of the move and sent a small force in the *Bianca* under John L. Durkee, a former city policeman turned Vigilante, which intercepted the *Julia*. Captors and prize then returned to San Francisco. Of the three prisoners, James McNabb was released. The others, J. R. (Rube) Maloney and John G. Philips, regarded as undesirable because of earlier records, were held briefly and then released.[29]

Durkee had arrived with his prize and prisoners early in the morning of June 21. By early afternoon the executive committee had reconsidered and had decided to rearrest Maloney and Philips. There have been various reasons advanced for this reversal. William T. Coleman does not explain the causes in his statement. Bancroft asserted that Maloney and Philips proceeded from one saloon to another, drinking and cursing the Vigilance committee and continued, "Of these proceedings the Executive had due notice. It was evident that these mighty men needed a lesson."[30] Another reason may have been that the committee realized that it might be charged with piracy for the seizure of the *Julia*. If such a development occurred, Maloney would be a good man to have

[28]"Law and Order View," XV, Pt. II, 78.

[29]Durkee statement, MS in the Bancroft Library, pp. 3-4.

[30]*Popular Tribunals*, II, 376. C. J. Dempster statement, MS in the Bancroft Library, p. 5.

in the custody of the Vigilantes, rather than as witness for the prosecution.[31]

The man selected to make the arrest was Sterling A. Hopkins, a member of the Vigilante police who had been the hangman in the execution of Cora and Casey. He heard that Maloney was in the office of Dr. Ashe, over the Palmer, Cooke & Company Bank, on the northeast corner of Kearney and Washington streets. As he headed for the building, Hopkins rather casually picked up several assistants.[32]

Meanwhile a number of men had gathered together in Dr. Ashe's office. One was David S. Terry, who early that afternoon had been talking with his friend, General Howard. They had concluded that it was hopeless to continue to resist the Vigilance committee without arms or funds. They agreed that Terry should go immediately to Sacramento to persuade the governor to issue an order deferring any further efforts on behalf of the militia until word could be obtained from Washington regarding the position that the federal government would take. Terry had then seen Secretary of State Douglass, who was returning to Sacramento, and they had decided to go on the same boat. While waiting for sailing time, the judge visited his friend, Dr. Ashe, in the latter's office. Unfortunately for Terry and Hopkins alike, the Vigilante entered the door a few minutes before the judge was ready to leave for the four-o'clock boat.

[31]*Judges and Criminals*, p. 56. Durkee and another Vigilante policeman were arrested for piracy. When the time came for Maloney's testimony as a witness, the deputy marshal was permitted to search the Vigilance building. Bancroft stated, "but no such person could be found." He was "found" by the Vigilance committee in time to be deported a week or so later. *Popular Tribunals*, II, 501-509. Durkee said of his own trial, "The Grand Jury was a packed jury, anti-vigilance men. The petit jury was a different thing. My counsel had the names of all the jurors before the trial; they knew who they were and all about them; they had the history of every man who came to the country. I knew when the first man got drawn on the jury I should not be convicted. He was a member of the Committee, and his name was Bayleys." MS in the Bancroft Library, p. 7.

[32]This account is drawn largely from sworn statements of witnesses, but it must be noted that the statements were in most cases by prejudiced persons, either for or against Terry. There are enough of them, however, to be checked against each other, and it is hoped that substantial truth has emerged. *Trial*, passim.

It was perfectly natural for Maloney to go to Dr. Ashe's office, for he was a member of Ashe's company, and in addition the doctor's office was being used as temporary headquarters by General Howard, who had sent Maloney and the men under him for the arms. Having been intercepted by the Vigilance police in the performance of his duties, Maloney returned to headquarters to explain the circumstances. McNabb may have been with Maloney, although there is a question on this point. Some time after three o'clock, Hamilton Bowie had gone to Dr. Ashe's room from General Kibbe's office. He had heard a rumor of the seizure of arms but did not know the facts. Maloney and others were describing the affair when they heard a knock on the door.

Dr. Ashe rose as the door opened and seeing strangers asked them what they wanted. Two men were there, Hopkins and Horace A. Russell. Hopkins became momentarily confused and asked for Mr. Roach instead of Mr. Maloney. He quickly corrected himself and said that it was Maloney he wished to see. Ashe told him to come inside and then shut and locked the door, leaving Russell in the hall. Hopkins next told Maloney to accompany him to headquarters, but Maloney demanded to see the warrant of arrest. Hopkins had none and hearing this fact Dr. Ashe said that since Maloney was a member of his company he was bound to give him protection. Hopkins, who was not lacking in courage, took Maloney by the collar to remove him forcibly. The others in the room went to Maloney's support, and Hopkins seeing that he was outnumbered left the room.[33]

Realizing that Hopkins would probably go for reinforcements, Dr. Ashe told Maloney to go to the armory of the Marion Rifles, a part of the militia being raised. It would be

[33]The testimony regarding events in Ashe's office is difficult to analyze, since all in the room but Hopkins were pro-Terry. The crucial point was whether or not Hopkins had a warrant. If he had had one either Russell or Barry would have seen it before or after Hopkins entered the room. Hopkins claimed that Terry drew a knife in the room, but others denied the charge. See Hopkins statement, ibid., p. 20.

easier to protect him there, and Maloney could report to General Howard, who was thought to be in the building. It was quickly decided that all who had been in Dr. Ashe's office should go to the armory, which was at the corner of Jackson and Dupont streets. Before leaving, the men armed themselves—some with guns, others with pistols, and Terry with a gun and his favorite weapon, a bowie knife.

As they went down the stairs and on the street, they passed Russell and Barry of Hopkins' posse, but neither side made a move toward the other. By the time Ashe, Terry, and the rest of the group had reached Jackson Street, Hopkins had returned. Borrowing Dr. Beverly Cole's horse, he had dashed to Vigilance headquarters for reserves.

It appears clear that neither side particularly wanted gunplay and bloodshed. Hopkins was intent on capturing his man; Terry, Ashe, and the others wished to avoid this result by reaching the armory. The situation unfortunately was an explosive one. The times were rough, feelings ran high, and neither side respected the authority of the other.

As the retreating group headed for the armory, Maloney and several others were in the lead. Behind them were Terry, Ashe, and possibly another man. The judge and his friend held their guns at Hopkins and his men as they approached as if to keep them from passing. After an exchange of words, Hopkins seized Terry's gun in an effort to wrest it from him. Another Vigilante, James S. Bovee, was seizing the shotgun held by Ashe. At the same time Russell, seeing a pistol in Ashe's pocket, extracted it with his left hand. He then raised his right hand and with a cocked pistol of his own made ready to strike Ashe's arms to force him to release the gun that Bovee was attempting to take from him.

Unfortunately, as Russell was about to use his weapon as a club, his arm was hit by another Vigilante who was entering the battle against Ashe. As a result Russell accidentally fired his pistol. The bullet passed through Vigilante Capprise's coat but hit no one. This shot apparently spurred Terry to the action for which he was later to stand trial by the Vigilance committee. To this point he had been struggling with Hopkins for possession of the gun he had been carrying. The well-known Terry temper was undoubtedly somewhat frayed. The judge knew that Ashe was wrestling with several Vigilantes, although the evidence seems to bear out the contention that his back was toward that group when Russell accidentally fired his pistol. Hearing the shot, Terry reasoned that at worst Ashe had been hit or at least that the struggle had turned into a murderous assault. Feeling his own life to be in danger, he drew his bowie knife and struck his assailant.

Hopkins fell back bleeding profusely and cried that he had been stabbed. By this time the Vigilantes had secured Ashe's gun. There was a further show of arms, but soon afterward Terry and Ashe reached the armory and went inside.

A running brawl such as this of course could not escape notice. There were numerous witnesses, and within a short time a crowd had gathered. The news of the stabbing of a member of its force soon reached headquarters and the Vigilance committee quickly went into action. At the toll of the bell from the fortress on Sacramento Street, hundreds of men rushed to the building, placed a white badge on the left lapel, and marched out again by companies. Up Sacramento Street and along Montgomery Street they went to the building of Palmer, Cooke & Company, in which Terry was rumored to be seeking refuge.

It soon became known that Terry was at the Jackson Street armory, and a delegation of Vigilantes made its way to this building. By this time the men inside had closed the armory and were preparing to ward off an attack. The odds were hopeless. Sixteen men, including Terry and Ashe, were in the building, and outside, milling about, was a mob of over a thousand people. Terry at this time did not know the identity of the man whom he had stabbed nor did he know whether Hopkins was living or dead. He did know, however, that as a result of his action the Vigilance committee sought him. He told the others that he would give himself up rather than see them risk their lives.[34] Ashe did not protest against this offer but pointed out that the first task was to escape the fury of the mob that might not await the orders of the Vigilance committee.

Not long after the crowd assembled, the representatives of the Vigilance committee arrived. The leader demanded the surrender of all in the armory and of the structure itself. Hoping to save as much as possible, Ashe reduced the discussion to writing. In reply to the demand for unconditional surrender, he wrote the following note:

San Francisco, June 21, 1856

Gentlemen of the Vigilance Committee—

If the Executive Committee will give us protection from violence, we will agree to surrender.

R. P. Ashe, Capt. Co. A.,
J. Martin Reese, 1st Lieut. Co. B.[35]

The delegation, giving a deadline of fifteen minutes for a reply, promised protection for persons and building if Terry, Maloney, Philips, and the arms and ammunition were surrendered.

Ashe and Reese next made a request for a specific guarantee for Terry and Maloney that they would "also be protected, while in your hands, from violence from persons outside of your organization." They stated in addition that Philips was not in the armory. When the Vigilantes had agreed, Terry and Maloney were placed in a hack and driven under guard to Fort Vigilance. The arms were loaded into three drays to swell the arsenal of the committee. Vigilance companies flanked the remaining prisoners and marched them to headquarters.[36]

[34]R. P. Ashe statement, *Trial*, p. 36.

[35]Wagstaff, p. 106.

[36]Bancroft, *Popular Tribunals*, II, 384-86; Dr. William H. Rogers statement, MS in the Bancroft Library.

Having made this forcible move against the militia, the Vigilance leaders decided to secure all the armament of the opposition. The next objective was another armory, on Kearney and Clay streets, to which with difficulty General Howard had made his way. Having only about sixty-eight men against a Vigilante force of more than 1,500, Howard reluctantly decided to surrender. The Vigilantes seized the arms in the building and jailed the men overnight for refusing to take an oath of allegiance to the Vigilance committee.[37]

With the seizure of the Kearney Street armory, the Vigilance committee had practically completed its aim of eliminating the militia as a military force. Vigilantes occupied the other armories in the city but found no arms. The committee then heard that a few state arms were being taken from Benicia to the state prison at San Quentin with a possible view to later use in San Francisco. A small Vigilante group detailed to seize these arms accomplished its objective with little difficulty.

[37]*Judges and Criminals*, pp. 61-65. A member of the Vigilance committee, T. J. L. Smiley, takes credit for the release of the men. Smiley statement, MS in the Bancroft Library, pp. 9-10.

Chapter III

The Prisoner in Fort Gunnybags

THE SEIZURE OF David S. Terry by the Vigilance committee was the climax of the exciting events of June 21,
1856. Public sentiment in the main had supported the
arrest and execution of the gambler Cora and the unsavory
politician Casey, but what would the people think of the incarceration of a justice of the supreme court of California?
William T. Coleman made no overstatement when he wrote
many years later that the Terry case constituted the "most
unexpected and severest task of the year."[1]

The situation was complicated by the fact that for a time
no one knew whether or not Hopkins would survive. If he
died, Terry was indeed in great peril. After receiving the
wound, Hopkins had told his men to continue their efforts and
although bleeding badly he was able to walk. An unknown
doctor first sought to help him, but on the wounded man's
insistence, Dr. Cole was called in attendance.

Fortunately for Hopkins, Dr. Cole arrived within ten minutes after the wound had been inflicted and immediately saw
that the real danger lay from loss of blood. The blow had cut
through the back of the neck into the throat and had severed
an artery. Although he requested other medical assistance, he
started the operation to check a second hemorrhage without
waiting for help to arrive.[2] It is curious that the doctor who

[1]Coleman, *Century statement*, p. 143. This document is taken from the MS
statement by Coleman in the Bancroft Library. Other statements of the Vigilance
committee cited in this chapter are from MSS in the Bancroft Library.

[2]Cole testimony, *Trial*, pp. 17-18.

saved Hopkins' life was the same man who charged that James King of William had died as a result of the malpractice of the attending physicians.

Although by his prompt action Dr. Cole had prevented the death of Hopkins, this fact was not realized for some time. To a very considerable degree, the executive committee delayed its decision regarding Terry until it knew the fate of his victim.

Meanwhile there were strong repercussions in the city and throughout the state. On the one extreme were the advocates of drastic punishment for the judge. The editor of the San Francisco *Bulletin*, who had already attacked Terry, stopped the presses to run an account of the stabbing of Hopkins. The article asserted that "If necessary for the public safety, Terry, Howard, and the other leaders of the law and murder faction, must be hung—and that without delay." By June 23 the *Bulletin* reached the position it was to maintain vociferously during the ensuing weeks:

If Hopkins dies, Terry will and must be hung. Should Hopkins live, which is extremely doubtful, Terry must be banished. His doom is unalterable; justice requires it. Salus Populi suprema lex—THE SAFETY OF THE PEOPLE IS ABOVE ALL LAW.

On the other extreme Terry's supporters quickly went to his aid. It was rumored that the governor might go to San Francisco, but wisely he remained in the capital. Leaving on the steamer *Constance*, Mrs. Terry arrived in San Francisco, Sunday evening, June 22. She obtained permission to see the judge, but shortly thereafter the executive committee reversed itself, possibly as a result of newspaper pressure, and withdrew this privilege.[3]

Mrs. Terry strengthened her husband's cause. Her devotion

[3]Bancroft asserts that the committee reversed itself because of rumors that an effort would be made to rescue Terry. On July 1 Mrs. Terry wrote a note to the Vigilance committee requesting to see the judge on purely business matters, and "if you require it in the presence of the whole committee." *Popular Tribunals*, II, 425-26; letter of Cornelia Terry to "Gentlemen," Terry MSS.

made a marked impression, and the judge's friends were not averse to making the most of it. As a result correspondence of the couple appeared in the newspapers. After the restriction on Mrs. Terry's visits, the judge wrote her a letter. Whether written with a view to publication or not, it stands as a remarkable document. Terry knew that his own life hung in the balance with that of Hopkins. He was a brave man, but he knew a tight situation when he confronted it. From his prison room in Fort Vigilance, Terry wrote:

San Francisco June 30, 1856

Dearest Neal

I received yours just now. Next to seeing you it is my greatest comfort to know that you are well and still keep up your spirits under the most distressing circumstances in which we are placed.

I have today been engaged in taking the testimony of the witnesses against me. The testimony is very conflicting as must always be the case when a no. of persons differing in temperament & excitabillity [sic] detail occurrences which they all witnessed.

Before any important tribunal even upon the evidence already adduced I would be held blameless—but it is not in human nature to judge our enemy fairly and impartially & the result must be as God wills. I have tried with a great deal of anxiety to read the characters of those who are at once my judges and accusers. I am inclined to think that a majority of them are men who desire to do right but considering the infirmity of human nature they are assuming an awful responsibility in sitting in judgment on a man against whom so much has been said to excite their prejudices. You desire to know if I am well & in Spirits. I am well & keep up my Spirits as well as could be expected. Do not fear that I will despond. My mind has been relieved from care for the future of my boy & I am now equal to any fortunes.

If I felt guilty of any crime I would despond but upon this point I am invulnerable. I know that I acted not from any feeling of malice towards any human being but solely from regard to a sacred principle, from a desire to prevent the consumation in my presence of an act which (though it may have been attempted from good motives & would certainly have worked no injury to the community, (as the man sought to be removed was a bad man)) was a violation of the Constitution of this state which I had *sworn* to sup-

44

port as well as the Constitution of the United States to secure the blessings of which to their posterity both my grandfathers fought & bled & toiled & suffered. I was educated to believe that it is the duty of every American to support the Constitution of his Country to regard it as a sacred instrument not to be violated in its least provision—& if necessary to die in its defense. The meanest criminal is under that instrument guaranteed the same rights as the noblest citizen & cannot without a violation of its provisions be deprived of his liberty, except by legal process—It was at this holy principle and the obligation of my oath I looked and not at the demerrits (?) of the man whom I knew to be a bad man—& I believe even those who are my self constituted judges will do me the justice to believe I would not defend him for his own sake. The matter stands thus with me actuated by the principles taught me in my childhood. I have done certain acts about the merrits [sic] of which men who are perhaps equally honest and patriotic differ. This must always be the case as long as mens minds are differently constituted. I feel that I am right & so feeling would lay down my life rather than deny these principles the same conciousness [sic] of the Justice of my cause which sustained old Nat Terry when wounded & a prisoner in Charleston & which nerved the heart of David Smith to refuse to release his fathers brother who had supported his tottering steps [in] infancy & whom he had made prisoner at King's Mountain must support me in this trial. If need be I can go out of this world feeling that I have done nothing in this life which would cause the spirits of those patriots & heroes to blush for their descendant.

So My Darling dont fear that I will falter.

I believe that if I am permitted to live out my three score years and ten I have those elements in me which would enable me to be of service to my country and to leave a name of which my children would be proud. I cannot doubt this when I look back in the past & see what I have already accomplished with so little effort.

By the death of my mother I was left at thirteen to my own guardianship, my only counsellor who had influence with me a brother but two years older. From that age I counted myself a man & associated with men aye and played a mans part in the struggle which secured the independence of Texas & gave to the union one of the brightest Stars in its constellation.

Acknowledging no controll [sic] upon my actions I could not sink from the Soldier to the Schoolboy so what education I have acquired above what a boy of twelve gathers at Common Schools I

45

acquired by reading at home all the books I owned or could borrow, during the time I was not engaged more pleasantly on the frontier.

With these disadvantages & without a very extraordinary amount of application I have maintained a respectable standing at the bar, enjoy an unblemished reputation for honor & integrity & at thirty three have been placed by the votes of the people of this state upon the Supreme Bench—

With proper industry what may not be accomplished in thirty years more but it is unprofitable now to consider of this.

If we should not meet again my love remember & say to my friends that the request I made to you and to Capt Lubbock remains still my wish. I know that sooner or later justice will be done to my memory, and that all good men who know my motives will respect them & me—

I cannot understand the allusion in your letter. Perhaps after a little while I may be able to do so. Keep up your spirits be hopeful for the future & rely upon the assurance that I will give our Son no reason to blush for the memory of his Father.

Remember me to all my friends. Say to them that their devotion is the best endorsement of my motives as it is not possible that a bad man should have *Such* Friends.

Good bye my only love. May God bless you & my Son

Your own forever

D. S. Terry

Upon reflection I think I do understand your allusion.

Mrs. Terry decided to publish this letter and accompanied it with one of her own which was in itself an excellent piece of special pleading. Both letters appeared in the sympathetic *Daily Herald*. Mrs. Terry sharply attacked the Vigilance committee for refusing to permit her to see her husband and recounted her continuing efforts to secure permission to visit him. She then charged that the committee kept her from Terry, "that my feelings may be so agonized that I shall be willing to entreat him to resign the office to which the voice of his fellow citizens called him." Such an aim was futile, for she wrote, "I cannot tempt him to dishonor. I know my husband too well to suppose that any influence would induce him to betray a trust confided to his care." The wife admitted, "He may err in his zeal in defending that trust, but he cannot be coerced into resigning it." At the same time she expressed the opinion that if through customary methods the "will of a majority of the whole people" was shown that Terry should resign, he would "yield a prompt acquiescence." Mrs. Terry ended her plea by commending her cause to "the people of the State and not to San Francisco alone" and she wrote, "If I do anything unwomanly in thus stating it, I beg that it may be remembered that an unheard of proceeding has deprived me of access to my protector and adviser."[4]

Dr. Beverly Cole attested to Mrs. Terry's firm support of her husband. Present when she first visited Terry, Cole later noted:

On the occasion of my visit, whilst the Executive Committee were endeavoring to induce him to resign his position of Chief Justice, Mrs. Terry raised her voice and said, "Judge Terry, I would rather see you hanged from one of those windows than to recognize that you were compelled to resign your official position!"—so distinguished was this lady for courage, decision and pride.[5]

Dr. Ashe, arrested with Terry, was less strong willed and eagerly sought parole and promised that he would remain neutral in word and in action. Fortunately for him he was an official of the federal rather than of the state government. Commander Boutwell quickly brought pressure in a letter for the release of the naval agent.[6] Since Ashe had injured no one and since his retention might carry the Vigilantes into open conflict with the federal government, the committee freed him on parole. Ashe soon realized his blunder and sought unsuccessfully to be released from parole.[7] Later the naval agent defended Terry in a letter to the press.[8]

[4]July 2. The *Daily Evening Bulletin* declined to print the letters.

[5]Statement, pp. 16-17.

[6]Boutwell to the executive committee of Vigilance, June 21, Ex. Doc. No. 101, 34th Cong., 1st Sess., pp. 21-22.

[7]Ashe's letter is quoted in the statement of W. T. Coleman, p. 99.

[8]*Daily Evening Bulletin*, July 22, 1856.

Among those greatly disturbed by Terry's arrest was Governor Johnson. The judge had been a principal aid to the governor in the fight against the Vigilantes, and Johnson made vigorous efforts to secure his release. One move was an attempt to persuade the naval authorities to intervene. Johnson knew Farragut's reluctance to act in civil matters and concentrated on Boutwell, a strong believer in states' rights and emotionally inclined to side with Terry. In a letter dated July 3, for example, Boutwell wrote, "The appeals of his distressed wife, and the fact that Judge Terry acted in self-defense, would have almost induced me to batter the city down, if I could have done so without destroying the lives and property of the innocent with the guilty."[9]

On June 27 Governor Johnson wrote to the commander stating that his proclamation of June 3, declaring San Francisco to be in a state of insurrection, had been ignored by that city. Terry had been "engaged in the due performance of his duties as a peace officer of the State, and in the defense of his lawful rights as a citizen thereof" when he was seized and jailed by the Vigilance committee. Terry's life was in "imminent danger and peril from the lawless violence of the said Vigilance Committee," and it was "Wholly beyond the civil or military power of this State" to protect him. Johnson then requested "at your hands, and with the power and means under your command" the protection of Terry from everything "except such punishment as may be inflicted on him in due course of law."[10]

Though he was deeply sympathetic, Boutwell answered that he could not act because with the feeling against federal action in San Francisco any direct action might endanger Terry's life as well as injure or kill many innocent people. He further expressed the hope that since Hopkins was apparently recovering, the committee would soon release Terry.

[9]Boutwell to J. C. Dobbin, secretary of the navy, Ex. Doc. No. 101, 34th Cong., 1st Sess., p. 21.

[10]Ibid., pp. 23-24.

Boutwell ended his letter, however, with the following promise: "If Hopkins dies, and the committee condemn Judge Terry to death, I will make an effort to save his life in such a manner as not to be offensive to my fellow citizens."[11]

Others joined in making appeals to Commander Boutwell. Among those who wrote to him were the collector of the port, the United States marshal of the district, Mrs. Terry, and the prisoner himself. Terry strongly denounced the Vigilance committee as a "powerful organization of men, acting in open and armed rebellion against the lawful authorities of this State." He further charged that some of its members "now openly threaten to seize the *forts* and *arsenals* of the United States as well as the ships of war in port, and secede from the Federal Union." The judge asserted that he had been handcuffed, his friends kept from him, and "all kinds of terrorism are resorted to to compel me to resign my office." Instead of attacking a Vigilante, he declared, "I acted solely in defence of my own life against their assaults on the public streets." As a result he was in "hourly danger of suffering an *ignominious death* at the hands of these traitors and assassins."

In asking Boutwell to intervene "with all the powers at your disposal, to protect my life from the impending peril,"[12] Terry noted that in 1853 another naval officer, Duncan Nathaniel Ingraham, had gained national popularity by threatening to attack an Austrian vessel to rescue a Hungarian revolutionist who was thought to be an American citizen.

Boutwell had already thought of Kostza, and in fact had mentioned the episode in a letter to the Vigilance committee, written June 28, on behalf of Terry. The naval officer told the committee that it was following one of two courses, "either in open rebellion against the laws of your country and in a state of war, or you are an association of American citizens combined together for the purpose of redressing an evil, real or imaginary, under a suspension of the laws of California." If

[11]Ibid., June 29, p. 24.
[12]Ibid., June 28, pp. 26-27.

following the first course, the committee should place Terry aboard the *John Adams* as a prisoner of war. If the committee felt that the laws were suspended, to avoid shedding blood, it should turn the judge over to the lawful authorities of the state. Boutwell then issued a veiled warning. Reminding the Vigilantes of the action of Captain Ingraham to save the life of Kostza, who was not an American citizen, he asked, "how much more necessary it is for me to use all the power at my command to save the life of a native born American citizen, whose only offense is believed to be in his effort to carry out the law, obey the governor's proclamation, and in defense of his own life." The naval officer concluded by expressing the hope that a peaceful solution could be reached.[13]

The committee made a noncommittal acknowledgment of the receipt of this communication.[14] Commander Boutwell on the next day received Judge Terry's letter and this may have prompted him to write a second letter, dated June 30, in which he requested an answer to his previous correspondence.[15] The committee neatly avoided a debate with Commander Boutwell by replying that they were submitting the correspondence to his "superior officer," Captain Farragut. As they anticipated, the result was a mild dispute between the two naval officers. The details were unimportant, but it is significant that although Farragut was more conservative and opposed to interference in civil strife, even he was critical of the action of the Vigilance committee. He replied to that body that he had read the correspondence forwarded to him and that while he differed with Boutwell as to methods, he agreed with him "that the release or trial of Judge Terry, in accord-

[13]Ibid., pp. 25-26. D. O. Shattuck of the superior court had advanced the "state of war" theory in the San Francisco press. Shattuck was highly regarded by all, but his views were challenged by the pro-Vigilante element. Bancroft goes to some length in an effort to refute Shattuck's theory. *Popular Tribunals*, II, 430-431.

[14]"33, Secretary" to Boutwell, June 28, Ex. Doc. No. 101, 34th Cong., 1st Sess., p. 26. The signature "33, Secretary" was that used by Isaac Bluxome, secretary of the Vigilance committee.

[15]Ibid., pp. 27-28.

ance with the Constitution of the United States, would be the readiest mode of attaining the great object we all have in view." The captain also politely but clearly showed that he believed the Vigilance committee to be a secret body acting in contradiction to the constitution of the United States.[16]

Despite his assurances to the committee that he favored a peaceful solution of the matter, Farragut made ready for possible trouble. On July 3 he ordered Commander Boutwell not to sail from San Francisco harbor without orders from him, and he told the captain of the *John Adams*, "You will receive on board Judge D. S. Terry, for his personal safety, should any arrangement be accomplished to that end."[17] On the same day Farragut wrote the Vigilance committee and ended, "With a sincere hope that some satisfactory arrangement may be made for the release of Judge Terry."[18]

By this time Captain Farragut had decided to advise his department of developments, and he forwarded the correspondence on the subject for orders. The navy department's instructions, from a practical standpoint, constituted a victory for the Vigilance committee. The federal government was not yielding to the Vigilantes, but neither was the navy to intervene in matters between the committee and the state. It was to act only to protect federal property and federal officers.[19]

These instructions were based upon a policy laid down by the secretary of state on behalf of the president, July 19, 1856.[20] Secretary William L. Marcy's statement showed that Governor Johnson had failed to persuade the president to in-

[16]Farragut to Messrs. Farwell and Case of the committee of Vigilance, July 1, ibid., pp. 18-19. Leading Vigilantes were convinced that Farragut was on their side. Statements of T. J. L. Smiley (p. 14) and James D. Farwell (p. 21). After an interview with Farragut, Farwell stated, "We found the old Commodore in sympathy with us, although he could not express himself very much in that direction."

[17]Loyall Farragut, op. cit., p. 184.

[18]Farragut to Coleman, Ex. Doc. No. 101, 34th Cong., 1st Sess., p. 20.

[19]Dobbin to Commander William Mervine, Aug. 2, ibid., pp. 13-15.

[20]W. L. Marcy to J. Neely Johnson, ibid., pp. 7-8.

tervene against the Vigilance committee. On June 19 Johnson had appealed to President Pierce for federal aid. R. Augustus Thompson, recently United States land commissioner for California, and Colonel F. Forman, postmaster of Sacramento, acted as lobbyists for the communication but were unsuccessful.[21] Attorney General Caleb Cushing, to whom the letter was referred, gave his opinion on July 19 in his reply to the president. His picture of the Vigilance committee was legal and unflattering. It had indulged in a public hanging "without law" of two alleged murderers. Cushing stated that he was not clear on the state of public opinion in San Francisco, but that that was immaterial, "since, whatever may be the local opinion regarding the committee, its organization and its acts do not the less constitute a lawless usurpation of the powers of the State."

The attorney general, therefore, agreed with the opinion of Johnson and others that the Vigilance committee was an illegal body acting in violation of the laws of the state. The crux of the matter, however, was the course of action the federal government should take. Johnson had insisted that it should intervene, but the attorney general disagreed. In the first place, Cushing stated, the Vigilance committee was not interfering with the laws or actions of the federal government, which, therefore, did not need to intervene on its own account.

The question was, then, when the federal government should intervene on behalf of a state. Not simply, said the attorney general, when the governor requested it. Instead the appeal should come from the legislature. Johnson's error, according to Cushing, was in failing to call the legislature in special session. Furthermore there was no actual armed clash between the state and the Vigilantes that might move the president to act.[22]

There were other pressures in Washington. One came from

21Letters of Johnson to Thompson and Forman, June 18, ibid., pp. 6-7.
22Cushing to the president, ibid., pp. 8-13.

Terry's former state, Texas, for his friends were excited and angered by his arrest. The Galveston and Houston papers ran accounts of the developments and published some of the Terry letters to relatives and friends. Terry's sister-in-law wrote that "Cousin Frank [Terry] is almost like a madman —he says if cousin Dave dies, one hundred men *die* for *him* —that he will make himself into the greatest desperado, that ever lived, will hide & skulk, not look in the face of man unless to shoot him until this fearful oath is fulfilled." Mrs. Sessums herself apparently did not consider these words extreme, for she added that Frank was not the only one who would die for David S. Terry, and she warned that it would be the most dismal day for San Franciscans "that ever dawned if one hair of his head, is *touched*—'vengeance is mine sayeth the Lord'—but I feel as if I could tare [sic] their *hearts out* —for treating him in the manner they have."[23]

At Austin the state legislature passed a resolution asking Congress to intervene in the matter. Senator Sam Houston, either more realistic or less sympathetic than his constituents, presented the resolution with the simple request that it be printed and referred to an appropriate committee. A few senators commented. Senator Albert G. Brown of Mississippi gave Judge Terry a strong recommendation and said that he had known him and his family for years. Senator John Bell of Tennessee voiced the only criticism. He praised Terry's character but expressed the opinion that Terry was hot tempered. Senator John B. Weller of California, one of Terry's firmest supporters in Washington, took issue with Senator Bell.[24]

Although both friends and enemies of the Vigilantes employed pressure politics in Washington, the issue was actually a minor one in the capital. The president and other leaders were preoccupied with far more important matters.

[23]Mary Sessums to Cornelia Terry, Aug. 8, Terry MSS.

[24]*Congressional Globe*, 34th Cong., 2nd Sess. (Washington, 1856), pp. 69-70. The discussion in Congress had no practical significance since Terry had already been released.

The new Republican party, with its colorful candidate, Frémont the Pathfinder, and its opposition to the extension of slavery presented a threat to the Democratic party in the coming presidential election. The question of civil strife in Kansas seemed far more vital than trouble in a city on the distant Pacific Coast. It must be remembered too that Franklin Pierce was not one of the nation's strongest executives.

Because of these factors the president no doubt received with relief the advice of his attorney general, and on the same day Secretary of State Marcy wrote the government's reply to Johnson's request for intervention. The president, he explained, had given the matter serious thought, but on the attorney general's recommendation had decided not to intervene. Optimistically Marcy wrote, "The President will not allow himself to believe that the prevalence of rash counsels and lawless violence still continues in California." He "confidently" trusted that by this time the people of San Francisco would have seen the error of their ways and returned to a conformity with the laws.[25]

Meanwhile the Vigilance committee had determined not to wait for Hopkins' death or recovery and on June 27 Terry found himself on trial for his life, not before a court of law, but before the executive committee of the San Francisco committee of Vigilance. Not only did committee members indict him for his resistance to Vigilance authority and his attack on Hopkins but in addition they tried the judge on numerous past charges that had been raised against him. As it developed Terry was actually retried for acts of violence for which he had already been found guilty and punished in an established court of law.[26]

[25]Ex. Doc. No. 101, 34th Cong., 1st Sess., pp. 7-8.

[26]Coleman's statement (p. 101), made some years after the event, differs from that of the writer. He asserted, "We included under the indictment specifications of other acts of violence for which no previous trial or punishment had been had, all his crimes or misdemeanors being a part of the proper charges and actions of the people against the accused, where ever the same may have been committed within the state."

The indictment of "The People vs. D. S. Terry" was as follows:

1. David S. Terry is charged with resisting, by violence, the officers of the Committee of Vigilance, while in the discharge of their duty.

2. David S. Terry is also charged with committing an assault, with a deadly weapon, with intent to kill Sterling A. Hopkins, a police officer of the Committee of Vigilance, on the 21st day of June, 1856. David S. Terry is also charged with breaches of the peace and attacks on citizens, when in discharge of their duties, as follows:

3. In 1853, an attack on Mr. Evans, a citizen of Stockton.

4. With an attack on Mr. Roadhouse, a citizen of Stockton, while in the Court House.

5. An attack on Mr. King, a citizen of Stockton, at the Charter election.

6. In 1853, resistance of a writ of Habeas Corpus, by which William Roach escaped from the custody of the law, and the infant heirs of the Sanchez family were defrauded of their rights.

7. In 1853, an attack on J. H. Purdy in the city of San Francisco.[27]

These charges having been read, Judge Terry was asked to answer to the question, "Guilty, or not Guilty?" He replied firmly, "I am not guilty of any crime whatever." The prosecution, conducted by T. J. L. Smiley, then opened its case. The men who had accompanied Hopkins in his effort to arrest Maloney were the principal witnesses, and of them the most important were Barry, Russell, and Bovee. Other casual witnesses gave corroborative evidence. Terry took advantage of the opportunity afforded him to question the witnesses. It became clear from the evidence that Terry had stabbed Hopkins. Other points were not as easily clarified. One of the most significant was whether Terry saw the accidental firing of Russell's pistol. The evidence seemed to indi-

[27]*Trial*, p. 3.

cate that he did not. Such being the case, one can explain, if not justify, Terry's subsequent action.

After the prosecution had made its case, Terry opened by making a statement which obviously he had prepared with care. By this time he had been able to observe his judges and had decided the nature of his defense. It was no time for bluster and threats, but for an appeal to fair play and the feeling of justice. This was not Terry, the Law-and-Order politician, feet on the table, hat down over the eyes, cursing the "d——d pork-merchants." This was Terry the lawyer with his own life at stake before an unpredictable jury operating on unknown law.

His first words consequently were almost deferential to the committee members. Although he could not reconcile their acts with his concepts of justice and right, "candor forces me to confess that the evils you arose to repress were glaring and palpable, and the end you seek to attain is a noble one." The question on which he and the committee disagreed was whether the end justified the means. This was a question that Terry did not discuss further in his defense, for he stated that it was one upon which honest men could differ.

Terry next denied that the Law-and-Order group consisted mainly of associates and sympathizers with "ballot-box stuffers and other disreputable characters." He asserted that he had consistently opposed this class of person and had been denounced as a bolter from the Democratic party because he had refused to support candidates whose nomination had been the result of fraudulent practices.

Having laid the groundwork with a temperate statement of the difference between his views and those of the committee, Terry moved to a consideration of the charges against him. He admitted that the charge of resisting the officers of the Vigilance committee was true, but declared, "I do not understand how it can be imputed as a crime that I, who am a sworn officer of the law, was not guilty of violating my duty as such officer." He noted that Hopkins did not have a warrant for the arrest of Maloney and, therefore, was not even operating under the procedure established by the Vigilance committee.

Responding to the charge of assaulting Hopkins, Terry asserted that he did not know that Hopkins was an officer of the Vigilance committee. He described the events as he had seen them, "I threw a glance over my shoulder and saw Dr. Ashe apparently confused and staggering. Thinking I would receive the next discharge, and seeing several pistols drawn, I thought it absolutely necessary for the preservation of my own life, to be rid of my persevering antagonist, who continued to struggle for the gun for the purpose, as I still think, of using it with fatal effect against me. With this view I struck with my left hand at the most exposed part of him, thinking to disable him."

Terry then lectured the committee on one of the dangers of its procedures, perjured evidence. He drew attention to an unfriendly witness, John Hanna, and contended that with no penalty for perjury in the Vigilance court false oaths would be sworn for personal reasons. In regular courts perjurers could be caught even at a later time and punished by prison sentence.

He also warned his judges "against being betrayed into injustice by the bloodthirsty appeals of a prostituted press." The *Evening Journal* was an abolitionist paper opposed to him because of his Southern birth. He could not account as easily for the "hostility and bloodthirstiness" of the *Bulletin* but suggested that it was because the editor "seems to be a sort of Ishmaelite; his hand is against every man." He hoped that the attempt to create prejudice in committee members' minds would be "treated with the contempt it merits."

The nature of the remaining charges, Terry said, forced him "to conclude that, having already determined to compass my ruin as far as possible, certain persons are anxiously striving to furnish some sort of plausible pretext, and, by reviving and falsifying transactions long past, excite as far as possible, the mind of the community."[28]

The minor charges served the purpose of prolonging the trial. Its termination did not depend on the completion of presentations by prosecution and defense; it rested on the condition of Sterling A. Hopkins. Consequently, while the executive committee waited to hear what this would be, it occupied itself with a detailed examination of Terry's earlier difficulties, interrogated witnesses, and read sworn statements.

As the trial continued Terry's appeal may have had a bearing on the executive committee's determination to use reason and justice. From the scribbled notations on some of the documents that remain, certain points appear. One is that some of the members at least were attempting to sift the evidence to secure the facts in the case. Another point that seems equally clear is that hard as they might try, the men judging Terry were not impartial. One note, crossed out after it was written, showed the reaction to the suggestion that Terry be turned over to the regular courts: "Try him according to law & will accept a verdict. His own mistakes prove that he was in the habit of taking the law into his own hands. Why should he then complain of our action." At least one member of the committee was sensitive regarding its usurpation of power. This note and others also demonstrated that the charges against Terry of earlier violence were quite damaging to him. The committee could rationalize its own actions by pointing to his past indiscretions.[29]

The trial was a secret, indifferently kept. Rumors of all sorts kept slipping out and appearing in the newspapers, which to a considerable degree were also trying Terry. Like the executive committee the press was no impartial jury. At one extreme John Nugent's *Herald* opposed the Vigilance movement and defended Terry, and at the other, the virulent

[28]Ibid., pp. 3-23.

[29]Rough notes in the San Francisco committee of Vigilance papers, MSS in the Huntington Library.

Bulletin paraded before the public the old Stockton accusations against the judge. The *Bulletin* published anonymous letters which charged Terry not only with his own mistakes but with acts of violence of his friends as well.[30] This paper customarily called him the "rowdy judge." It accused him of following the "brutal instincts of his nature" toward the Indians while living in Texas, and of killing them "with the same gusto, as Nero, his prototype killed flies." A few typical extracts show the extremes to which the *Bulletin* went: "true to his bloody instincts"; "his various midnight rowdying excursions" in which he made the night "hideous"; "Terry satiated his brutal thirst for revenge upon his poor helpless victim." "Judge David S. Terry, still breathing slaughter, bathed his bowie-knife in the blood of an unarmed witness."

On July 8 the *Bulletin* ended a list of charges against Terry with the following trenchant allegations:

8. Judge David S. Terry, seeing a favorable opportunity to gloat on human gore even to satiety, came to San Francisco, with the sworn purpose of making our streets run with the blood of our innocent citizens.

9. Judge David S. Terry, as the last crowning act of his bloodthirsty nature, plunged his bowie-knife into the neck of S. A. Hopkins, one of the Committee's most active and most efficient Police officers.

Blood, blood, blood, seems to be the only substance in nature capable of slaking the thirst of this man-beast.

One of the most controversial aspects of the trial was the charge that the committee attempted to force Terry to resign his judicial position. As early as June 24 General Kibbe transmitted to Governor Johnson the rumor that "if Hopkins lives Terry will be released on condition that he and

[30]Among the most extreme charges were those made by a writer from Stockton, using the pseudonym "Vigilance." R. P. Ashe and S. H. Brooks wrote an answer, assuming the responsibility for some of the acts of violence charged against Terry. "Vigilance" calmly admitted that he had been mistaken in some accusations but produced new ones. July 17, 22, 25.

Murray [chief justice] both resign their offices."[31] In his effort to free Terry, Johnson worked not only officially but unofficially. Privately he asked his father-in-law, James C. Zabriske, to attempt to reach a compromise with the committee. Apparently Johnson hoped that the committee would turn Terry over to the courts for trial, return state arms to the governor, and then disband. In return Johnson would advise the courts not to prosecute any of the Vigilantes, or if they were prosecuted and found guilty, the governor would grant them an unconditional pardon. Zabriske, a well-known San Francisco attorney, agreed to make the attempt and took with him James Allen and C. B. Zabriske. Their efforts failed. The executive committee would not negotiate unless Terry first agreed to resign from the supreme court. The judge is reported to have told his wife, who reluctantly took the suggestion to him, "If I leave this building alive, I shall leave it as justice of the Supreme Court of this State, and no power on earth can make me change this resolution."[32]

A. C. Crittenden, a close friend of Terry, was persuaded by Zabriske and his associates to speak to the judge. Bancroft asserts that Terry made something of a compromise offer, and quotes him as saying, "Let the offenses charged against me be submitted to a public trial before an impartial jury, as speedily as may be. If I am found guilty of any offense whatever I will at once resign." If Terry made such an offer, the executive committee rejected it. Possibly they, like Bancroft, suspected that "there would be little danger to the high official in this, as Judge Terry's friends were the court party."[33]

The Zabriske venture failed, therefore, and from it came little but bitterness. When the story leaked out, the governor, not wishing to be public party to an unsuccessful plan, denied

[31]"Law and Order View," XV, Pt. III, 148.
[32]Wagstaff, p. 121.
[33]Popular Tribunals, II, 454.

60

any share in the matter. By this action he disgraced himself with his father-in-law, who was made to look either the liar or the fool. Zabriske and his colleague, Allen, consequently aired their side in the newspapers, to the obvious pleasure of the anti-Johnson press.

The Vigilance committee, as well as the defendant, found itself subjected to pressures. Later, and still with irritation, one of the leading Vigilantes, C. J. Dempster, declared that "Social efforts of every kind" were made to "work in the minds" of the members of the executive committee. Even their wives found social calls turning into appeals for Terry. Businessmen attempted to influence Dempster, and he asserted, "I have never known or heard of a case where a man's friends worked so hard in his behalf."[34]

Committee members were sensitive to the rumors that began to spread. It was not that they were frightened, but they did not wish to be caught unprepared. The rumor that some 500 Texans had banded together in the interior and pledged themselves to rescue Terry was the immediate cause of the erection of sandbag breastworks to protect the Vigilance building, and of the search of every room. Talk that the *John Adams* might fire on the city led to careful plans for an assault of the vessel by Vigilante forces if necessary, although the committee wanted no clash with federal authorities. Another rumor allegedly caused one committee member to change his mind toward Terry's guilt. It was said that Sheriff Scannell and the Law-and-Order men planned to arrest executive committee members singly as they went home from headquarters at night. As J. W. Brittain walked cautiously homeward with pistols cocked in anticipation of an attempted arrest, he thought that if he had been in Terry's place he would have acted as Terry did. Thereafter, this Vigilante worked to set Terry free.[35]

[34]Dempster statement, p. 10.

[35]George W. Frink statement, p. 17.

According to still another rumor, a man remained on guard for several weeks in a saloon on the northeast corner of Front and Sansome streets. He was armed, and if Terry should be sentenced to hang, from his vantage point the man planned to sever the rope with a rifle shot and let Terry drop.

The crux of the Terry trial was the condition of Hopkins. If he had died shortly after receiving the wound, in all likelihood the Vigilance committee would have hanged Terry and taken its chances on the consequences. Later statements by Vigilantes are agreed on this point. Hopkins, however, did not die. After the operation by Dr. Cole, he remained in a critical state for a time, and then made an amazingly rapid recovery.

Hopkins had exhibited courage and persistence in his attempt to arrest Maloney. Aside from these characteristics, there was little for which he could be recommended. Even pro-Vigilante Bancroft wrote, "Hopkins was poor material, truth compels me to say, for a first-class martyr."[36] His wife and mother were a marked contrast to Mrs. Terry and her mother, who worked zealously for Terry's release. Hopkins' wife's moral standards were not above reproach, and evidently both women anticipated financial betterment as a result of the husband's misfortune, since San Francisco citizens had contributed $30,000 to the relief of the family of James King of William. While Dr. Cole was attending the wounded man he heard Hopkins' mother say to the wife that if her husband died she would be a "rich widow."[37] The fact that Hopkins also heard the remark may have accounted for his rapid recovery.

Like his mother, Hopkins was interested in money. As soon as he was well advanced toward recovery, he appeared before the Vigilance committee which was still conducting the trial of Terry. Hopkins calmly suggested that the whole

[36]*Popular Tribunals*, II, 399.
[37]Ibid.

matter could be settled easily between Hopkins and Terry—on a financial basis. Some time later Hopkins applied to the committee for a pension.

Hopkins' recovery split the committee. Even the *Bulletin* no longer could demand the death penalty for Terry, but it continued to insist on banishment. Actually both sides had been delaying, the committee to see what happened to Hopkins, and Terry in the hope that public opinion would rise against the Vigilance committee or that he could secure federal aid.

Ultimately federal assistance of a sort did arrive. Although probably not decisive, it had a bearing on the outcome. Captain Farragut had remained aloof, had declined to co-operate with the governor, and had endeavored to restrain his more impetuous fellow officer, Boutwell. In spite of his caution, which sorely disappointed Johnson and the Law-and-Order men, Captain Farragut was irritated by the Vigilance committee's actions.

Early in August Farragut advised the secretary of the navy of a new development. Friends of Terry had been exerting pressure on Judge M. H. McAllister, of the circuit court of the United States, to issue a writ of habeas corpus for the imprisoned judge. The purpose of such action was to involve the federal government in the San Francisco picture. Hearing of the move, the Vigilance committee appointed a three-man committee to secrete Terry should such a writ be presented.

Judge McAllister hesitated to issue the writ, in part because he did not know whether he could obtain naval backing. A mutual friend, Senator William Gwin, brought Farragut and McAllister together for a conference. As a result of this meeting, Farragut made certain moves that to the outsider looked very much like preparation for military action.

Another factor prompted the naval officer. Federal authorities had become increasingly concerned for the safety of government property in San Francisco, especially funds amounting to about $4,000,000 in the branch mint. Farragut, the sub-treasurer, and the superintendent of the mint had reached a tentative decision to remove the funds from the mint to the more easily defended Mare Island. Not only was the *John Adams* in the bay, but two vessels at Mare Island, the *Decatur* and *Warren,* made ready for action with their batteries in good working order.

When Farragut went to see Gwin and McAllister on July 21, he received a message from the sub-treasurer announcing that he had reconsidered and would not release the funds without a written request from Farragut. Judge McAllister at this time suggested another use for the naval forces. He told of the possible issuance of the writ for Judge Terry and asked Farragut, as the latter expressed it, if he would "give the United States Marshal the necessary assistance on the water to prevent the abduction of Judge Terry from the harbor of San Francisco by the associated mobites styling themselves a Vigilance Committee." Farragut replied that if McAllister could make it clear that he had a right to issue the writ, the naval officer would support him. Farragut added that although he was not willing to move in the matter he would "support the Constitution and the laws of the Union to the extent of my power."

McAllister convinced the naval officer of his right to issue the writ. Farragut accordingly gave Commander Boutwell instructions he no doubt was glad to receive. He was to go to the aid of Terry to protect him from seizure once such a request came from the United States marshal. To assist Boutwell, Farragut sent over the fast schooner, *Fenimore Cooper,* to lie alongside the *John Adams.* As Terry's trial drew to a conclusion, therefore, members of the executive committee knew that two naval vessels lay off San Francisco and that two more were being prepared for action at Mare Island.

Terry's trial came to a close July 22, after twenty-five days, and now it was up to the executive committee to reach

64

its decision. Each committee member was required to take the following oath:

We hereby pledge our sacred honor to God and ourselves, never to divulge the votes taken in our verdicts rendered in the trial of David S. Terry to any living being outside this room. So help us God.[38]

Having agreed that a three-fifths vote would be necessary to convict, the committee considered each of the charges raised against Terry. He was found guilty of the first charge of resisting the officers of the Vigilance committee. The second charge proved to be a stumbling block and was passed temporarily. On all but one of the remaining charges dealing with Terry's earlier activities, he was found not guilty and the charges dismissed. The committee found Terry guilty of the last charge, an attack on Purdy. The meeting lasted nine hours without a substantial break. The members, exhausted, then adjourned and did not meet until the next evening. After prolonged discussion of the second charge, "committing an assault, with a deadly weapon, with intent to kill Sterling A. Hopkins," the committee compromised by finding Terry guilty of a reduced charge of assault only.

After the question of punishment had been decided, the committee sent its recommendation to the board of delegates. This body consisted of representatives of the various divisions of the Vigilance committee and was empowered to ratify the executive committee's decision.

The board assembled Friday, July 25, at eleven in the morning. William T. Coleman, president of the Vigilantes and a member of the executive committee, presided over the hundred delegates present. Such was the seriousness of the case that after the roll call the doors were closed, no one was to be admitted, and no motion except for recess was to be in order until the Terry matter was settled.

The board then heard a detailed summary of the case, including the arguments and extended testimony for prose-

[38]Ibid., 468.

cution and defense. The executive committee next presented its recommended verdict to the board and made the unusual recommendation that after finding the defendant guilty of certain charges he should be released. In explanation, the committee wrote:

That David S. Terry, having been convicted after a full, fair and impartial trial, of certain charges before the Committee of Vigilance, and the usual punishments in their power to inflict not being applicable in the present instance, that the said David S. Terry be discharged from their custody.

The executive committee further resolved, "That in the opinion of the Committee of Vigilance the interests of the State imperatively demand that the said David S. Terry should resign his position as Judge of the Supreme Court."[39] The committee must have realized that this statement constituted no more than an expression of opinion.

If the executive committee members hoped their resolutions would be unchallenged they were quickly disappointed. The board of delegates defeated a motion to concur and decided to vote on each point separately. On the crucial second charge, the attack on Hopkins, the board reversed the executive committee and found Terry guilty of the entire charge and not merely of assault. It virtually upheld the other decisions, although for some reason, instead of finding Terry guilty of the assault on Purdy, the board expunged the entire charge from the record.[40]

The recommendations of the board of delegates had to go back to the executive committee. The latter was in no hurry to act, and it was the board that made the next move. On the evening of July 31 the larger body voted that if the executive

---

[39]Ibid., 469.

[40]In the *Trial* (p. 73) it is stated that on charge no. 3, Terry was found guilty by the executive committee and had the charges dismissed by the board of delegates. Hittell and Bancroft both say, in contrast, that the executive committee found Terry not guilty of the charge involving an attack on Mr. Evans. Hittell, *History of California*, III, 602; Bancroft, *Popular Tribunals*, II, 469.

committee concurred Terry should be banished from the state under the usual penalty of death if he should return.

Some years later W. T. Coleman admitted that the difference of opinion between the executive committee and the board was "embarrassing." He explained:

The Executive felt that it were better that their conclusions should be maintained and carried out, but the spirit of the whole organization was that of harmony and unity of action, and the Executive did not want a divergence on this most important case.

Coleman continued, "The fact was that Hopkins had recovered, and any severe penalty on Terry was impossible." Terry's "long incarceration and trial, which had weighed heavily upon him, was a severe punishment to him and sufficient to wellnigh compensate for his ill-advised interference with our affairs." The rank and file of the Vigilantes, Coleman explained, did not share this view and "were still enraged against him, and not inclined to lessen any former conceived measures of punishment or penalty." The delegates "shared largely" in the latter opinions, although they recognized the force of the "views and actions of the Executive."[41] Under these circumstances, the executive committee procrastinated and conveniently found other business to prevent action on the recommendation of the board. On August 5 Hopkins appeared before the committee with his embarrassing suggestion that he and Terry reach a financial solution of the matter. That evening the board of delegates met again. An effort was made to reconsider the recommendation for banishment but opinion was turning against it. On the following day, by a vote of forty-four to thirty-six, the board of delegates agreed to concur in the punishment that had been recommended by the executive committee.

There still remained the actual release of the prisoner. Virtually forced by Hopkins' recovery to free Terry, President

[41]Coleman statement, p. 115.

Coleman at least hoped to cause the judge some public embarrassment. He planned that "Terry should be formally discharged in broad daylight, in the presence of the whole Committee, assembled for the occasion, and escorted by the military from his place of imprisonment." The Vigilante leader justified this public chastisement on the ground that the "proceeding would have been more in accordance with the character and dignity of the Committee than that actually pursued by the minority of the Executive."[42]

Coleman's last comment indicates the bitterness that resulted from the method of Terry's release. Other members of the executive committee feared that a public dismissal might result in mob violence and perhaps the lynching of the released prisoner. A mob, if it seized Terry, would not be punished for any acts of violence it might perform. Instead, Vigilante leaders realized, they would be held to blame.

Committee members thinking along these lines concluded that since Terry was to go free, the sooner that release came the better. There had been a late meeting of the board of delegates on the night of August 7. Some time after adjournment a special meeting of the executive committee was called. This meeting had a distinctly clandestine air. As soon as a quorum of eleven was present, the committee called Terry in and read the verdict and punishment to him. Members of the committee then took the judge to the home of his friend, Duncan W. Perley, where Mrs. Terry was staying.

Miers F. Truett, who had acted as Terry's attorney in the trial, was one of the leaders of the truncated committee. He believed and continued to believe that Terry had stabbed Hopkins because "he was convinced, and any other person would have been convinced, that his life was in danger." Later Truett explained the action of the abbreviated committee by stating, "A quorum of the Executive Committee was obtained, as there was danger of Terry's being attacked, as we thought,

[42]Ibid., pp. 125, 128. Coleman asserted that his plan would have protected Terry.

by members of the Committee and we thought it best to discharge him as soon as possible."[43]

Satisfied with their action, Truett and the others retired. Within an hour they were awakened and told that the news of Terry's release had spread and that a thousand persons were searching for the missing judge. Realizing the tragic possibilities of their action, members of the executive committee rushed to the protection of their former prisoner. I. Bluxome, Vigilance committee secretary, took a squad of men to Perley's home on Dupont Street, in which despite the lateness of the hour Terry and his friends were celebrating his release. Bluxome informed the judge of his new peril and offered him the use of his own apartment as a sanctuary. Having more confidence in Truett than in the other Vigilantes, Terry said that he would follow his advice and board the *John Adams* as soon as possible. The two men went to Broadway and down to the waterfront where friends had procured a boat.

Members of the Vigilance committee who had not been party to Terry's sudden release were indignant, and as one Vigilante expressed it, "There was the devil to pay."[44] Coleman bitterly accused the others of taking advantage of a rule that had been set up for emergencies, that some twelve persons in a body of about thirty could constitute a quorum "by night in cases of danger or emergency, and proceed accordingly." The president clearly felt that no such emergency existed on the night of August 7, and stated that the action was "very ill advised, very hasty, very unfortunate, very undignified, not in good taste, nor becoming the Vigilance Committee." The deed, however, was done. The other members of the committee could complain, but as Coleman admitted, "While we could not approve we had to abide by what was done."[45]

[43]Truett statement, pp. 4-5.
[44]George W. Frink statement, p. 18.
[45]Quoted in Bancroft, *Popular Tribunals*, II, 476-77.

Such organs as the *Bulletin* were strongly critical. King, who had supported the committee to this point, spoke of the "first False Step" of the executive committee, which had "seen fit to let loose upon our community the rowdy judge, D. S. Terry, in the farce of trying whom this body has been for some time engaged." Admitting that he did not know the facts, the editor suggested that the committee had released Terry because it was "awed by the influence of Terry's friends and swayed by a regard to his position."[46]

Commander Boutwell cordially greeted Terry aboard the *John Adams*. The following day the steamer *Helen Hensley* left the dock at San Francisco for Sacramento, carrying among her passengers Mrs. Terry and numerous exuberant friends of the judge, "law and murder bloods," as the *Bulletin* contemptuously termed them. As the steamboat neared the sloop, a small vessel put out from the naval craft and transported Terry and some other persons to the *Helen Hensley*. When the river steamer passed the *John Adams*, the latter gave a one-gun salute. This act of Commander Boutwell was almost the last straw for the anti-Terry faction, and they wrote bitter letters of protest to the *Bulletin*.

The salute did not disturb the ranking naval officer at Mare Island. In fact Farragut's letters to the secretary of the navy make one feel that he was pleased at the outcome. He described the events of the night of August 7, and wrote that he had heard that one of the reasons for Terry's release was the war preparation of the naval vessels. He hastened to remind his superior that the arming was to protect treasury funds, but he slyly said of the persons who had told him this rumor, "I did not think it proper to undeceive them, and said nothing on the subject." Of the salute by the *John Adams*, Farragut reported that it was merely a signal to friends on shore that Terry had left the vessel.[47]

---

[46]Aug. 7.
[47]Farragut to Dobbin, Aug. 19, in Loyall Farragut, op. cit., pp. 187-88.

Chapter IV
The Judge

D AVID S. TERRY was neither a great nor a mediocre judge. A bitter critic declared, "He never wrote an opinion, prepared a brief that we ever heard referred to as worth reading a second time."[1] An admirer answering the charge that Terry was not eminent as a jurist asserted, "Probably that criticism was due to the fact that Terry wrote opinions to decide the very cases before the court without indulging in legal essays for the purpose of showing learning. . . ."[2]

When Terry took office both the state and the court were new. Despite its youth the supreme court experienced numerous changes in personnel during the first decade. Also, as we have seen, procedure in the lower courts was often rough, and probably some of the crudeness at times crept into the functioning of the supreme court.

The California supreme court of the 1850's consisted of three justices. Two of these could hold court. During part of 1856 circumstances brought the operations of the court to a halt. Early in the year Associate Justice Solomon Heydenfeldt secured a leave of absence to take a European trip, on assurances by the other judges to the legislature that they could handle the court's business. No one of course anticipated Terry's imprisonment by the Vigilance committee during the summer. The result was that while Terry was in Fort Gun-

[1] *Alta California* (San Francisco), May 30, 1879.

[2] J. W. Terry to Dumas Malone, Sept. 17, 1934, MS in the Bancroft Library, p. 5.

nybags and Heydenfeldt was in Europe, Chief Justice Hugh C. Murray was unable to hold court.

A native of Illinois, Murray had fought in the Mexican War and then joined the rush to California. His rise to prominence was phenomenal, and he was first appointed to fill a vacancy in the supreme court at the age of twenty-six. Unfortunately there were charges that drunkenness and gambling counterbalanced his native ability, and before Terry's difficulty with the Vigilantes it was Murray who was being excoriated by the press. His temper was at times undisciplined, and he became involved in at least two brawls of record. Murray's health was poor after he came to California. It forced him at one time to request a leave of absence from the court and it brought him to his death at the age of thirty-two.[3]

Much less aggressive than Murray was Solomon Heydenfeldt. An unsuccessful candidate for United States senator in 1851, he had secured election in the same year to the supreme court. Actually since the chief justice was selected on a seniority basis, Heydenfeldt had a better claim to the post than did Murray, but he did not wish a fight over the matter.[4]

During his service on the court Terry had a number of other colleagues. Peter H. Burnett succeeded Heydenfeldt. The first governor of the state of California, Burnett is generally considered to have been well-meaning and honest but not exceptionally able. There was no question of the ability of Stephen J. Field, who ascended the bench after Murray's death. Joseph G. Baldwin succeeded Burnett. Baldwin was ranked by an authority as taking "second place only to Field."[5] Like Field, he was to be the object of bitter charges of corruption.

Certain concepts of government stand out in Terry's decisions. He believed strongly for example in separation

[3] E. W. Camp, "Hugh C. Murray, California's Youngest Chief Justice," *California Historical Society Quarterly*, XX (1941), 365-73.

[4] Oscar T. Shuck, *Bench and Bar in California* (San Francisco, 1888), pp. 79-91.

[5] Carl W. Swisher, *Stephen J. Field, Craftsman of the Law* (Washington, 1930), p. 74.

of powers. In one of his earliest cases he stated of a certain action, "Such a course would, we conceive, be a usurpation of functions properly belonging to another department of government."[6] Later he wrote a dissenting opinion when his colleagues declared the Settlers Act of 1856 unconstitutional and expressed a similar view.[7]

Terry not only favored separation of powers but he exhibited little interest in unduly increasing the authority of the supreme court at the expense of the lower courts. In one case Terry noted that the questions presented in the case had been questions of fact, "and the verdict depended upon the weight which the jury attached to the testimony of each witness." Modestly the judge continued:

Upon this point, the jury, having heard the testimony and observed the manner of the various witnesses produced before them, had better opportunities of forming a correct judgment than the Appellate Court from merely reading the statement of evidence; and we are not disposed—although this is an equity case, and the verdict of the jury is not binding on the Court—to interfere with the verdict and ruling of the Judge who tried the case.[8]

This opinion by no means indicated that Terry thought the supreme court should be weak or that it should refrain from judgment on the actual operation of the various branches of the government. In fact one of the contributions of the supreme court during the fifties was to clarify the functions and limitations of office. Numerous cases for example arose over the proper duties of the sheriff, and Terry did not hesitate to deliver opinions defining the tasks and responsibilities of this and other officials.

As a practicing attorney Terry had disliked corrupt judges, and as a judge he showed a belief that holding an office involved both honesty and efficiency. In one case a notary public was sued for damages resulting from alleged negligence on

[6]Johnson v. Fall, 6 Cal., 361.
[7]Billings v. Hall, 7 Cal., 19.
[8]Ritter v. Stock, 12 Cal., 402.

73

his part. He sought to solve the matter merely by returning his fee. Terry, with Field concurring, held that the notary, Joseph W. Finley, was responsible on his bond, and he wrote:

The condition of the bond executed by the defendant is that Joseph W. Finley would "well and truly perform and discharge the duties of notary public according to law."

Finley, according to the judge, had "held himself out to the world as a person competent to perform the business connected with the office," and he had "given a bond to indemnify those who should suffer by the unfaithful or unskilled performance of his duty."[9]

Terry showed more than once that an official's bond was a thing to be used if the occasion arose. In another case he declared, "The decree in this case is clearly erroneous. Admitting the allegations in the plaintiff's bill to be true, it shows that he has a perfectly adequate remedy at law by an action, on the official bond of the clerk. And he must pursue his legal remedy."[10]

Like other judges, Terry considered it a part of his duty to develop and regulate legal practices. Confused conditions in the fifties made such direction especially necessary, for lawyers had come to the area from all parts of the world. The judges had to reduce both procedure and the law itself to some sort of uniformity. Numerous cases attest to their efforts to guide people in legal action.[11] The case just cited is one in point. A narrow line had to be drawn between meticulous observance of the rules on the one hand and the use of common sense on the other. Terry made a serious effort to walk this line. On the side of strict observance of the laws Terry

[9]Fogarty v. Finley, 10 Cal., 239, 244-45.

[10]Miller v. Sanderson, 10 Cal., 490.

[11]Even Bancroft, who is sharply critical of most of the early judges, wrote, "Yet, it would be altogether unfair to withhold from Murray and his associates the credit of having done much, while dispensing justice, to frame the judicial system of California, which became for equity and soundness unsurpassed by any of the older states." *History of California*, VII (San Francisco, 1890), 226.

held in one case that since a complaint had been filed late, an order of arrest was void.[12]

On the other side Terry showed a commendable tendency to use common sense. A convicted murderer attempted to use a technicality to plead double jeopardy; Terry discarded the argument.[13] A lower court had limited arguments in a larceny case; Terry upheld the action and stated that the establishment and enforcement of such rules were matters "resting in the sound discretion of the Court, and are often necessary, to prevent the time of the Court from being wasted in useless and unprofitable discussion."[14]

Terry was impatient of legal tricks. In a case in which one party sought by a technicality to avoid payment of a note, Terry affirmed the judgment for payment and stated, "I know of no instance where a Court of equity has interfered to enjoin a judgment not manifestly wrong, simply because of a defect in the evidence."[15] On another case Terry wrote sharply, "The objection, that there was no tender of a certificate of sale, is frivolous; the question has already been twice decided by this Court." He followed with a comment that appeared more than once in the decisions of the fifties: "The appeal was without merit, and was evidently taken for delay."[16]

In another decision Terry showed his impatience with what was either inefficiency or trickery by attorneys who had raised an objection that the lower court had erred in refusing a new trial on the ground of newly discovered evidence. In his opinion the judge noted with obvious scorn that the so-called "newly discovered evidence" consisted of two items, a deed that had been recorded in the recorder's office "more than twelve months prior to the trial," and the record of a judgment in the same court in which the case was tried. Terry commented, "and we are not able to perceive why this

[12]*Ex Parte* Cohen, 6 Cal., 318.
[13]The People *v.* March, 6 Cal., 543.
[14]The People *v.* Tock Chew, 6 Cal., 636.
[15]Pico *v.* Sunol, 6 Cal., 295.   [16]Harvey *v.* Fisk, 9 Cal., 95.

evidence could not as well have been discovered before the trial, by the exercise of the slightest degree of diligence."[17]

Terry was not disposed to consider inconsequential errors. In a murder case that had been appealed he stated, "The question proposed to the witness . . . to which exception was taken, was not strictly proper, but the answer to it could not possibly have prejudiced the case of the defendant." The supreme court consequently affirmed the judgment of the lower court.[18]

The court attempted not only to regularize judicial practices but also to bring concepts of law into a semblance of uniformity. The problem was complicated for there were involved common law, the American practice of statute law, and the Mexican law that had obtained before the United States acquired the territory. Terry agreed that statutes could supersede common law, but that caution should be employed. For example he stated that an act to regulate interest on money was "in derogation of the common law, and must be strictly construed."[19]

In view of Terry's trouble with the Vigilance committee and some of his later experiences, his comments in a murder case are of interest. The case was up on appeal on the ground that there had been a partial juror who evidently had declared himself in favor of lynch law. Terry wrote, "One of the dearest rights guaranteed by our free Constitution, is that of trial by jury." This guarantee "would be entirely worthless" if biased persons got on the jury, for

A man who could so far forget his duty as a citizen, and his allegiance to the Constitution, as to openly advocate the taking of the life of a citizen without the form of law, and deprive him of the chance of a jury trial, would not be likely to stop at any means to secure, under the forms of a legal trial, a result which he had publicly declared ought to be accomplished by an open violation of the law.[20]

[17]Weimar *v*. Lowery, 11 Cal., 113.   [18]The People *v*. Plummer, 12 Cal., 256.
[19]Raun *v*. Reynolds, 11 Cal., 19.
[20]The People *v*. Plummer, 9 Cal., 308-13.

On another occasion Terry stressed not only the importance but the difficulty of securing impartial jurors:

It is well known that there is in the minds of most men a desire to be thought consistent, which induces them to adhere with tenacity to views once entertained, and expressed; the law has therefore wisely ordained that the life or liberty of a citizen shall not be committed to the decision of those whose prejudices and pride of opinion are enlisted against him.

In addition, he continued:

Few men will admit that they have not sufficient regard for the truth and justice to act impartially in any matter, however much they may feel in regard to it, and every day's experience teaches us that no reliance is to be placed in such declarations.[21]

Terry at this time was not as much concerned about the partiality of a judge, and in one of his opinions he stated that the law had established different rules for the selection of judges than for juries. The reason for the difference, he explained, was that the judge's actions were subject to correction by the higher court.[22]

As might be expected from his background, Terry strongly defended states' rights. This point of view did not affect the majority of the opinions he delivered. In one dissenting opinion, however, Terry made it perfectly clear where he stood on the question. Baldwin and Field concurred in declaring that the twenty-fifth section of the Judiciary Act of 1789 was constitutional. This section involved the right of the United States Supreme Court to review decisions of state supreme courts upon a writ of error. In contrast to his usual brevity, Terry wrote at some length in dissent.

Admitting that claims of federal jurisdiction had been acquiesced in by courts of various states, the judge nevertheless attacked the principle and noted that it had never been admitted in Virginia, had "always been repudiated by Georgia," and had "lately been questioned in several other states."

[21]The People *v*. Gehr, 8 Cal., 362.   [22]Macauley *v*. Weller, 12 Cal., 500-533.

The section embodied the principles of a party that had passed away and its principles were "directly opposed to those adopted by the same tribunal in the late case of Dred Scott." Terry argued that the federal and state judiciary systems were entirely separate and that one did not have a supervisory power over the other. In many cases the jurisdiction was concurrent, "and in all such cases the judgment of the highest Courts of the system first acquiring jurisdiction is final and conclusive." The right to determine controversies of her citizens was "an essential element of sovereignty, which was possessed by each State before the adoption of the Constitution, and this right was not surrendered by that compact."[23]

For the most part, cases that came before the supreme court dealt with the everyday life of men and women in California. Perhaps the most important question that arose was the ownership of land, a problem complicated by Mexican law. In these cases Terry attempted to take into account background and local conditions in his effort to mete out justice. On occasion he even prefaced his opinions with a brief summary of life in California.

Considerable litigation centered around the holdings of Captain John A. Sutter and his son, John A. Sutter, Jr. Legal complications had developed from the sale of 2,200 lots in Sacramento by the younger Sutter to five men for $125,000. Questions arose concerning the deed, and it was to this phase of a difficult problem that Terry addressed himself. In case of doubtful wording of a deed, he wrote, the first inquiry was "what was the intention of the parties?" In his opinion the judge showed that he was taking into consideration time and circumstances surrounding the deed, for he declared:

Taking the deed from Sutter to Brannan and others as a whole, and testing it by the above rules, it is clear that Sutter intended to convey all his real estate in California; but, in view of the state of affairs then existing, he was unwilling to part with the legal title until his vendees had fully complied with the conditions of the sale.

[23]Ferris v. Coover, 11 Cal., 182-86.

Terry continued with a description of local conditions:

At the time of making the contract California had just completed the organization of a State Government; the operation of the judiciary system adopted had not been tested; the population was unsettled; sudden changes in the fortunes of individuals were constantly occurring, and personal security was of little value. It was, therefore, natural that a party disposing of valuable real estate should retain the legal title in himself as the best possible security for the payment of the purchase-money.[24]

In one of his cases Terry showed his interest in the small landowner in California as opposed to the land speculator. He wrote:

In order to prevent speculation, the possession of each settler is restricted to one hundred and sixty acres, and he is required to make affidavit that he has taken no other claim under the Act. If this could be done by proxy, the intention of the statute would be defeated, and the public lands of the state be monopolized by speculators, instead of furnishing farms to *bona fide* settlers.[25]

Later in private practice Terry was hostile to the railroad companies as he was in two opinions delivered during the fifties. Supported by Heydenfeldt, Terry held that if building a railroad made it necessary to erect fences "on either side of the line in order to protect crops," the farmer's land would be "injuriously affected to that extent," and the railroad should pay the costs of fence construction.[26] A man sued the railroad company when his horse, running at large, had been killed by a train. The lower court had refused to let the plaintiff prove that it was the custom of the state to allow animals to roam at large and instead held the owner to be guilty of negligence. Once again Terry delivered an opinion in the light of what he considered to be the surrounding circumstances. Declaring the action of the lower court to be in error, he wrote:

[24]Brannan *v.* Mesick, 10 Cal., 105-107. For details of this and related cases, see *John A. Sutter, Jr., Statement Regarding Early California Experiences,* ed. A. R. Ottley (Sacramento, 1943), pp. 36-37, and passim.

[25]Sweetland *v.* Froe, 6 Cal., 147.

[26]Sacramento Valley Railroad Company *v.* Moffatt, 6 Cal., 75-76.

The rule of common law which requires owners of cattle to keep them confined by their own close has never prevailed in California. Before the discovery of gold mines this was exclusively a grazing country; its only wealth consisting in vast herds of cattle, which were pastured exclusively upon uninclosed lands. This custom continued to prevail after the acquisition of the country by the United States, and has been in various instances recognized by the Legislature.[27]

The so-called "water-lots" in San Francisco caused great controversy. These were really slips along the water front. In 1851 the legislature had granted the land along the water front to the city of San Francisco. A struggle for the water slips developed when the plaintiffs in the action claimed title to the lots through purchase from the state land commissioner and the defendant set up title through the city under the act of 1851. Terry decided in favor of the latter,[28] but the matter was not settled, and when it came before the courts again bitter charges were made that Judges Field and Baldwin had financial interest in the outcome.[29]

A few miscellaneous cases give added insight into Terry's attitudes and opinions. His opinion in a case arising from the Homestead Act of 1851 indicated that women had a considerable distance to go before reaching equality under the law. The judge's attitude was one of protection rather than equality.[30]

The question of mining rights came frequently before the court. Terry delivered no momentous decisions on this problem, but rather followed his usual practice of dealing with such cases as they came in a practical fashion. He held the view of many Californians of his day toward the Chinese.

[27]Waters v. Moss, trustee of the Sacramento Valley Railroad Company, 12 Cal., 538.

[28]Hyman v. Read, 13 Cal., 444.

[29]The strongest charges were in an anonymous leaflet said to have been written by former Governor John McDougal, *The Gold Key Court or the Corruptions of a Majority of It* ([n. p., n. d.]), pp. 1-4.

[30]Pease v. Barbiers and Wife, 10 Cal., 440.

State legislation earlier had provided that no Indian or Negro could testify as a witness in a case involving a white man. This was a regulation with which Terry, a staunch Southerner, had no quarrel. Then, when the Chinese had become numerous and sentiment rose against them, the supreme court, in a decision written by Chief Justice Murray and concurred in by Judge Heydenfeldt, held that the term "Indian" used in the statute included the Chinese or Mongolian race. Murray went to some length to show common origin of the Chinese and Indians. In 1859 Terry, with Judge Field concurring, handed down a decision based on the earlier case and expressing a similar view.[31]

Like every judge, Terry occasionally found his judgment reversed. In 1858 he declared a Sunday-observance law unconstitutional. Field delivered a dissenting opinion. After Terry left the court, the issue came up again, and Terry's decision was reversed.[32]

Whatever opinion one may have of Terry's ability as a supreme court justice, there seems to be no doubt as to his integrity. The anonymous author of *The Gold Key Court*, who charged Baldwin and Field with corruption, had only the following to say of Terry: "At one time a certain Attorney was employed to bribe Terry, but Terry obstinately refused to sign the opinion. . . ." Even the San Francisco *Bulletin* during Vigilante days, it will be recalled, had admitted that Terry was personally honest. As far as rough behavior was concerned he was probably on the same level as his legal associates. A former Vigilante making a statement in the 1880's declared of Terry, "He was a rough fellow, and, sitting on the Supreme Court Bench, he would take out his pistol and lay it on his desk, and sit with his heels as high as he knew, and behave very ungentlemanly."[33] Further evidence is needed before one accepts this picture. A study of Terry's

[31]Speer *v.* See Yup Company, 13 Cal., 73.
[32]*Ex Parte* Newman, 9 Cal., 502; *Ex Parte* Andrews, 18 Cal., 678.
[33]Charles V. Gillespie statement, MS in the Bancroft Library, p. 10.

decisions indicates very clearly that he took his position seriously and respected its dignity.

There may be a little more truth in an episode recalled some forty years after the event. It was said that one day Terry was listening to the arguments of two lawyers of equal prominence. The controversy became heated and the two men finally came to blows. The bailiffs rushed in and separated the belligerents. The chief justice, however, made no motion and said nothing when the attorneys resumed their oral arguments. Later the attorney general, who had witnessed the affair, asked Terry why he had not stopped the fight. Somewhat startled by the question, the judge admitted that he should have intervened, but he said, "I assure you I didn't think of it; you see, they were both about the same size, and it was a fair fight, and I thought—well, perhaps, I ought to have interfered." One's confidence in this story is of course shaken by the narrator's assertion that there were *six* justices on the bench in addition to Terry.[34]

[34]Fred S. Myrtle, "Gleanings from Bench and Bar," *Bulletin* (San Francisco), June 20, 1896.

Chapter V

The Duelist

THE ACT for which David S. Terry is most widely known came as a tragic aftermath to a great political struggle in which he had played a secondary role. The titans in the California political arena during the 1850's were William M. Gwin and David C. Broderick. Two more dissimilar men could not easily have been found.

Gwin, about fifteen years older than Broderick and eighteen years the senior of Terry, was a Southerner by birth and training. His father, like Terry's grandfather, David Smith, had been an Indian fighter and friend of Andrew Jackson. Young Gwin received a good education for the times and in fact prepared for two professions, law and medicine. He practiced the latter until 1833 and then turned to politics in his home state, Mississippi. He soon gave evidence of his ability as a leader and by shrewd manipulation and management overcame a natural weakness as a public speaker. At the conclusion of a single term in the United States Congress, Gwin left politics for a time, apparently for financial reasons, and went into business in New Orleans.

When the gold rush to California started, Gwin, like others, saw in the new region possibilities of political reward. Standing before the Willard Hotel in Washington to watch Zachary Taylor's inaugural parade in March, 1849, Gwin told Senator Stephen A. Douglas that he was leaving for California and planned to return soon as a senator from the new state.[1] The Southerner made his way to the West Coast and with little

[1]Jeremiah Lynch, *A Senator of the Fifties* (San Francisco, 1911), p. 89.

difficulty moved into top political ranks. Attending the constitutional convention at Monterey, armed with copies of the Iowa and New York constitutions, he became a leading figure in the convention.

California, it will be recalled, had not waited for congressional action to prepare for statehood. Weary of the procrastination of the federal government, Californians held their convention, drafted a constitution, and selected members of congress, whose first task was to help lobby California into statehood. The two senators were John C. Frémont, who had gained a reputation as a pathfinder and who had participated in the military struggle in California during the Mexican War, and William M. Gwin. The latter not only secured the post he coveted, but when the two men drew lots for the longer term, the former Mississippian won.

The struggle in congress for statehood was protracted and bitter, but it was successful. Gwin, because of his ability and experience, soon controlled the federal patronage for his state. So effective was he in obtaining offices for impecunious sons of the Southern aristocracy that the San Francisco Customs House came to be known as the "Virginia Poor House."[2]

Such political control did not rest long unchallenged. Many men were ambitious for power in California, but the politician who began to emerge as the real threat to Gwin's supremacy was David C. Broderick. This California leader came from an entirely different social and political background than that of either Gwin or Terry. A native of Washington, D. C., he was essentially a product of New York City. On the death of his father, a stonemason, Broderick at the age of fourteen began the craft of his parent. He drifted into politics and as a member of the volunteer fire department became an apprentice in ward politics. Husky and of a truculent disposition, at times he used brawn as well as brain in the practice of his new trade.

In addition to increasing in experience and prominence

[2]John Currey, *The Terry-Broderick Duel* (Washington, D. C., 1896), p. 5.

in the Tammany Hall organization, Broderick became a saloon owner, although he was personally temperate. Though dissimilar in other ways, Broderick and Terry had one attribute in common, the ability to gain the friendship and support of a heavy-drinking, hard lot of men without participating in their excesses.

Broderick moved with some success up the Tammany ladder and in due course received its nomination for the house of representatives. Then he encountered reverses. He lost the election, his mother died, and his brother was killed in an accident. With his political rise checked and his family ties removed, Broderick eagerly embraced the opportunity for advancement in the rush to California. Like his great rival, Gwin, Broderick reportedly told a friend that he would return as a senator from California.

When Broderick arrived on the West Coast he found that a branch mint had not yet been established in California and that while there was plenty of gold in dust and nuggets there was a scarcity of coins and other customary media of exchange. Broderick and an associate, therefore, began the private production of gold coins. Since they made five-dollar gold pieces at a cost of four dollars and ten-dollar pieces for eight, and since the demand was ample, the partners for a time made satisfying profits.

But Broderick, like Gwin, had not come to California simply to acquire wealth. The former New Yorker soon began to put into practice the techniques he had learned so thoroughly at Tammany Hall. A volunteer fire department became the basis for the building of a political machine. Appointed to a vacancy in the California state senate in 1850, in the succeeding election Broderick secured the post in his own right. In 1851 he was elected president of the senate when the lieutenant governor became governor on the resignation of the incumbent Peter H. Burnett.

From the start Broderick's aim was the senate of the United States and not that of the state of California. While in the latter body and after he left it in 1852, the San Francisco politician worked steadily toward his goal. Unable to prevent the election of John B. Weller to succeed Frémont in 1851, Broderick concentrated on becoming the successor of William M. Gwin. The task, in view of Gwin's capabilities, was formidable. In 1854 Broderick made a daring and unorthodox attempt to bring about the election of a successor to Gwin a year before the expiration of the senator's term. His supporters gave as an excuse for the action the possibility that the legislature might fail to elect a senator in 1855, and California would be without one of its representatives in congress.

By a narrow margin the Gwin forces and other enemies of Broderick prevented his plan from succeeding. In the following year Broderick's prediction came true and the senate became deadlocked and elected no one to succeed Gwin. The story repeated itself in 1856. During this period Broderick was not yet strong enough to secure the election for himself, but he was able to keep anyone else from obtaining the post.

By 1857 Broderick knew that at last the goal he had been seeking was in reach. The passage of time had produced an unusual development, for in 1857 there were two senatorial posts to be filled. Senator Weller's term was expiring, whereas the post vacated by Gwin had been unfilled for two years. Normally upon meeting, the state senate would be expected to vote first for Gwin's successor, but Broderick was strong enough to select the long term. As a result when the senate convened it elected Broderick to replace John B. Weller for the six-year term.

The next problem was that of a successor to Senator Gwin. Of the numerous candidates the real contenders were Gwin and Milton S. Latham, collector of the port of San Francisco. Latham was a shrewd and able politician who in a few years by clever manipulation was able to reach his goal.[3] He was

[3] E. E. Robinson, "The Day Journal of Milton S. Latham," *California Historical Society Quarterly*, XI (1932), 3-28.

only thirty years of age in 1857, and was perhaps not as desperate for the senatorship as was his older rival, Gwin.

Broderick was in an enviable position. He was not only senator-elect, but he had the power to select the other senator as well. He and Gwin had no liking for each other; in fact their rivalry had contributed greatly to the split of the Democratic party in California. At the same time Broderick was not noticeably enthusiastic about Latham. The younger man had a strong will and would not easily be anyone's tool. Perhaps Broderick sensed that Latham's ability and ambition might constitute a menace to him. It is also possible that Broderick had no personal objection to Latham, but simply preferred another candidate. His real choice seems to have been a member of his own political organization, Joseph W. McCorkle. This little politician had an intense hatred for Latham, who not only had defeated him in the congressional race in 1852 but who in the suit for a young woman had emerged victorious as well. McCorkle was also a bitter opponent of Gwin and had fought a duel with him in 1853.

In 1857 McCorkle was not strong enough to obtain the election even with Broderick's help. It began to appear that the victor must be either Gwin or Latham if the post was to be filled. Broderick was in no hurry. He enjoyed his position and is said to have told a friend, "It is my turn now; and not one of them shall get his head to the front until I have pulled out his claws and put my brand on him."[4]

William M. Gwin was an astute politician. Much as he might dislike Broderick personally or detest his Tammany Hall tactics, he realized that if he expected re-election he must come to some sort of an understanding with the senator-elect. He was also secretive enough in his own political ways to wish as few persons as possible to know of any overtures he might make. Instead of meeting Broderick openly, he sought him secretly in the night. By careful prearrangement on Sunday night, January 11, 1857, Broderick met him in

[4]O'Meara, *Broderick and Gwin*, pp. 158-59.

his room in the Magnolia Hotel. Broderick no doubt enjoyed the meeting, for he believed that he was pulling Gwin's claws and putting his brand on him. When the older politician left the room he took with him a verbal promise of support by Broderick. In return he had written two letters, one for the public and one for Broderick. Each contained a pledge that Gwin would no longer attempt to control the patronage if re-elected.

Broderick's next move is a little more difficult to explain. It appears that he went to Latham and endeavored to exact a similar pledge in return for his support. It is impossible to know what Broderick actually planned to do, for Latham declined to make such a promise. One suggestion is that Broderick intended to double-cross either Gwin or Latham. Another is that he sought to outwit both of them by making public the pledges of each and then profiting by their discomfiture to put McCorkle into office.[5]

Having failed to brand Latham, Broderick fulfilled his pledge to Gwin and for that and other reasons Gwin won re-election. Shortly thereafter California newspapers published the statement Gwin had prepared at Broderick's insistence. Writing that the struggle over patronage had caused a great deal of friction and nearly cost him two elections, Gwin continued, "From patronage, then, and the curse it entails, I shall gladly in future turn, and my sole labor and ambition henceforth shall be to deserve well of the State." He concluded with an open acknowledgment of the support given him by Broderick.[6] The letter produced a sensation, and among the disappointed candidates and their friends there were angry charges of a corrupt bargain. There was nothing they could do, however, for the voting was over and the principals had no further comments to make.

Toward the end of January, 1857, the California senators

[5]John S. Hittell, *A History of the City of San Francisco and incidentally of the State of California* (San Francisco, 1878), pp. 299-300.

[6]Quoted in O'Meara, pp. 184-85.

left by vessel and the Isthmus route for the national capital. In Washington Broderick soon found that he had underrated his colleague. Although skilled in state politics, Broderick was a fledgling senator. Gwin on the other hand was on familiar ground and among friends, not the least of whom was the newly inaugurated president, James Buchanan. The struggle for control in Kansas had increased the bitterness between the North and the South. Buchanan, although from Pennsylvania, had strong ties of friendship with Southern politicians. Essentially conservative and a lover of the Union, he attempted to keep peace and harmony by leaning over backward in his attitude toward the South.

In making appointments to federal posts in California it was to be expected that the president would observe "senatorial courtesy" and follow the recommendations of the senators from that state, since he and they were Democrats. As a result of Gwin's pledge, Broderick thought he had the patronage firmly in his grasp. He counted without Buchanan and he counted without Gwin. The president soon became unfavorably disposed toward the junior California senator. Broderick lost little time in becoming outspoken on the issues of the day, and he lustily took the extreme Northern view. He was especially critical of the president's stand on Kansas. Then, because of Broderick's own stubbornness, Buchanan found the excuse for refusing to follow his recommendations regarding the patronage. In his eagerness for office Broderick had made many promises. It is possible that he had given pledges of support to different men for the same positions. At any rate, when the president requested Broderick to make his recommendations in writing, the senator refused. Buchanan, therefore, declined to take the recommendations.

The explanation of Broderick's failure to control patronage is more complex than a difference of opinion over written recommendations. If Broderick had sought to double-cross Gwin by going to Latham in California, the senior senator neatly returned the favor in Washington. Outwardly Gwin remained completely aloof from the struggle for patronage. He deluded Congressman C. L. Scott, a devious politician of no mean order himself. Scott wrote, "Old Gwin has been merely a looker on, & B seems to have him by some spell or charm, for he does not even make a show of a fight."[7] Gwin's inaction was having its desired results. The California members of the house of representatives were anti-Broderick, and when they saw Broderick's action and Gwin's passiveness, they organized and carried the patronage fight against Broderick. Scott explained, "McKibben, Denver, Weller, myself & others have made a fierce fight against Broderick."[8] In view of the circumstances it was not necessary for Gwin to enter directly into the patronage struggle. Others were fighting it for him. In one instance, however, Gwin very definitely broke his pledge of abstinence from seeking positions for his friends. On March 19, 1857, he wrote his good friend, J. W. Mandeville, that he was the only one the senator would work for, and on April 3 he wrote that in his case he was going directly to the president to recommend him for a federal post.[9]

President Buchanan seems to have been aware of what was transpiring. Gwin, without comment but undoubtedly with pleasure, reported to Mandeville a conversation he had had on April 4 with the president: "I spent yesterday in visiting the Cabinet and the President with whom I had talks they will not forget it especially the latter. It was our first of which I informed him when he replied that it was true I did not come near him was committed to no appointment and yet how the devil did it happen that all my friends were appointed. I replied because they were the best men."[10]

Disgusted with the turn of events, Broderick left on April

[7]Scott to J. W. Mandeville, Mar. 18, 1857, Mandeville MSS in the Huntington Library.

[8]Ibid.

[9]Mandeville MSS. On Apr. 3 Gwin wrote, "I intend to see the President in the morning and make a strong personal appeal to him."

[10]Apr. 5, Mandeville MSS.

5 to return to California. Gwin accurately commented, "His object is to carry the State Convention, nominate his friends for the State offices & censure the Administration for the appts. made."[11] Broderick failed in his effort to gain ground politically in California, and the state offices went against him in the ensuing election. Returning to Washington, he made the cleavage between himself and the president even wider as the Democratic party split on the question of Kansas. He aligned himself closely with Senator Stephen A. Douglas of Illinois, who emerged as the leading Democratic critic of the administration. By this time Broderick had definitely lost the patronage, which was dominated primarily by Congressman Scott and Senator Gwin.

The conflict within the Democratic party reached a climax in 1859. At that time both senators returned to California to take part in the campaign. Gwin sponsored the election of state officials who would support the national administration and the pro-Southern Lecompton constitution for Kansas. Broderick backed candidates who took the opposite view. However, his forces were handicapped to a certain extent by the entry of a new party into national politics. Since the Republicans held similar views on the Lecompton issue to those of the Broderick or anti-Lecompton Democrats, the danger existed that they might split the Northern vote and let the Lecomptonites win.

The relationship between Gwin and Broderick had changed completely since the former had announced his debt to Broderick in 1857. By 1859 the junior senator was convinced that Gwin was a traitorous scoundrel who had violated his pledge. Broderick was not an especially good speaker, but he took the stump for his candidates. The result was one of the most bitterly contested campaigns in California history.

Broderick partly compensated for his weakness in oratory by turning to thunderous denunciation and even invective. His main target was of course Senator Gwin. Forgetting or

[11]Gwin to Mandeville, Apr. 3, Mandeville MSS.

ignoring the fact that he had publicly stated that there had never been a bargain between the two senators, Broderick now openly charged that Gwin had violated his agreement. On August 9, 1859, speaking in Sacramento, Broderick declared, "I come tonight to arraign before you two great criminals, Milton S. Latham and William M. Gwin."[12] On another occasion he said, "Gwin was dripping with corruption."[13] As the campaign became more heated Broderick produced the second letter Gwin had written to secure re-election. The first had been written to the public; the second was to Broderick himself, and in it Gwin flatly promised, "Provided I am elected, you shall have the exclusive control of this patronage, so far as I am concerned."[14]

Like Broderick, Gwin was no great public speaker, but like Broderick, he could muster strong words when the occasion arose. He could not deny the authenticity of the letter but he could say that he had made a mistake and that if the bargain was corrupt Broderick had a part in it as well. He declared that Broderick's version of the senatorial election was "a tissue of falsehoods from beginning to end," and he said of his colleague, "He deceived me, and then tried to ruin me."[15] Among those supported by Gwin was Milton S. Latham, Lecompton candidate for governor.

The speech made by David S. Terry that was to have such tragic consequences seems mild in comparison with the public charges made by Gwin, Broderick, and other participants of the campaign. Two factors had militated against Terry's political career. His experience with the Vigilance committee alienated certain voters. The charges thrown at him, whether true or false, had left their scars. Other voters, fewer in numbers, were impressed by what they considered to have been his fight for the preservation of law and order under the constitution.

[12]O'Meara, p. 208.   [13]Ibid., p. 211.
[14]Ibid., p. 212; Lynch, op. cit., pp. 194-98.
[15]O'Meara, p. 213.

Far more important than his involvement with the Vigilantes was the fact that Terry was not only a Southerner, but an extreme Southerner. Gwin for example was more moderate in his aims and actions. He was a strong sympathizer with the South and its customs, but when he came to California he made no effort to transplant slavery, but instead helped bring California into the Union as a free state. Terry on the other hand was an avowed believer in the doctrine of states' rights. He later wrote:

I was born and reared in a southern state and believed in the doctrine of the ultra states' rights men of the South. I desired to see the government of this state in the hands of those whose political opinions coincided with my own.[16]

Terry believed as strongly in the right to own slaves in the South and hoped to extend that right to California:

I desired to change the Constitution of the state by striking out that clause prohibiting slavery and for several years entertained strong hopes of effecting this object or, failing in that, to divide the state and thus open a portion of California to Southerners and their property.[17]

Since Broderick represented views diametrically opposed to those held by Terry, it was natural for the latter to work against Broderick's candidates in 1859. Being a member of the supreme court, he did not campaign actively, but he did make one speech. His term of office was drawing to a close, and he sought re-election. The Lecompton Democrats held a convention in the Congregational church in Sacramento on June 22. Terry and the other candidates whose names were placed in nomination were called upon to explain their views on the current issues.

[16]Charles R. Boden, "David Terry's Justification," *The Wasp*, LV (1933), 3. This article contains a statement written some years after the event by Terry justifying his actions in the duel. Hereafter cited as *Terry's Justification*.

[17]Ibid.

In his address to this convention Terry attacked both the Republicans and the anti-Lecompton faction of the Democratic party. The Republican party, he asserted, was distinctly a sectional party, "based on no principle, excepting the abusing of one section of the country and the aggrandizement of another." The judge then declared of the anti-Lecomptonites that they were the "miserable remnant of a faction sailing under false colors, trying to obtain votes under false pretenses." He charged that they were "the followers of one man, the personal chattels of a single individual, whom they are ashamed of. They belong, heart and soul, body and breeches, to David C. Broderick." The members of this faction were "yet ashamed to acknowledge their master" and called themselves Douglas Democrats. With satirical bitterness, the speaker then declared that if they sailed under the flag of Douglas it was not that of Stephen A. Douglas, but "the banner of the black Douglass, whose name is Frederick, not Stephen."[18]

Terry had explained his views. Possibly they were too strong, or perhaps other factors affected the voting. Whatever the cause, the convention passed over Terry and nominated W. W. Cope for justice of the supreme court. There had been a stiff fight for the congressional nomination, and on June 24 the *Bulletin* suggested that the supporters of the victorious candidate, C. L. Scott, had traded votes with Cope's followers.

The Sacramento *Union* reported extensively Terry's address. A few days later, on the morning of June 26, David C. Broderick sat at breakfast in the dining room of the International Hotel in San Francisco. Nearby were Mr. and Mrs. A. A. Selover and across the way, within easy speaking distance, the wife of Colonel James was talking to Judge Terry's former law partner, Duncan W. Perley. Broderick was reading the Sacramento *Union* and when he saw the account of Terry's speech he said to Perley, "I see your friend Terry has

[18]Quoted in O'Meara, pp. 218-19. The *Daily Evening Bulletin*, highly critical of Terry, complimented the convention for rejecting Terry and did not report his speech.

94

been abusing me at Sacramento." Perley asked for particulars and Broderick continued, "The damned miserable wretch, after being kicked out of the convention, went down there and made a speech abusing me." The senator then declared, "I have defended him at times when all others deserted him." Broderick was referring to the Vigilante affair and claimed that he had paid three newspapers to defend Terry. The senator concluded by saying of Terry:

I have hitherto spoken of him as an honest man—as the only honest man on the bench of a miserable, corrupt Supreme Court— but now I find I was mistaken. I take it all back. He is just as bad as the others.[19]

Perley had a temper that was almost the equal of Terry's. He asked, for verification, whom Broderick was calling a "wretch" and when Broderick repeated the charge, Perley said that he would tell the judge of the remarks made. Broderick told him to do as he wished. The discussion became increasingly heated and before it was over Perley challenged Broderick to a duel. He had some difficulty finding anyone who would carry the formal challenge to the senator, but finally S. H. Brooks consented to bear the document.

Since Broderick had already fought one duel, it could not be expected that he would refuse on moral grounds. Broderick's reply, dated June 29, could hardly have soothed Perley's disposition. The senator declined to meet the challenger. The reasons given were somewhat unusual. He told Perley, "Your own sense of propriety should have taught you that the positions we relatively occupy are so different as to forbid my acceptance of your challenge." Broderick noted that only a few days earlier, Perley had announced that he was a subject of Great Britain. "The giving or accepting a challenge could not therefore affect your political rights, as you are not a citizen of the United States." Apparently what the senator was saying was that an American citizen could fight only

[19]O'Meara, p. 220.

another American citizen in a duel. The second reason for declining the challenge had more validity. Broderick wrote that under no circumstances would he engage in a duel during the political campaign. If he accepted Perley's challenge, others might challenge him also, "for the purpose of accomplishing a political object, or to obtain public notoriety."

Some people have interpreted one statement in Broderick's letter as bait for a later challenge. Having informed Perley that he was not good enough to fight him, Broderick wrote, "If compelled to accept a challenge, it could only be with a gentleman holding a position equally elevated and responsible." There are those who say that possibly Broderick was thinking of the other senator from California. It is probably safe to say that he did not have Terry in mind.[20]

Perley informed Terry of Broderick's verbal assault. If Terry's later comments are to be believed, he had meant no personal attack on Broderick in his speech at the Lecompton convention. He explained:

At the time I had not the most distant idea that those remarks could be construed into a personal offense by anyone and least of all by Mr. Broderick. No personal offense to anyone was intended and, if I had been called upon, I would have so stated readily and with pleasure. I spoke of a political party and of him as its leader and not one word was said as to his private character or which could possibly be regarded as a reflection upon his honor or integrity.[21]

On the other hand Terry became convinced that Broderick had made personal charges against him in his talk to Perley. He determined that he could not let the matter rest, but since Broderick had stated that he would accept no challenge during the campaign, Terry waited.

[20]In a letter to *The Overland Monthly* (2nd Ser., XIII [1889], 105), John S. Hittell asserted that Broderick wrote the letter to Perley to draw a challenge from Gwin and declared this purpose to a friend, Frank Soulé, saying that he "wanted to kill old Gwin." Hittell stated that he received this information from Soulé. The *Daily Evening Bulletin* (Sept. 9, 1859) wrote of Perley as "the recipient of a gross insult at Mr. Broderick's hands at the public table of the International Hotel in June last."

[21]*Terry's Justification*, p. 23.

The temptation to let the matter drop must have been great. There was nothing personally to be gained from a duel. His Vigilante experience made him well aware of the vilification the press and segments of the public were capable of hurling at him. His term as a supreme court justice would close at the end of the year and once again he would have to build up his legal practice. Good will was essential to success, and unfavorable publicity arising from a duel might well block this professional comeback. Then there was his family to consider. Cornelia Terry had stood by him through the ordeal of the San Francisco imprisonment. Should he subject her once more to the mental torture of knowing that his life hung in the balance or to the glare of publicity that would accompany a duel? Intensely fond of his three boys, he must have pondered the question of their welfare should he be killed in the duel. But there were even more powerful factors involved. His heritage and training perhaps led him inexorably toward a showdown with Broderick. Back in 1847 old Hiram Runnels had written of young Terry, "If high toned chivalry and unquestionable integrity serve as a recommendation he has them." What seems to have swung the balance toward disaster was the fact that the press had given publicity to the matter. The judge noted bitterly that the press which had been so outspoken against dueling had seen fit to broadcast the news of the affair throughout the country. If the news had not gone beyond California, Terry stated, he might have been constrained to let the matter drop. "It had reached my early home, had been read by those whose good opinion I prize above all things. I could not endure that those friends should hear of the slander and not hear also that it had been retracted or atoned for."[22]

Mrs. Terry went to their friend, Sam Brooks, and begged him to dissuade the judge from the step she feared he would take. Brooks made the effort, but by that time Terry had reached his decision. "Never before has any politician or

[22]Ibid.

paper, in all that has been said about me, cast a reflection upon my integrity," he told his friend, and he added, "No one shall do it."[23] When Brooks asked what he intended to do, Terry replied that if Broderick did not apologize by the end of the campaign he would challenge him.

The campaign was bitter, and if Broderick thought of anyone it was of Gwin, Latham, or Scott, for Terry had not taken an active role in the campaign. The Lecompton Democrats had profited by the split in Northern sentiment between the anti-Lecompton Democrats and Republicans to make nearly a clean sweep of the offices. Milton Latham, who had been strongly supported by Gwin, had been elected governor.

On election day Terry wrote a letter of resignation from his judgeship that was to expire in a month or two and gave it to friends to keep until the course of events became known. He then went to Oakland and consulted with two or three friends. Sam Brooks evidently made another conciliatory effort and then acquiesced in Terry's decision. The judge had already selected two men to act as seconds in case Broderick refused to retract his statements. They were both San Franciscans, Colonel Tom Hayes and Calhoun Benham. Benham, who had been an active member of the Law-and-Order party in 1856, was an aggressive and impulsive individual who may have helped push Terry toward the duel. On the other hand when the event finally came Benham proved to be a most efficient second. Brooks apparently did not become a second because of his official position as state controller.

Although he had determined to challenge Broderick, Terry still hoped that Broderick would find it possible to retract. The best view of the preliminary steps leading to the duel is through the letters of the interested parties. The first came from Terry to Broderick, who had returned to San Francisco after the campaign. Terry wrote:

[23]Carroll Douglas Hall, *The Terry-Broderick Duel* (San Francisco, 1939), pp. 27-28. This is probably the most satisfactory treatment of the duel.

Sir: Some two months since, at the public table of the International Hotel in San Francisco, you saw fit to indulge in certain remarks concerning me, which were offensive in their nature. Before I had heard of the circumstance, your note of 20th of June, addressed to Mr. D. W. Perley, in which you declared that you would not respond to any call of a personal character during the political canvass just concluded, had been published.

I have, therefore, not been permitted to take any notice of those remarks until the expiration of the limit fixed by yourself. I now take the earliest opportunity to require of you a retraction of those remarks. This note will be handed to you by my friend, Calhoun Benham, Esq., who is acquainted with its contents, and will receive your reply.[24]

Broderick discussed the challenge with friends, some of whom advised him to retract. The senator, however, came to his own decision and that evening sent his reply to Terry. "The remarks used by me in the conversation referred to may be a subject of future misrepresentation; and for obvious reasons, I have to desire you to state what were the remarks that you designate in your note as offensive, and of which you require of me a retraction."

The reply was hardly conciliatory. On the other hand, if there was to be a duel over words, it was legitimate to know precisely what the words were. After all, several months had elapsed since the incident in the International Hotel. Terry complied, and told Broderick that the remarks he was said to have made were, "I have heretofore considered and spoken of him (myself) as the only honest man on the Supreme Court bench, but I now take it all back." "Thus," continued Terry, "by implication reflecting on my personal and official integrity." The precise words, he told Broderick, were not important. "What I require is a retraction of any words which were used calculated to reflect on my character as an officer or a gentleman."

[24]Most of the correspondence preceding the duel was published by Calhoun Benham and Thomas Hayes in the *Democratic Standard* (Sacramento), Sept. 16, 1859. A convenient source for the letters is Ben C. Truman, *The Field of Honor* (New York, 1884), pp. 406-10.

That evening Broderick's reply came. It showed that Broderick, like Terry, had reached a decision. He would not retract.

Sir: Yours of this date has been received. The remarks made by me were occasioned by certain offensive allusions of yours concerning me made in the convention at Sacramento and reported in the *Union* of June 25. Upon the topic alluded to in your note of this date, my language, so far as my recollection serves me, was as follows:

"During Judge Terry's incarceration by the Vigilance Committee I paid two hundred dollars a week to support a newspaper in his (your) defense. I have also stated, heretofore, that I consider him (Judge Terry) the only honest man on the Supreme Bench; but I take it all back."

You are the proper judge as to whether this language affords good ground for offence. I remain, etc.

To David S. Terry there could be but one answer to such a letter.

Sir: Some months ago you used language concerning me, offensive in its nature. I waited the lapse of a period of time fixed by yourself before I asked reparation therefor at your hands. You replied, asking specifications of the language used which I regarded as offensive. In another letter I gave you the specification and reiterated my demand for a retraction. To this last letter you reply, acknowledging the use of the offensive language imputed to you and not making the retraction required. This course on your part leaves me no other alternative but to demand the satisfaction usual among gentlemen, which I accordingly do. Mr. Benham will make the necessary arrangements.[25]

Broderick replied by stating that arrangements for him had been placed in the hands of his friend, J. C. McKibben.

The principals were out of the picture briefly while the seconds made the necessary preparations. Benham and Hayes met with McKibben and Broderick's other second, David Colton, former sheriff of Siskiyou County. After some disagreement, the four men worked out plans. Since Broderick

[25]Truman, pp. 408-409.

100

had been challenged, it was his right to determine the type of weapon and order the terms of the combat. Consequently his seconds presented the following rules and regulations:

1st. Principals to be attended by two seconds and a surgeon each; also by a person to load the weapons. This article not to exclude the drivers of the vehicles. If other parties obtrude, the time and place may be changed at the instance of either party.

2nd. Place of meeting, on the farm adjoining the Lake House ranch. The road to the farm house leaves the old Lake House road, where you strike the first fence on the Lake House property, about a mile before you reach the Lake House. There you take a road to the left, which brings you to the farmhouse, on the upper end of the lake (Laguna Merced), occupied by William Higgins. This is in the general neighborhood; the precise spot to be determined when the parties meet.

3rd. Weapons, dueling pistols.

4th. Distance, ten paces; parties facing each other; pistols to be held with the muzzles vertically downwards.

5th. Word to be given as follows, to wit: The inquiry shall first be made, "Gentlemen, are you ready?" Upon each party replying "Ready" the word "Fire" shall be given, to be followed by the words "One, two." Neither party to raise his pistol before the word "Fire," nor to discharge it after the word "two." The intervals between the words "Fire, one, two," to be exemplified by the party winning the word, as near as may be.

6th. The weapons to be loaded on the ground in the presence of a second of each party.

7th. Choice of position and the giving of the word to be determined by chance—throwing up a coin, as usual.

8th. Choice of the two weapons to be determined by chance, as in article 7th.

9th. Choice of the respective weapons of parties to be determined on the ground, by throwing up a coin, as usual; that is to say, each party bringing their pistols, and the pair to be used to be determined by chance, as in article 7th.

Time, Monday, 12th September, 1859, at 5½ o'clock A.M.[26]

[26]O'Meara, pp. 232-34.

Terry's seconds objected to some of the suggested regulations. They opposed conducting the duel in either San Francisco or San Mateo counties, and they protested at the arrangement of fire, which was to stop at "two" instead of the customary "three." Benham and Hayes thought the suggestion of a short count was designed to give an edge to Broderick, who was not only an excellent shot but also was in the habit of firing rapidly. When Terry heard of the rule he decided to raise no objection lest he be charged with attempting to withdraw from the duel on a technicality. The place of meeting likewise remained as Broderick's seconds had stipulated.

News of the impending duel spread rapidly, and a number of friends of both men attempted to effect a compromise. John Nugent, editor of the San Francisco *Herald*, and A. C. Crittenden were among those who made the effort, but all were unsuccessful. During Saturday and Sunday the friends of Broderick boasted that he would be victorious. Colonel A. J. Butler reportedly turned away would-be peacemakers with the comment, "It is no use. You are too late. The fight has got to come, and this is the best time for it." He predicted, "Broderick never had a better chance, and he isn't going to get hurt. He can hit the size of a ten-cent piece at his distance every time. These 'Chivs' have got to learn that there is one man they can't back down." Even Broderick himself, before leaving for the field Monday morning, told his friend John White, "Don't you fear, John; I can shoot twice to Terry's once; beat him shooting every time."[27]

Judge Terry spent Sunday night at the home of his second, Colonel Hayes; Broderick, at the house of a friend. At one or two in the morning, Terry, Brooks, and Benham rode by horseback along the Cliff House road and over to the ravine which they thought was to be the rendezvous. The night was cold, and they wrapped saddle blankets around their legs as they waited. Finally Benham decided to look for the other

[27]Ibid., pp. 235-36.

party and found that they had been waiting in another ravine.

Since news of the duel had spread, a large number of witnesses braved the morning chill. One of the spectators, Martin J. Burke, chief of police of San Francisco, stepped forward, armed with appropriate legal documents from San Francisco and San Mateo counties, and arrested the would-be duelists for disturbing the peace. The two men submitted to the officer and later in the day appeared before Judge Coon. Since there had been no duel as yet there was no breach of the peace, and after some deliberation the judge dismissed the case.[28]

Burke's action merely delayed matters. The *Bulletin* predicted, "It is supposed they will fight within a day or two." Actually the seconds met Monday and determined to carry the duel through the following morning.

The delay caused a change in Terry's attending physician. Dr. Dan Aylette, a friend from Stockton, had accompanied him on Monday morning and took with him another physician, Dr. William Hammond, not previously known to Terry. When Burke interrupted the proceedings, Dr. Aylette thought the duel would not take place for several days and went home to Stockton. After the decision was made to meet Tuesday morning, Terry asked Dr. Hammond to be his physician and the latter accepted.

The duel was scheduled for seven in the morning. Terry and his friends spent the night at a nearby farmhouse and breakfasted before leaving for the ravine. Broderick and his seconds passed what was apparently a miserable night at the Lake House. This was a little-used inn in which the cots were hard, the bedcovering insufficient, and the fleas multitudinous. To add to the discomfort, the party was unable to secure so much as a cup of coffee before leaving for the rendezvous.

The second time and place of meeting were as poorly kept secret as had been the first. Between sixty and seventy persons

[28]Burke was anti-Terry, possibly in part because he had been a member of the executive committee of the Vigilance committee of 1856. Burke statement, MS in the Bancroft Library.

had traveled to witness the event.[29] This time, however, Martin J. Burke was not present. He had been so annoyed by the judge's release of the two men that he "determined to take no further part in the proceedings."[30]

The dueling pistols used have provoked sharp controversy. Friends of Broderick have charged that he was deliberately maneuvered into the use of pistols with which Terry was familiar and he was not, and that more than this, the particular pistol that he was handed to use had a faulty mechanism.[31] The view of Terry's supporters is that the pistols were alike and that Terry had fired them but once or twice.[32]

Each side had brought pistols. Terry's seconds won the toss for choice of weapons and selected those they had brought. These were pistols owned by Dr. Aylette. Jo Beard, at one time clerk of the supreme court, was their former owner. They were French dueling pistols, light in weight, and with a barrel about a foot in length. They possessed hair triggers, and it was charged by some and denied by others that one was more delicately adjusted than the other.

As the time for the duel drew near, tension noticeably increased. Broderick's physician did not contribute to equanimity. Dr. Hammond had sat quietly down on the grass, with none of his equipment in evidence. Dr. Loehr on the other hand had with him a large sack from which protruded a saw, and which rattled as he walked. Broderick's seconds had won for him the choice of ground and the giving of the word. They

[29]An anonymous witness wrote probably the most detailed account of the duel. Reprinted in Shuck, op. cit., pp. 287-91. This witness, whose account is dated Sept. 14, 1859, counted 71 persons present, including the participants.

[30]Burke statement, MS in the Bancroft Library.

[31]Judge John Currey was especially bitter on this subject, and charged not only that one of the pistols had a trick trigger but that Terry had practiced frequently with the pistols. Op. cit., pp. 24-29. For an opposite view see J. W. Terry to Dumas Malone, Sept. 17, 1934, MS in the Bancroft Library.

[32]O'Meara (p. 234) declared that the pistols had "hair-triggers, evenly and equally adjusted," that they had been used previously in duels, and that no difference had been seen in their shooting qualities. He stated that Terry had fired the pistol only twice prior to the duel.

gave their man the advantage of a rising sun to his back. Colonel Hayes stepped off the ten paces, a distance that to one spectator looked "murderously close."[33]

It is probable that as the two men faced each other Terry had a physical and psychological edge on his opponent. It was not a matter of courage. Broderick, however, was run down physically, and this weakness tended to make him more susceptible to the terrible strain to which both were exposed. The recent political campaign possibly had been more nerve-racking for Broderick than for Terry, although it must be remembered that Broderick's own position had not been at stake and Terry had lost his. It is true that Broderick had not been accustomed to the barnstorming type of electioneering in which he had been engaged. One writer states that he may have had pneumonia;[34] another flatly asserts that at the time of the duel the senator had both diarrhea and piles.[35]

Sam Brooks loaded Judge Terry's pistol, and a gunsmith, Bernard Lagoarde, who had brought the unused weapons for Broderick, loaded the pistol for the senator. Then came the customary procedure of searching the participants for armor of any kind. In the earlier duel with Smith, Broderick's watch had stopped the bullet and saved his life. McKibben, Broderick's second, made a perfunctory move at Terry. Benham on the other hand went to Broderick and made a thorough check. One is tempted to agree with Broderick's friends, who insist that the second was trying deliberately to irritate the senator, although Benham was acting within his rights. Broderick had already handed his watch and money to McKibben, and Terry had given the contents of his pockets to Benham, who casually tossed the change on the ground.

Throughout the entire proceedings, Terry's seconds conducted themselves in a fashion that contributed to the psycho-

[33]Shuck, p. 289.
[34]Lynch, p. 216.
[35]Hittell, *History of San Francisco*, p. 309.

logical edge held by their principal. They went at their work as if they thoroughly knew their business and at all times had an air of complete confidence. Broderick's seconds in contrast seemed unsure of themselves and have been charged with acts of omission and commission. Even the senator himself was later critical of his seconds. Leonidas Haskell, one of Broderick's friends, was noticeably nervous.

The worst failure of the Broderick seconds, according to their critics, was in permitting the use of the Beard dueling pistols. When criticized later, however, McKibben drew attention to the fact that Terry's seconds had won the toss and had their choice of weapons. McKibben examined the pistol to be used by Broderick and pronounced himself satisfied.[36]

The morning had been cool, and the participants wore their overcoats until the preliminaries had been completed. At last they took their positions as indicated by Benham. The men removed their overcoats and took their pistols. Terry held his weapon for a moment behind his back, then brought it around and rested it before him on his left hand. According to an unfriendly witness, "Mr. Terry's lips were compressed, his countenance darkly sallow, and his whole appearance betrayed that of a man without fear, as well as without religious constraint." The same spectator observed that Broderick "on being handed the pistol, anxiously examined it, and at intervals measured with his eye the ground between himself and his adversary." His frock coat bothered him, and the spectator thought that if someone had offered the senator a pin to pull the front tails together he would have accepted the gift. This witness wrote of Broderick: "The muscles of his face were strong, and his visage unrelaxed in every particular. His lips, when not conversing, were compressed, and his whole bear-

[36]Shuck, p. 289. J. W. Terry quotes Brooks as saying "Terry was no better acquainted with them [the pistols] than was Broderick." He also quoted a statement by McKibben printed in *The Washington Post*, Aug. 16, 1889, that "the pistols were sent for a month or two previous by Senator Broderick who had [sent] for them at that time and were thoroughly examined!" J. W. Terry to Dumas Malone, Sept. 17, 1934, MS in the Bancroft Library.

ing was that of a man who was about to meet a great issue, and who was firmly prepared for it."[37]

Calhoun Benham read the terms of the duel as agreed upon. Broderick's seconds had won the toss for the inquiry, as it was called, and David Colton prepared to put the question to the contestants. Benham noted that Broderick was holding his pistol at an obtuse angle instead of vertically, as the articles had prescribed. McKibben adjusted the pistol as requested. Then either Benham or Brooks stepped to Terry and whispered something to him. The judge's enemies hint that he was told at this time that Broderick had a faulty pistol. Others are of the opinion that Terry was simply advised to raise the brim of his hat for better sight. Whatever was said, Terry adjusted his hat.

"Gentlemen, are you ready?" asked Colton.

Terry answered immediately, but Broderick was still apparently adjusting the pistol to the feel of his hand and delayed for a moment before answering, "Ready."

In measured tones, the ex-sheriff of Siskiyou said, "Fire— one—two."

Almost immediately on hearing the "one" Broderick fired. The aim was straight, but the bullet plowed into the ground nine or ten feet in front of him. Before Colton had said "two" Terry fired. There appeared what a witness called "a slight show of dust on the right lapel" where Broderick had been hit. With a convulsive move, the senator fell to the ground.[38]

If Broderick's seconds had been poor, his physician was utterly inadequate. It was not until Terry's physician offered his services that Broderick began to get medical attention. The senator rallied so well after bandaging and taking a little brandy that Dr. Hammond retired from the scene under the impression that the wound was not fatal. Friends started to

[37]Shuck, p. 289. After the duel the *Daily Evening Bulletin* published extracts from several other papers stating that Broderick had been nervous and Terry calm. Sept. 14.

[38]Shuck, pp. 290-291; Hall, op. cit., pp. 72-74.

take Broderick to the home of Leonidas Haskell, whose nervousness prior to the duel now seemed to have been well grounded.

After the shot, not knowing the seriousness of the wound, Brooks told Terry to remain where he was. The judge has been credited with making a number of statements on seeing Broderick fall. One was that he told Benham that he had shot too high or too far out. Terry's critics have used this alleged statement to attempt to prove that Terry was a crack shot. Others assert that Terry made a loud remark upon hitting Broderick. The unfriendly witness, however, who had described Terry as a man showing no religious constraint, stated that the judge made no comment that was audible to anyone except his second.

Benham was convinced that Broderick was at least dangerously wounded and that the duel was at an end. Terry, therefore, left the scene of the engagement. Colonel Hayes's brother had secured a boat, and in it Terry crossed the bay to Oakland.

On the long, hard ride back to Haskell's home near the Golden Gate, Broderick complained of a great heaviness in his chest. Physicians soon realized that the wound was serious, but through Wednesday and Thursday they still hoped that he might recover. By the end of the second day, however, it was clear that he was weakening, and at nine-twenty on the following morning the senator died.

Almost immediately the senator's friends raised the charge that the dueling pistols had not been alike, and that Broderick had been given one with a light trigger. Bernard Lagoarde, the gunsmith who had taken the other pair of pistols to the duel, made the accusation at the inquest, and the pro-Broderick press took up the cry. Whether or not it was true that Lagoarde found fault with all guns save his own, it would seem that he should have spoken earlier or not at all. Broderick's own seconds rose quickly to challenge him, and the Broderick newspaper, the San Francisco *News*, printed the following "card":

We are requested by Mr. McKibben and General Colton (the seconds of Mr. Broderick) to state that Mr. Lagoarde, the gunsmith, did not tell them, when on the ground, as he testified at the inquest, that there was any difference between the pistols used by Mr. Broderick and Judge Terry; and, that as far as their own careful examination of the weapons was concerned, there was no perceptible difference in the tightness of the triggers.[39]

More important was the charge that Broderick had been killed not so much for himself as for the cause he represented. As he lay dying, he allegedly said, "They have killed me because I was opposed to a corrupt administration and the extension of slavery." Whether or not he said these exact words, it appears that, as he became delirious toward the end, he expressed the fear that he was being persecuted.

The picture of Broderick as a martyr was further fixed in the public mind by the funeral ceremony. The popular speaker, Edward D. Baker, who was soon to leave San Francisco and win election to the United States Senate from Oregon, delivered the oration. He emphasized the theme that Broderick had been deliberately sought out and murdered for his beliefs. Lauding Broderick, Baker quoted the words attributed to the dying politician and elaborated eloquently on the theme. Broderick's death "was predicted by his friends; it was threatened by his enemies; it was the consequence of intense political hatred. His death was a political necessity, poorly veiled under the guise of a private quarrel." Baker then attacked the principle of dueling as a "shield blazoned with the name of chivalry to cover the malignity of murder."[40]

The charge that Broderick's death resulted from a Southern plot to remove him has been repeated so often that it must be examined. Broderick's real opponent was Gwin, who was certainly more of a leader of the Lecompton element than Terry. If there had been a plot, one would think that Gwin

[39]Quoted in *San Joaquin Republican*, Sept. 21. See also McKibben's testimony in ibid., Sept. 20, and a MS biography of D. C. Colton in the Bancroft Library.

[40]Lynch, pp. 229-38.

would know of it. Gwin spoke out clearly and definitely. "Not a word ever passed between him and Judge Terry on the subject," and no one was more surprised than he to hear of the impending duel.[41]

The case against Terry as a member of a plot to murder Broderick is not convincing. The only thing he could possibly hope to gain from the duel would have been lost if there had been tampering with the pistols, for what he sought to defend was his personal integrity.[42] The fact that the judge adhered to an extreme view of the code of chivalry is an indication that he would not violate that code by attempting to place a defective weapon in the hand of his opponent. It must be remembered that Broderick had the choice of weapons and selected the type with which he was the most proficient. The senator, as a matter of fact, had a better reputation as a pistol shot than did Terry. Broderick's seconds had prepared the terms of the duel, which were objected to in part by Terry's seconds but acquiesced in by the judge.

The duel was fairly fought and fairly won. Both men were brave, but Broderick was taut while Terry was relaxed. One fired prematurely, as a consequence; the other did not. The duel was a tragedy to both contestants. Broderick was dead, a symbol of the Northern point of view and a martyr to the cause. Terry was alive, but thereafter a symbol of murderous chivalry in the eyes of many and a man whose political career had come to an abrupt stop.

[41]"Memoirs of Hon. William M. Gwin," ed. W. H. Ellison, *California Historical Society Quarterly*, XIX (1940), 347.

[42]J. W. Terry wrote to Dumas Malone, "Terry told me, as he stated to others, that he did not have any desire to kill Broderick, and he sent the challenge solely for the purpose of vindicating his personal honor according to the usages of those days." Sept. 17, 1934, MS in the Bancroft Library.

Chapter VI

The Washoe Lawyer

FRIENDS met Terry when he arrived in Oakland after the duel. On hearing a false report that Broderick had already died, the judge showed that he, like Dr. Hammond and others, had not realized that the wound was fatal. He told John Freanor that he had shot "too far out," but that if he had had a moment's deliberation he would have fired to inflict no injury at all.[1] Broderick's reputation as a fast shot contributed to his death, for Terry as a consequence wasted no time in shooting and fired before he sensed that the senator's bullet had missed its mark.

Instead of returning to Sacramento, Terry went from Oakland to Stockton. He probably rode to his own ranch some distance from the city, although he may have remained for a time at the ranch of John McMullin, who had come to California with Terry in 1849 and had become a cattle rancher. He and his wife were close friends of the Terry family.

Broderick's death and the resultant attacks in the press made life very unpleasant for Terry. Instead of being termed the victor in an affair of honor, the judge found himself damned as a murderer. He resented the charges and determined to clear himself at least legally. When, therefore, a warrant was issued for his arrest, he welcomed the opportunity to face the courts.

It was hardly to be conceived that Terry would be punished for his participation in the duel. Broderick, Nugent, Gwin,

[1]O'Meara, p. 242. J. W. Terry states that his uncle later told him much the same thing. J. W. Terry to Dumas Malone, Sept. 17, 1934, MS in the Bancroft Library.

and other prominent California politicians had fought duels and Terry's engagement with Broderick was neither the first nor the last in California. Terry's difficulty arose from the prominence of the loser and from the fact that there had been rising public sentiment against duels. The code was on its way out, and as a late exponent of it he received unusual criticism.

Since dueling was illegal, Terry faced the charges of both San Francisco and San Mateo counties, although the duel had been fought in the latter county, not far from the boundary.[2] San Francisco police officers, however, sought the judge on his farm, and without protest he went to San Francisco. Three men, two from Stockton and one from San Francisco, stood as his surety, and he was released on a bond of $10,000. Bonds were also posted for him in San Mateo County.[3] By this time Terry was no longer a member of the California supreme court, for the resignation he had written in advance was forwarded to the authorities on the day following the duel.

The trial arising from the duel was to be long delayed, and Terry turned to the disheartening task of rebuilding his private practice. He had many friends, but some feared to show their friendship. Sectional bitterness had increased, and people throughout California were aligning themselves according to their places of former residence. Northern sentiment predominated, and moderate pro-Southerners watched their language and their friends.

Not everyone deserted Terry. On the day after the duel, Dr. Samuel Langdon wrote congratulating him on the "successful termination" of his "late difficulty." He stated, "The confidence I entertained in your superiority over B both as a marksman and as possessing more courage and nerve relieved

[2]Herman Schussler, *The Locality of the Broderick-Terry Duel* (San Francisco, 1916), passim.

[3]Wagstaff, pp. 215-17. Signing the bond with Terry were B. Walker Bours, G. W. Trahern, and M. F. Truett.

my mind of much anxiety I should have otherwise felt, knowing that you had right and justice on your side."[4]

The Terrys had already planned for the family to visit Texas. Now that the duel was over, Mrs. Terry and the boys took their departure and went east by way of Panama. In a letter written from his ranch, Terry gave his wife an indication of his next course of action. If business would not come to him in Stockton, he would go to it. In following the gold rush to California in 1849 he had found prosperity in the law. Perhaps in 1860 he could join the miners' rush to Nevada and gain legal success once again. Consequently he wrote, "Everybody is crazy about Washoe and I will probably go over there next week." He even had financial support. D. W. Perley, who had started a train of tragic events by eating breakfast near Senator Broderick in the International Hotel, had sold an interest in a claim and offered Terry $5,000 to invest in a joint account in Nevada.[5]

Pushing into Nevada is a spur of the Sierra Nevadas known as the Washoe Mountains. Before it finally dwindles into the Carson Sink, there are cut into its sides numbers of depressions, Truckee Meadows, Washoe, Pleasant, and Eagle valleys. The highest point in the spur is Mt. Davidson, or Sun Peak, as it was first called, which is gashed by deep canyons. In their lusty search for gold the California forty-niners had spread into these ravines and made placer strikes.

Later in the fifties a wandering sheepherder, "Old Pancake" Comstock, turned to the search for gold from sheer destitution. By coincidence he ran across the cabin and effects of the ill-starred Grosch brothers, who had been cheated by death from capitalizing on a rich find they had made. Comstock and others began to work the eroded material that surrounded the hard lode that was to bear his name. Finally

[4]Sept. 14, Terry MSS.

[5]Terry to Cornelia Terry, Mar. 9, 1860, Terry MSS. The *Alta California* (Jan. 21, 1860) mistakenly reported that Terry had left with his family, but the *Daily Evening Bulletin* exposed the error on the same day.

113

someone assayed the black rock that resisted so obdurately and its great wealth in silver and other minerals was disclosed.

The rush to Washoe differed considerably from the early rush to California. The forty-niners had sought placer gold with pan, rocker, or long tom. Nevada mining was for quartz, and was more comparable to California mining toward the end of the fifties than with that of the earlier period. For several reasons, claims in Nevada were highly speculative. One could not be sure where a vein went under the surface. Another complicating factor was that mining law was still fluid, and the proper method of determining legal right to a mineral deposit was still in doubt.[6] It was this last point that encouraged Terry to move his practice to Nevada. Of the lawyers who flocked to the Nevada mining regions, two emerged as the ablest and certainly the most spectacular. One was the dueling judge, David S. Terry, for whom Nevada was but a passing episode of the early sixties. The other, to whom Nevada was to become home and a place for political and financial prosperity, was William M. Stewart.

Like other great strikes, the rush to Nevada was a frenzied one. J. Ross Browne has lampooned himself and others who were infected by the lust for mineral wealth:

But, softly, good friends! What rumor is this? . . . As I live, it is a cry of Silver! Silver in WASHOE! Not gold now, you silly men of Gold Bluff; you Kern-Riverites; you daring explorers of British Columbia! But Silver—solid, pure Silver! Beds of it ten thousand feet deep! Acres of it!—miles of it!—hundreds of millions of dollars poking their backs up out of the earth ready to be pocketed! . . . "Sir," said my informant to me in strict confidence, no later than this morning, "you may rely upon it, for I am personally acquainted with a brother of the gentleman whose most intimate friend saw the man whose partner had just come over the mountains, and he says there never was the like on the face of the earth."[7]

[6]One of the best accounts of Nevada mining is in Eliot Lord, *Comstock Mining and Miners* (Washington, 1883), passim.

[7]J. Ross Browne, "A Peep at Washoe," *Harper's Magazine*, XXII (1860), 5. Reprinted in *Comstock Bonanza*, ed. Duncan Emrich (New York, 1950), pp. 6-48.

People from nearby regions flocked immediately to the scene, but most Californians waited for spring to thaw the heavy snows in the mountain passes before leaving for Nevada. David S. Terry was one of the early migrants, and left Stockton probably in middle or late March. With him went a number of friends, including Captain John Russell, Lance Nightingale, and William Burns.[8] Aside from the fact that they undoubtedly went on horseback and J. Ross Browne walked, they probably covered the same route as that taken by the writer who so amusingly described his experiences in "A Peep at Washoe."

The road to Nevada was a rough one, beaten down by pack trains headed for the mines with all types of supplies, mainly alcoholic, if Browne is to be believed, and pack trains returning to California with the wealth of Washoe. By the side of the road lay the inevitable decorations of an immigrant trail, broken wagons, discarded boxes, shattered kegs. The scenery was magnificent; the human habitations along the way stood in sordid contrast. Men crowded into rooms at Strawberry to cram down "Pork and beans, cabbage, beefsteak, sausages, pies, tarts, coffee and tea, eggs." Farther along the road, near-starvation replaced this plentiful fare. If inclement weather forced Terry and his associates into wayside inns, they were lucky if they secured "lay-outs," or the right to occupy a certain spot on the floor. The same type of crowded accommodations existed in the mining towns. In the main hotel in Virginia City, the "Indication" or "Hotel de Haystack," as Browne called it, each night "three hundred live men" jammed themselves into this "tinderbox not bigger than a first class hen-coop." And every morning there stumbled out three hundred men swearing at the fate that had directed them to the spot—"every man a dollar and a pound of flesh poorer."[9]

[8]William M. Stewart, *Reminiscences of Senator William M. Stewart of Nevada* (New York and Washington, 1908), p. 129; Wagstaff, p. 221, incorrectly states that Terry made the trip in the fall of 1860.

[9]Browne, op. cit., *Harper's Magazine*, XXII (1861), 17, 156.

When Terry arrived in Washoe, the mining boom was in full swing, and the usual accoutrements were in evidence in the towns. Quartz mining had brought with it stock speculation. One bought a share in a vein not yet well uncovered, and paid from several thousand dollars a foot in the Comstock Ledge to a few cents a foot in the more speculative Grizzly Ledge, Hell Roaring, or Gouge-Eye. Even if one bought stock, he did not know what he had because of the uncertainty of the mining laws. Although economically and socially a part of California, Nevada was at this time a part of the Territory of Utah. As lawyers poured into the region and as the possibilities for litigation increased with the multiplicity of claims, the demand grew for the establishment of a court of law.

President Buchanan had appointed John Cradlebaugh, a lawyer who had gone early to Nevada, judge of the second judicial district, Territory of Utah. On September 3, 1860, he opened court at Genoa, a town in the Carson River Valley, some distance south and west of Virginia City. Facilities were bad, and the only place available for the court was a poorly lighted room above a livery stable. Lawyers, interested parties, curious spectators, prospective jurors filled the town beyond its capacity. Men paid premium prices for a bundle of straw on which to sleep, and as one writer described the scene, "the judge slept contentedly between rival attorneys, while the humbler attendants spread their blankets on the sage brush." Interest centered especially on the "Middle Lead Boys case," officially known as Ophir Company *v.* McCall *et al.*

William M. Stewart, who had arrived at about the same time, associated himself with the Ophir Company. Terry and the men with him came to be known as the "Middle Lead Boys."[10] Unfortunately the account of succeeding events comes almost exclusively from Stewart and may reflect only the point of view of that extraordinary gentleman. Although planning to practice law, Terry was interested in mining

[10]Lord, op. cit., p. 101.

116

claims. Realizing that possession was important, he and his friends not only occupied strategic points in the vicinity of the Comstock Ledge but, according to Stewart, erected fortifications.

Mining litigation was involved and need not concern us in its details. Basically, there was a conflict between two theories. The Ophir Company, the assignees of Comstock and his partners, advocated the single-ledge theory, which maintained that there was but one great ledge of ore in the region and that, therefore, the Ophir Company owned it all. The smaller prospectors and speculators naturally believed in the many-ledge theory, which held that there were numerous ledges. The matter came to an issue when the "Middle Lead" company began to develop a rich body of ore. The Ophir and an allied "Mexican" company immediately claimed the deposit.

The case provided color and tension but decided nothing. Stewart and Alexander Baldwin as counsel for the plaintiff opposed Terry and James Hardy for the defense. Both the attorneys and the jury showed a strong respect for the spectators, for some three or four hundred miners, well armed, listened carefully to the proceedings. They were not casual observers; rather, as one writer stated, they were "excited partisans, and an unguarded expression might at any moment bring on a collision which would cover the floor with bleeding bodies." No wonder then that the attorneys, Terry included, weighed their words carefully, were "markedly courteous in their personal allusions," and even showed a "deference" for the rulings of the court that made the presiding judge's heart swell with pleasure. Neither was it strange that the jury, confronted with armed partisans on each side of the question, chose the middle road and "appeared unnaturally obdurate in refusing to agree upon a verdict."[11]

Although the dispute over conflicting ledge theories continued unsolved, the mining companies went ahead with their

[11]Ibid.

work. The legal situation became further complicated in January, 1861. President Buchanan removed from office Judge Cradlebaugh, who for some time had been unpopular in Utah because of his opposition to the Mormons,[12] and appointed in his place R. P. Flenniken, a former minister to The Hague. The president's action precipitated another quarrel, for there was a sharp difference of opinion as to whether the president had the power to remove a judge under the act of congress organizing the Territory of Utah. Among those who questioned this use of presidential power was Judge Cradlebaugh, who despite Buchanan's move, opened court January 28, 1861. He gave two reasons for his action. First, the president had no right to remove him. Secondly, the government had not yet paid him, and a friend had advanced money to him on his salary to March 4. The judge, therefore, said that he owed it to his creditor to serve his full term. He evidently was not too sure of his right to hold court, for he announced that any lawyer could withdraw his suit, provided answer had not yet been filed. If a case had gone beyond this point, consent of both parties was necessary to a dismissal.

Since Flenniken had not arrived, a number of lawyers, including Terry, apparently decided that a judge whose status was in question was better than no judge at all. A test case was appealed from a decision of his to the court at Salt Lake City, and Terry, Stewart, and others began new suits. Terry soon came to feel that Judge Cradlebaugh's concepts of mineral rights were nearer those of Stewart than of his own. He announced consequently that he would recognize the authority of Judge Flenniken, who by this time had arrived in the region.

The new judge may have been an excellent diplomatic representative in the Netherlands, but he was no man to attempt

[12]Judge Cradlebaugh felt strongly that the Mountain Meadow Massacre was the work of Mormons. In 1859 he visited the site of the tragedy to attempt to discover the facts and in 1863, as a representative from Nevada, he was to fight against the admission of Utah as a state.

to preside over a Nevada court of the sixties. Described as an "elderly and somewhat pompous" individual, he apparently had seized in full ignorance upon the judgeship as a sinecure for his declining days. He made a bad start psychologically by appearing in Carson City in a fine silk hat, said to be the only one in western Utah territory.

Under these inauspicious circumstances, the ledge question once again came to the fore. The companies involved were different, but the issues were the same. Two mining companies, the Rich and the Lucy Ella, laid claim to a certain ledge on a hill near Devil's Gate, Gold Canyon. Some two hundred feet below another company, the Saint Louis, was cutting into the same ledge. Stewart, on behalf of the latter company, was holding to the single-ledge theory, and Terry, the opposing counsel, was forwarding the many-ledge theory that would leave his clients free to continue their mining operations.

Having swung over to the single-ledge theory, Judge Cradlebaugh on January 4, 1861, had issued an injunction restraining the Rich and Lucy Ella companies from mining the disputed areas. Before this injunction was enforced, the Rich and Ella companies had separated; the Rich Company remained, and the representatives of the other company left at the point of a gun. Shortly afterward the sheriff arrived with his injunction and dispossessed the Rich Company. The show of force, however, had not yet ended. When they learned that the president had removed Cradlebaugh, the members of the Rich Company defied the injunction. Pushing aside the deputy left to guard the ledge, they took possession again, erected a fort, and challenged the St. Louis Company to attempt to remove them.

Stewart did not remain inactive. He secured a warrant from Judge Cradlebaugh for the arrest of the Rich Company men for violation of the injunction. He then held the injunction until the judge's position could be clarified, and a stalemate lasted until February 15. At that time the stage from Salt

Lake brought information that the supreme court of Utah had recognized Cradlebaugh's right to hold office despite the action of the president. Hearing this news, Judge Flenniken informally told acquaintances that he would not contest the decision of the supreme court. When he heard of this statement, Stewart delivered the warrant he had been keeping to Sheriff John L. Blackburn with instructions to ride with a posse the next morning to Devil's Gate to arrest the garrison.

Stewart was awakened the following morning by a junior colleague with the news that later the previous night Flenniken had changed his mind and planned to contest the court's decision. The lawyer, according to his own account, was highly incensed. Searching for Judge Flenniken, he found him in front of one of the many saloons in town. Stewart seized the former minister to The Hague by the collar and, drawing a pistol, marched him to the nearby telegraph operator in Flyshacker's store. There the perspiring judge was forced to send four or five messages at the dictation of the angry lawyer to key persons in the region. The essence of the communications was that Cradlebaugh and not Flenniken was judge.

Meanwhile the sheriff's posse had gone to Devil's Gate and arrested the garrison which evidently had not heard of Flenniken's first change of mind. Having succeeded in evicting the members of the Rich Company, Stewart had nothing further against them and made a shrewd political move. When the prisoners appeared in court, Stewart rose unexpectedly to their defense. They were good citizens, he said, who had been misled by a usurper named Flenniken. He moved that the case be dropped and the men discharged. The judge hastened to comply with the recommendation.

One wonders if David S. Terry with his training in the rough ways of frontier courts would have been able to forestall the action of Stewart. Unfortunately he was absent on a trip to San Francisco when the events just recorded took place. When he returned he saw that the decision of the supreme court, the action of Stewart, and the flabby nature of Judge

Flenniken rendered hopeless his client's cause. He was a good loser. Going to Stewart's office he said that he and his party had been taught a valuable lesson, never to go to war without one's general in his own camp. "You had both generals in your camp," he told Stewart, "and you won the victory."[13]

Some writers have charged that in addition to practicing law and concerning himself with mining claims, Terry engaged in activities hostile to the interests of the United States. One of these described Terry going to the mines with five fire-eating Chivalry friends, armed with rifles, to capture Nevada for the South and for slavery.[14] This charge appears to be based only on rumor originating in Nevada and disseminated by the San Francisco *Bulletin*, hardly an unimpeachable source of information on Judge Terry.[15] The fact upon which the rumor was based was that as hostilities between North and South drew near in Nevada as elsewhere in the West there was great tension.

In the early days of the war Nevada was one of the few areas of the West in which there were sufficient numbers of Southerners to permit open manifestations of sympathy for the Confederacy. Furthermore, in this fluid, new mining frontier, men who bore arms in defense of mining claims might be expected to keep and perhaps use these arms in support of their country, whether it be the Union or the Confederacy.

In the spring of 1861 a number of pro-Unionists organized what they called the Committee of Safety of Nevada, on the ground that Southerners were uniting in this region. The committee's secretary, John A. Collins, on May 26 wrote to the army post, Fort Churchill, for aid. He reported that a hundred secessionists had organized under S. A. Means, former

[13]Stewart, *Reminiscences*, p. 139. A similar account is in Lord, p. 108.

[14]George D. Lyman, *The Saga of the Comstock Lode* (New York, 1934), p. 57.

[15]E. M. Mack, *Nevada, A History of the State from the Earliest Times through the Civil War* (Glendale, 1936), p. 278. J. W. Terry doubted that Terry held such a commission from Jefferson Davis. J. W. Terry to Dumas Malone, Sept. 17, 1934.

state treasurer of California.[16] In this letter and others it appears clear that Collins and those with him suspected Judge Terry of being the real leader in the secession moves in Nevada. The following are typical statements in the correspondence of the period: "Terry is expected soon." "It is also rumored that Judge Terry has the commission of Governor of the Territory from Jeff. Davis, and is only waiting the proper opportunity to act." "Terry is to join them soon . . . ."[17] The commanding officer of the Nevada fort forwarded the rumors and resultant requests for arms and ammunition to his superior officer in San Francisco. In his first report of the secessionist organization he wrote, "What reliance can be placed upon it I cannot say. The persons whose names are subscribed to it are said to be reliable men."[18] In his reply the assistant adjutant general in San Francisco stated for his superior, "The general does not much credit the existence of any deliberate plan for the object stated although there may be in certain quarters such a disposition."[19] At the same time the commanding officer at Fort Churchill was warned to be on guard.

No evidence has been found in the *Official Records of the Union and Confederate Armies* or elsewhere to support the charges that Terry engaged in activities against the federal government in Nevada or that he had a commission from the Confederacy for such action. One can in fact without much hesitation discard the latter accusation. The lukewarm attitude of the Confederate government toward military operations west of the Mississippi makes it unlikely that as early as May, 1861, there was any official Confederate sanction for actions of Southern sympathizers in Nevada. On the other hand it can be assumed that Terry knew what the secession-

[16]Collins to Brig. Gen. E. V. Sumner, May 26, 1861, in [U.S. War Dept.], *The War of the Rebellion: A Compilation of the Official Records of the Union and Confederate Armies*, Ser. I (Washington, 1897), Vol. L, Pt. I, 490-491. Hereafter cited as *O. R.*
[17]Ibid., pp. 490-491, 499.
[18]Capt. T. Hendrickson, Fort Churchill, to Capt. R. C. Drum, asst. adj. gen., San Francisco, May 26, 1861, in ibid., p. 490.
[19]Ibid., p. 493.

ists were doing in Nevada. He was in and out of the region on business during 1860 and 1861 and was acknowledged to be one of the most important Chivalry men in Nevada. At the very most Terry may have thought that Nevada could be secured for the Confederacy by force of arms. More probably he saw in flag waving and other signs of Southern sympathy an opportunity to create tension and perhaps cause a diversion of troops to the area. In any case, whatever the aims or actions of Terry were, even the rumor of his possible leadership in Nevada had a positive effect. The army officials gave moral support to the Committee of Safety of Nevada and encouraged its organization into companies and other military units. By early June General E. V. Sumner, commanding officer of the Department of the Pacific, was convinced that there was a secessionist threat in Nevada and agreed to increase the garrison at Fort Churchill by one or two companies of infantry If Unionist Californians were making life unpleasant for David S. Terry, he was, intentionally or not, making matters uneasy for them.

Terry returned to California from time to time during his residence in Nevada. The warrants against him arising from the duel hung over him until the summer of 1860. Quite understandably he did not wish to be tried before a court in San Francisco. Friends attempted to help him by introducing a bill in the state legislature amending the existing act concerning courts of justice. The significant change was that cases of persons indicted for dueling were to be transferred from the court of sessions to the district court. The sponsor of the amendment in the assembly calmly stated that its purpose was to protect Terry from a trial in San Francisco. There was little opposition; the amendment passed and became law February 14, 1860.[20] The next step was to seek a change of venue to a court away from San Francisco. The matter continued for months, but from one standpoint the delay was desirable,

[20]California. *Legislature. Assembly. Journal* . . . 11th Sess. (Sacramento, 1860), p. 288.

since it might allay public sentiment. However, particularly for the sake of his family, Terry was anxious to have the legal blot removed.

Mrs. Terry and the three sons had received a warm welcome in Texas and returned to California in the late spring or early summer of 1860. Texans had been deeply interested in the duel, and Terry's friends defended his actions. Frank Terry was worried about the trial. He wrote his brother that he could secure no California newspapers or letters and pleaded, "For God's sake write me and relieve my anxiety."[21] On June 8, 1860, Terry wrote from San Francisco to his wife who had returned to Stockton. He was optimistic and told her that on the following Monday Judge Hager would decide on a change of venue. He wrote that the judge "plainly intimated that he would grant the motion and unless the parties agreed on some county would send the case to the nearest Dist Court which was free from objection." Terry explained, "This will take the case to Marin and will suit me exactly [as] the Court sets there on the first Monday in July and a few weeks longer will rid me of all further trouble & you of anxiety."

As Terry had predicted, the case was transferred to Marin County. If a San Francisco court would have been prejudiced against Terry, the court before which he finally appeared was equally biased in his favor. Judge McKinstry, who normally occupied the bench in the seventh judicial district, was touring Europe. His replacement was Judge James H. Hardy of the sixteenth judicial district, a close personal friend of the defendant. One account asserts that the witnesses were on a boat that was becalmed on the way across the bay from San Francisco, and the judge, tiring of the delay, dismissed the case.[22] Another strongly anti-Terry source charges that the courtroom clock was set ahead an hour, and that for this reason the witnesses were late and found the case dismissed

[21]Jan. 31, Terry MSS.
[22]Franklin Tuthill, *History of California* (San Francisco, 1866), pp. 567-68.

by the time of their arrival.[23] Whatever the details, Terry clearly came to trial before a judge of strong Southern sympathies,[24] who no doubt held views similar to those of Terry toward the settlement of questions of personal honor. At the same time it is probably true that no judge at that time, in view of the prevalence of duels, would have decided the case against Terry. The court at Redwood City used the action in Marin County as a precedent, and when action was brought against Terry in San Mateo County the judge ordered a verdict of not guilty.

The courts of law had exonerated Terry. From the court of public opinion, however, he did not emerge uncondemned or unpunished. Since the preponderance of sentiment in California was pro-Northern it was also anti-Terry, and the view that he had murdered Broderick for his political views became widespread. For example Andrew J. Stone, a miner at Forest City, wrote to his brother, Wesley, in New Hampshire hotly describing the duel. Calling Broderick "an extraordinary smart man and, what you probably never saw, an honest politician," Stone wrote that the administration party was against the senator and was "determined, it is thought to kill him if they can. The man that challenged him is a ded [sic] shot, for he has killed several." The angry miner wrote of the state administration:

There is about a dozen of the leading Democrats of this State that I would like to see their guts cut out, they are the vilest and most damnable of the human race, and rule the politics of the state, but Mr. Broderick was too smart for them and they are dtermined [sic] to get him out of the way for the future God d—m them . . . . [25]

[23]Tinkham, op. cit., I, 296.

[24]In 1862 Judge Hardy was impeached on a variety of charges, including his conduct of the Terry trial. He was found guilty of only one charge, using seditious and treasonable language, and was removed from office. Later the California state senate expunged the Hardy matter from the record. See Hittell, *History of California*, IV, 300-302, 431-33.

[25]Sept. 14, 1859, Stone MSS in the Huntington Library. Stone wrote his brother another angry letter at the time of the dismissal of the case against Terry. This letter is dated Sept. 2, 1860.

With the advent of the Civil War, Terry's position became even more difficult. The popular feeling against him in California made it hard to rebuild his practice in that state. He had shown his legal ability in Nevada, but a shrewd lawyer, William M. Stewart, and a combination of circumstances had placed him on the losing side in the interpretation of mining law.

Then, as the war progressed, Terry suffered a serious personal blow. He had always held his brother, Benjamin Franklin Terry, in the highest regard. By 1860 the latter had become a person of prominence in Texas. His plantation, Oakland, was one of the show places in the Oyster Creek-Sugarland region, with its imposing mansion and huge fields of cotton and sugar cane. The bond between the brothers is attested to by the fact that of the six children of Frank and Mary Terry one was named David S. and another Cornelia, and of David and Cornelia Terry's children two were called Frank.

When war came, after a brief interlude with the Confederate army in Virginia, Frank Terry returned and raised a company of mounted Texans. A commanding personality, like his brother David, he was a large man and by customary standards probably the more likable of the two. He was bluff and hearty, whereas his brother was more self-contained. As Frank Terry rode away from his plantation he took with him the prestige of the past and the promise of the future, for strapped to his side was the sword that Uncle Ben Fort Smith had used at New Orleans, and by his side rode his eldest son, David S. Terry, Jr., not yet out of his teens.[26]

In his first encounter with the enemy in Kentucky, Colonel Frank Terry was killed, after demonstrating not only his courage but his recklessness.[27] One account states that

[26]Clarence R. Wharton, *History of Fort Bend County* (San Antonio, 1939), pp. 160, 170-171.

[27]J. K. P. Blackburn, "Reminiscences of the Terry Rangers," *Southwestern Historical Quarterly*, XXII (1918), 49-50.

when the prisoners were rounded up, a young German-American was pointed out as the soldier who had shot Terry. The Rangers then in their grief at the loss of their beloved colonel, let young Dave Terry shoot the man who had killed his father.[28] Probably the best tribute to Frank Terry's leadership and popularity was the fact that although he was killed in the first skirmish with the enemy, the company was known as "Terry's Texas Rangers" throughout the war.

[28]Wharton, p. 171n. For an official account of Terry's death, see *O. R.* Ser. I, Vol. VII, 20-21.

Chapter VII

The Confederate Colonel

THE NEWS of Frank Terry's death came as a great blow to Judge Terry, for the bond between the two was strong. When it appeared that the break with the Union was coming, Frank had written that he would like very much to have his brother with him. At that time in May, 1861, however, he still hoped that the North would not fight and he advised the judge "not to make too great a sacrifice" to go to Texas.[1]

Financial reasons in part held Terry in California after the outbreak of the war, for he had a wife and three children to support. In late 1860 or early 1861 being pressed for funds, he had asked his brother to sell his holdings in Texas, probably his share in the family properties. Frank Terry made the sale, not for cash but about $14,000 in notes at 12 per cent. In normal times such a transfer would have produced a good income for the value of the land, but with the war in progress the notes were of little value, especially outside Texas. In addition, as we have seen, the Nevada venture was not fulfilling hopes, and the Civil War hit hard at Terry's legal practice in California. In view of the responsibility to his family and of the stringency of his financial position, Terry may have rationalized to himself that he was serving the Confederacy more in the West than he could do on the battlefield. Certainly Terry was a thorn in the side of the Army of the Pacific as long as he remained in the region. In addition to

[1]May 13, Terry MSS.

believing that he was the leader of Southern resistance in Nevada, army officials came to think that Terry was carrying a similar role in California.

In September, 1861, a perturbed captain of infantry reported to headquarters that there was considerable secessionist strength in southern California. The centers of this feeling, he asserted, were in the Los Angeles area, around El Monte, and in San Bernardino County. In the last region the Mormons, who were numerous, were supposed to be anti-Union because of treatment they had received from the United States. El Monte on the other hand was pro-Southern because many of its residents had come from Texas. Captain Davidson told of secret meetings of armed men at El Monte and wrote, "Judge Terry is said to be at the head of the organization."[2]

Paradoxically, although Terry was a source of irritation for the military authorities, they did not wish him to leave the state. Some prominent Southerners had left for the Confederacy. General A. S. Johnston for example had gone overland from Los Angeles and had escaped being seized, although orders had been issued for his arrest. Senator Gwin had been arrested en route east by way of Panama. Daniel Showalter, a pro-Southern politician who had killed the Northerner, Charles W. Piercy, in a duel early in 1861, attempted to lead a group of men to the Confederacy in November, 1861. Colonel James H. Carleton, commanding officer of the army in southern California, on November 4, 1861, issued orders to his officers in outlying posts to be on the lookout. Carleton told E. E. Eyre, the ranking officer at San Bernardino, that if he caught Showalter he should order him to swear allegiance to the government, and "If he refuse, hold him good. I will send him to Alcatraz; same of Judge Terry. Be on the qui vive. There are plotters all about us, without a doubt." In his orders to Major E. A. Riggs at Camp Wright, near Los Angeles, Carleton was even more explicit. Showalter if caught was to

2J. W. Davidson to R. C. Drum, Sept. 16, 1861, in O. R., Ser. I, Vol. L, Pt. I, 621-22.

be searched and forced to take the oath. "We have had enough of the bullying and treason of such men." The colonel then ordered, "If Judge Terry tries to pass, he must go through the same ordeal. There must be no child's play with him."[3] Showalter was caught and imprisoned for a time at Fort Yuma. Later he made good his attempt to reach the South and became a colonel in the Texas forces.

Frank Terry's death apparently impelled a younger brother to action. Clinton Terry had built a promising legal practice in Brazoria, Texas. His partner, John A. Wharton, had already gone to war and sometime after Frank Terry's death had become the leader of Terry's Texas Rangers. After his brother's death, Clinton Terry decided to join this force. As he left Texas, he may have had misgivings about his own future but none concerning that of the Confederacy. He drew up his will and advised his executors to sell his land and invest in slaves, since he felt the latter to be a safer business venture.[4] Clinton Terry's war experience was brief. Joining the Rangers shortly before the Battle of Shiloh, he had not only the courage and dash of his eldest brother but his ill luck as well. He was shot down as the Rangers rode into an ambuscade and died shortly thereafter.

Meanwhile David S. Terry carried on his practice in California. The rumors circulated about him in the early months of the war began to appear unfounded since Terry engaged in no activity that could be held against him. There is some evidence that his practice improved as time went on. People in need of an attorney knew that whatever Terry's views on the war might be he would handle their case honestly and effectively.[5]

Apparently the death of Clinton Terry was the determining factor causing his brother to decide to leave California and

[3]In ibid., 700-701.

[4]Wharton, p. 168.

[5]During part of this period Terry was in partnership with A. C. Bradford. *San Joaquin Republican*, June 25, 1862.

offer his services to the Confederacy. It is difficult to determine accurately the date of his departure. As Wagstaff commented, Terry was not a man to advertise his actions, and for obvious reasons he was cautious in his preparations to leave California. Dan Showalter's experience demonstrated the difficulty of taking a party of any size across the border into Arizona or Mexico. The best chance seemed to be to board a vessel for the coast of Mexico and then cross overland to Texas.

The decision to leave Mrs. Terry and the three boys must have been difficult. Another son, Jefferson Davis, had been born in 1861 but he did not live out the year. There was another child on the way. Terry could not take his family with him for fear that the departure could not be kept secret.

Consequently he left them in Stockton and boarded a vessel for Mexico early in 1863. With him went seven or eight men, at least one of whom, Duncan Beaumont, was to serve under him in Texas. The group had planned its departure carefully, and the first news of the party came from Mazatlan. Fact was difficult to separate from rumor, as no doubt Terry would have wished it. He was said to be carrying a brigadier general's commission with him, to have a uniform that had been made for him in San Francisco, and to have taken with him a horse valued at $2,000, presented to him by Confederate sympathizers throughout the state. A Stockton editor, incensed by this last rumor, asked "Who gave Terry the $2,000 war horse but sneaking rebels, who are likely to be the most loud and free in prating union on every occasion?"[6]

According to newspaper reports reaching California, Terry and his party left Mazatlan, February 20, 1863.[7] Experienced in frontier travel, the men had carefully selected supplies and mounts before starting across Mexico. As they neared the eastern coast Terry went through country in which he had fought during the Mexican War. It is related that two travelers caught up with Terry's party in Monterrey. They were Ne-

[6]*Stockton Daily Independent*, Mar. 12, 1863.
[7]Ibid., Mar. 10.

groes, taken to California as slaves by Terry and freed by him
when the region became a free state. Devoted to their former
master, they heard of his departure, followed him, and served
him throughout the war.

The party stopped briefly in Texas on the plantation that
had been the proud possession of Frank Terry and arrived in
Houston on April 15, 1863.[8] Terry crossed the Mississippi
when Northern forces were beginning their pressure on Vicksburg. Some distance to the east were the troops of General
Joseph E. Johnston, and Terry paid a call on a friend, Captain
W. W. Porter, who was on the general's staff. Porter introduced the judge to Johnston, who in turn invited Terry to
become a temporary member of his staff. Terry accepted and
was with Johnston's forces as they made token resistance to
Grant. After Vicksburg fell, Johnston attempted to hold
Jackson but, unable to secure reinforcements, evacuated the
city.

When events had reached this unsatisfactory stage, Terry
continued on his way to Richmond. Unfortunately, as is the
case with much of Terry's Civil War career, detailed information is scarce, and what exists is open to question as to
accuracy. It is rumored that when Terry reached the war
department he requested a top rank and was rejected with
the answer that such appointments went only to men who
had distinguished themselves on the battlefield.[9] Throughout
his life Terry gave little evidence of a consuming desire for
personal gain or glory. He was thoroughly devoted to the Confederate cause and had lost two brothers in the war. The judge
may well have had plans for the Confederacy, such as the
conquest of California, but it is doubtful that these schemes
were for his own advancement.

Whatever conversations Terry may have had with the war
department or others high in the Confederate government,

[8]J. W. Terry notes for Klette, p. 22.

[9]Wagstaff, p. 227. The charge is denied by J. W. Terry to Dumas Malone, Sept.
17, 1934, MS in the Bancroft Library.

one result is known. He received a commission to raise a regiment in Texas.[10] On his way back to that state Terry experienced the only significant military action of his Civil War career. Passing through Tennessee he ran across his brother's old unit, Terry's Texas Rangers. John A. Wharton had moved ahead and commanded a division of which the Rangers were a part. Once again Terry became a temporary aide. While he was with them the Rangers became involved in the Battle of Chickamauga, and in this engagement Terry received a wound in the arm. The injury was slight, and Terry resumed his journey to Texas.

Terry's subsequent action in the Civil War falls into two categories. One was his connection with proposals for reconquest of the Southwest, and the other was his actual military service in the Confederate army.

Several schemes were presented to Confederate officials for military activity in the Far West. In 1843 Judge L. W. Hastings had led a party to California in the hope of winning the region from Mexico. Now, twenty years later, he proposed a plan for the reconquest of the Southwest by the Confederacy. He presented his recommendations to the secretary of war, James A. Seddon, and made certain headway. Although Seddon declined to furnish troops or funds, he gave the judge a letter to General E. K. Smith, in command of Confederate forces west of the Mississippi. The letter stated that Hastings had been commissioned a major to raise troops in Arizona and that in addition he had been authorized to proceed with a plan to raise troops in California. Hastings had suggested that funds might be raised through the export of cotton to Mexico. Hastings' plan was to be carried out only as far as Smith considered it practicable. Seddon himself expressed doubts since Hastings was inexperienced in military affairs. The secretary of war, therefore, ordered Smith to select the proper assistants for the venture or to turn it over to a competent officer. Seddon clearly had one person in mind, for he wrote, "I should be

[10]O. R., Ser. I, Vol. XXXIV, Pt. II, 1048.

pleased if a gentleman of the known character and spirit of Judge Terry would undertake its guidance."[11] Nothing came of the plan, for a Northern force under General N. P. Banks made an unsuccessful but disturbing thrust into western Louisiana toward Texas.

Just how closely Terry was involved in the Hastings proposal is not known. Actually during the early part of 1864 there was another plan for action in the West that competed with the Hastings scheme. Henry Beaumont of the quartermaster's office of the trans-Mississippi department of the Confederate army nominally headed the second proposal. Beaumont's brother Duncan had made the trip from California with Terry and was serving under his command in Texas. The two brothers and Terry submitted a plan to General Smith for the reconquest of the Southwest that was similar to that of Judge Hastings. Terry and his friends were to furnish cotton to be exported to Mexico. Using the funds secured from the sale of cotton, the men would go into Sonora and draw from Arizona and adjoining regions men who would fight for the Confederacy. Hastings had anticipated that he could raise a force of five hundred; Terry and the Beaumonts more optimistically predicted that a thousand could be recruited.

General Smith and his leading adviser were inclined at first to support the Terry-Beaumont proposal, but then decided against it in favor of the Hastings scheme, for the reason that Hastings possessed a commission from the Confederate government. However, after securing authorization, Judge Hastings for some reason failed to go ahead. By fall Beaumont determined to try again. This time he addressed the government at Richmond instead of the commanding officer of the trans-Mississippi department. His letters found their way to Richmond and nearly a month and a half later

[11]Ibid., Ser. IV, Vol. III, 76. Prior to the Mexican War, Hastings sought to increase American interest in California by writing an emigrant guide and leading parties to the region.

the reply was sent. The year was drawing to a close and so was the Confederacy. To the sorely tried officials in Virginia, it probably seemed of little moment whether Arizona or even California came within the Southern orbit. Secretary of War Seddon's answer was brief:

Our resources are fully taxed and our attention so engrossed by nearer and more pressing interests that I must forego enterprises of this distant and contingent character, or leave them to be arranged by the judgment of the commanding general of the trans-Mississippi Department.[12]

There was still a third proposal to invade the West. John R. Baylor had commanded Confederate forces in a temporarily successful thrust into Arizona early in the war. He was convinced that the area could and should be retaken, and in December, 1864, wrote a letter to the secretary of war. In some ways his scheme was the most optimistic of all. He stated that men like Judge Terry and Colonel Showalter had told him that a force of from 15,000 to 20,000 men could be raised in southern California if a route could be opened to the coast, but Baylor modestly placed his estimate at from 5,000 to 10,000. In order to open the way to California and release this sizable body of men it would be necessary to send an invading force of 2,500. The time was ripe, he urged, for such a move. The trans-Mississippi region was relatively free of the enemy, and the Confederate forces could be mainly cavalry and live off the land.[13] Although Seddon did not give the Baylor proposal the cavalier treatment accorded the Beaumont plan, he probably forgot it under the pressure of other matters.

Meanwhile, although he was interested in the proposals regarding the Far West, Terry carried on his regular military duties. It will be remembered that he had been commissioned to raise a force in Texas. After being wounded at Chicka-

12Ibid., Ser. I, Vol. XLI, Pt. IV, 1011.

13Dec. 21, in ibid., Ser. IV, Vol. III, 960-962.

mauga, he left the Rangers and proceeded to Texas. Recruitment was relatively slow. Enthusiastic Southerners had answered the first call to war, and a recruiting campaign conducted in late 1863 and early 1864 met with passive resistance.

At the outset military authorities evidently anticipated the raising of several regiments and expected that Terry would command a brigade and receive a brigadier general's commission. In March, 1864, however, Terry received orders to organize "one of his regiments" as quickly as possible and take a post at Beaumont, Texas.[14] Prior to his assignment he had probably spent most of his time in Houston, which was thriving as headquarters for the military forces in the region.

Terry did not remain long in Beaumont, if indeed he went there at all, for in April he was stationed at Fort San Jacinto in Montgomery County, not far northwest of Houston.

An unpleasant feature of military service in this area was the continual intrigue for rank and preference. The rancor did not come out into the open until late in the war, but no doubt it was present much earlier. Personal friendships were important in promotions and assignments to duty. Whether or not he wished it, it seems that Terry was involved in the rivalry. At one time he took command of a brigade, but only in an acting capacity and without advancement in rank. Shortly thereafter a brigadier general was assigned to the post, and Terry was left with the command of his own regiment. These shifts do not appear to cast any reflection on Terry's abilities, but resulted from either political maneuverings or the chaos of the last months of the war. There is some evidence that Terry demonstrated marked ability in the organization and training of troops. One writer states that Terry was given a commission as brigadier general just before the close of the war, but that it did not reach him until after the conclusion of hostilities. It is certain that as late as

[14]Special Orders, No. 76, Hdqrs. Dist. of Tex., N. Mex., and Ariz., Houston, Mar. 16, in ibid., Ser. I, Vol. XXXIV, Pt. II, 1048.

April 28, 1865, Terry was still regarded as a colonel by his commanding officer.

Terry's name became involved in one of the tragedies resulting from army intrigue. One of his closest friends was Major General John A. Wharton, former law partner of Clinton Terry, and on whose staff Terry had served briefly at Chickamauga. Tragically, Wharton's friendship with Terry indirectly cost the general his life. Like Terry, Wharton had been transferred to Texas, and it was he who had assigned Terry to the command of a brigade. Another colonel, George W. Baylor, objected strenuously to the appointment, mainly because of a feeling that he had been passed over. He quarreled with Wharton on the matter once, and refused to obey orders. Encountering his commanding officer in the Fannin Hotel in Houston, the colonel shot and killed the general.[15] Another version of the quarrel asserts that Baylor had been chafing for some time under what he considered high-handed treatment by Wharton and finally lost control of himself. This version makes no mention of Terry's appointment as a cause of the controversy.[16]

The last weeks of the war in Texas were hectic. Lack of communication facilities delayed arrival of the news of Lee's surrender at Appomattox on April 9, 1865. Rumors reached Texas first and contributed to the destruction of morale. The military leaders attempted to maintain control, but desertions were producing a rapid disintegration of the armed forces. Some of the Confederate leaders determined to stay and struggle through the reconstruction of their regions. Others, although the Confederacy for which they had been fighting had failed to leave the Union, decided to make the break themselves. The logical destination of such men serving in Texas was of course Mexico.

That country had been going through a strain nearly as

[15]J. W. Terry notes for Klette, pp. 12-14.

[16]*Houston, A History and a Guide* (Houston, 1942), p. 225. No correspondence relating to the matter is to be found in *O. R.*

severe, if not as bloody, as that experienced by the United States. With French backing, the Hapsburg Maximilian had become emperor of Mexico. He was, however, unable to exercise jurisdiction over the whole country, and in outlying regions supporters of the ousted Mexican leader, Benito Juárez, and other revolutionary groups were in virtual control.

During the Civil War, Confederate diplomats had attempted to use friendship toward Maximilian to secure French and possibly British aid, but generally speaking their effort had failed. Now that the Confederacy was collapsing, some of the leaders in the West contemplated moving in force across the border. On May 2, 1865, General E. Kirby Smith directed Robert Rose to make unofficial overtures to the Mexican emperor. He was to suggest the value of an alliance with the Confederate states and point out that the United States government would probably have aggressive designs on Mexico. Rose was to inform the imperial government that in Smith's command and elsewhere in the South were thousands of men, "daring and gallant spirits . . . to whom a state of vassalage to the Federal Government would be intolerable, and who would gladly rally around any flag that promises to lead them to battle against their former foe."[17] It does not appear that any such understanding was reached, but when the flight from the fallen Confederacy began, many men moved across the border into Mexico. One of them was Terry.

About two weeks before General Smith formally ended hostilities in Texas by capitulating at Galveston, June 2, 1865, Colonel Terry received orders to transfer his regiment. Formerly based at Richmond near the region of his youth, he was ordered to move his troops by rail through Houston to Navasota, some distance to the northeast.[18] This was the last military order to Terry that is on record.

Terry decided to go to Mexico and like other officers un-

[17]*O. R.*, Ser. I, Vol. XLVIII, Pt. II, 1292-93.

[18]Special Orders, No. 140, Hdqrs. Dist. of Tex., &c., May 20, in ibid., Ser. I, Vol. XLVIII, Pt. II, 1315.

doubtedly put the matter up to his regiment. Some of the officers and men were his personal friends. He had considerable success in persuading men to follow him. Since the gulf coast and the mouth of the Rio Grande were under federal control, Terry and his volunteer force of over six hundred men made their way across Texas farther north and crossed the river into Mexico far above Brownsville.[19] They had moved carefully and to this point had encountered no great difficulty. Their good fortune was not long to continue.

As Terry turned away from the fallen Confederacy and headed for the Rio Grande and beyond, he must have had misgivings concerning the future. Once again he was leaving his family behind him, for Mrs. Terry had joined her husband in Houston. The trip had been difficult. Taking her small sons, Sam, Dave, Clint, and the baby, Frank Cheatham, born late in 1863,[20] she had gone by sea to San Blas, on the west coast of Mexico. Somewhere on the trip overland across Mexico, the baby died. One account states that because of her desire to find a proper burial spot the mother traveled for several days carrying the dead infant on her horse.[21] It is also said that Mrs. Terry was twice robbed by bandits, but that in each case Mexican authorities recovered the stolen property. Terry was probably with his family throughout much of the war period. But now the Confederacy had collapsed. Deep as was his love for Texas, he had no desire to remain and endure the domination of the former enemy.[22] Better to try Mexico. It was the long chance, but he had always been ready to face the unknown.

[19]P. H. Sheridan to U. S. Grant, Aug. 9, 1865, in ibid., 1174.

[20]Samuel Langdon to Cornelia Terry, Nov. 28, 1863, Terry MSS.

[21]Wagstaff, p. 229.

[22]J. W. Terry stated, "There was nothing peculiar about Judge Terry going to Mexico. The Vigilance Committee and the Broderick duel had nothing to do with it. He went to Mexico because he did not wish to live in a conquered country." Notes for Klette, p. 14.

Chapter VIII

The Cotton Planter of Jalisco

B Y MOVING across Texas some distance inland, Terry and his party avoided contact with Northern forces. They were not as successful in evading Mexican units after they crossed the Rio Grande. The northern part of Mexico, along the United States border, was one of the regions that Maximilian did not control. Conditions verged on anarchy, although a guerrilla chief, Juan N. Cortina, maintained sporadic order. Where the ultimate loyalties of this Mexican general lay was somewhat uncertain, but in any case he was opposed to Maximilian. In April, 1865, he came out openly against the emperor and he was busy building military forces when Terry's party appeared in the area.

Now that the Civil War was over, the federal government began to look more sharply at the situation in Mexico. Secretary William H. Seward hoped by peaceful means to persuade the French to leave. Others, including General Grant, believed that a judicious show or even use of military force might hasten the departure. General Philip H. Sheridan, in command of the region west of the Mississippi, concluded that one method of undermining Maximilian was to make overtures to Cortina. In spite of a sharp protest from the French minister, therefore, the army worked rather closely with the Mexican guerrilla leader.

In return Cortina attempted to prevent the passage through his domain of large bodies of Confederates who might be headed for Maximilian's court. A body of six or seven hundred men, such as that led by Colonel Terry, could hardly escape notice. When Cortina, with more than a thousand men in arms under him, stopped the Terry party, the latter group had the choice of submission or fighting for their lives against heavy odds. Under the circumstances, since the aim of the men was not to fight Mexicans but start a new life, Terry and his force did not resist Cortina. According to a message sent by General Sheridan to General Grant, the Confederates were shorn of their arms and their transportation.[1] How complete the seizure was is not known, but at least the intervention broke up the party.

What the specific aim of the Terry group had been is not clear. Members of the party told Cortina that they were headed for Sonora, and possibly some of them planned to continue to California. On the other hand they may not have informed the guerrilla chief of their real intentions. Another group of Confederates went through the region in such numbers that Cortina did not dare attempt to stop them. This force, led by General Joe Shelby, was headed for Mexico City. Terry and his men may have had the same objective. Whatever the original goal of the group may have been, many of the members went to Monterrey after their interception by Cortina's forces. Shortly thereafter Terry and about twenty-five men who had remained with him proceeded to Parras, a small town some distance west. There he met with numbers of prominent Southerners as they passed through with General Shelby.[2]

Terry no doubt enjoyed sitting around campfires talking to these men, but his real aim in the Monterrey area was to secure the right to move westward. While in Monterrey he met an individual whom he had known well in California. Former Senator William M. Gwin was making a last effort to become a colonizer. In 1863 he had gone to Europe and in

[1]Aug. 9, 1865, in *O. R.*, Ser. I, Vol. XLVIII, Pt. II, 1174.

[2]Jennie Edwards, *John N. Edwards, Biography, Memoirs, Reminiscences and Recollections* (Kansas City, 1889), pp. 307-308.

Paris had made the acquaintance of Gutierrez de Estrada, a Mexican royalist who was seeking French support for the establishment of a European monarchy in his native land. Gwin's scheme was to settle some thirty thousand Americans from the Confederacy in northern Mexico. The settlers would make a formidable buffer against any aggression by the United States and at the same time through their efforts in mining and agriculture would strengthen the economy of Mexico as a whole.

Convinced of both the feasibility and the desirability of the plan, Gutierrez de Estrada sought to win Maximilian to the idea. The archduke was never enthusiastic. He had some knowledge of American expansionism, and when the Mexican enthusiastically exclaimed that Gwin was a "real pioneer," the Austrian commented, "Yes, a pioneer for the South."[3]

Gwin, meanwhile, unaware that Gutierrez was making overtures to Maximilian, had reached the ear of the French ruler. Napoleon was receptive to the colonization scheme, took it, and then shaped it to his own purposes. Frenchmen as well as Americans were to be settlers, and the valuable silver deposits were to be under the control of Frenchmen.[4]

Maximilian, who had not favored the original proposal, was no more favorable to the French revision. Gwin, still hopeful, went to Mexico in 1865 but could not get an audience with Maximilian. After a short trip to France, Gwin was again in Mexico in May, 1865. The emperor would have none of the matter, and on June 26, 1865, repudiated the Sonora venture. Since the American Civil War was over, the

---

[3]Daniel Dawson, *The Mexican Adventure* (London, 1935), p. 336. This account is drawn mainly from correspondence in the *Wiener Staats Archiv*. Gwin's memoirs place him in a more favorable light. He wrote, "The Archduke Maximilian was fully advised of the deliberations and conclusions of the French Government. The plan of colonization was sent to him by special messenger, and after deliberate examination of the same, it met with his unqualified approval. . . ." Gwin memoirs, MS in the Bancroft Library, pp. 220-221.

[4]Dawson, p. 358.

former Californian determined to go to the United States and seek safe conduct to France.[5]

On his way north Gwin met Terry in Monterrey and apparently had some sort of an understanding with him. If Gwin still had hopes of success he soon lost them and wrote to Terry explaining his failure. The emperor, he reported, "fears the Anglo-American spirit, believing that it is my intention, with that of others, to play a ruse in order to usurp the empire and dethrone [him]." Because of his fears Maximilian refused to allow Gwin to use the military support of the French which had been promised by Napoleon. Deprived of this military backing, Gwin felt that it would be impossible to go ahead, for, he told Terry, "the small force under your orders would not be sufficient to check the ravages of the Apaches." Nor could Terry seek to increase his own force since that action would be viewed as filibustering by both Mexico and the United States. Gwin concluded by stating that he was abandoning the project and returning to the United States. As for Terry, he wrote, "Your excellent judgment, my dear colonel, will be your best guide as to your future movements."[6]

Terry's "excellent judgment" dictated that he remain where he was for a time. Gwin's plan failed, but there was another that gave more indications of success. The leader of the latter venture was a well-known American hydrographer. Matthew Fontaine Maury, as a commander in the Confederate navy, had developed the art of torpedo warfare and mining of waterways to a degree hitherto unreached. Late in the war he went to England to purchase torpedo materials, and he remained abroad until almost the conclusion of hostilities. On his return he learned that the armies and government had collapsed. At Havana, while considering the next step to take, he received advice from friends

[5]Hallie Mae McPherson, "William McKendree Gwin Expansionist," MS doctoral diss. (Berkeley, 1931), pp. 259-68.

[6]July 2, 1865, quoted in Wagstaff, pp. 235-36.

not to go to the United States until feeling in the North had subsided.

Always an admirer of Maximilian, Maury decided to offer his services to the Austrian who by this time was on the throne in Mexico. Both the emperor and the empress gave him a warm welcome. Maury declined the offer of a post in the cabinet but accepted an appointment as director of the imperial observatory. His real interest, however, was in colonization, and his plan envisaged the movement to Mexico not only of Southern whites but of Negroes as well. Plantation owners whose slaves had been loyal throughout the war should make a bargain with their former slaves. In effect Maury was recommending bond service for the Negroes for seven years. During this time, while contributing their labor, the Negroes would be learning the language and preparing themselves for freedom. The scientist vigorously denied that he was plotting either to reopen the slave trade or reintroduce slavery to Mexico. It was his belief that his plan would bring prosperity both to the immigrants and to Mexico.

Maximilian had mistrusted Gwin as an aggressive Southern expansionist; he viewed Maury in a different light. When the latter presented his plan, the emperor accepted it and appointed the scientist imperial commissioner for colonization. Optimistically Maury launched his program, as Maximilian on September 5, 1865, issued a decree announcing the liberal terms of the new immigration policy.[7]

The immigration scheme was destined to early failure. Maury's own friends and relatives for the most part were unsympathetic, and General Robert E. Lee told him politely but clearly that he thought the place for loyal Virginians was in Virginia, not in Mexico. For a time Maury ignored the criticism and continued his work. He wrote a propagandist pamphlet and endeavored with some success to have

[7] D. F. M. Corbin, *A Life of Matthew Fontaine Maury* (London, 1888), pp. 233-34.

it reprinted in whole or part in American newspapers.[8] His son, Richard Maury, and General J. B. Magruder aided him in the project.

Under their auspices a few colonies started operation. On November 27, 1865, Maury wrote to his wife that he was selling lands around Cordova to immigrants at a dollar an acre on five years' credit just as fast as the land could be surveyed. The land was fertile and on the rail line from Veracruz to Mexico City. General Shelby was one of about forty purchasers of land in the Cordova project, which Maury named the Carlotta colony in honor of the empress. Early in the spring of 1866 Maury went to England. After his departure enemies of the program influenced the emperor, although he still wrote cordially to Maury. The scientist himself did not return to Mexico and he may have lost interest partly in the excitement of helping to lay the first transatlantic cable.[9]

The Carlotta colony was the only immigration venture with which Maury seems to have been directly concerned. He was, however, interested in other colonial enterprises, and his office of colonization was to a considerable degree a propagandist agency. It sought to persuade Southerners to go to Mexico and then merely gave them advice on methods of acquiring land. In his publicity letter of February 7, 1866, Maury urged, "It is best for every such company of immigrants to send some of their number ahead to select a place, and bargain for it themselves." The commissioner then noted that several parties had already followed this procedure; "Bryant from Arkansas has established a colony in Chihuahua. Mitchell of Missouri another on the Rio Verde in the Department of San Luis Potosi. Terry of Texas another in Jalisco."

[8][Letter regarding colonization], Feb. 7, 1866. (Photostat in the Huntington Library. Across the copy of the letter is written, "Please let this appear in one of your daily papers. Col. Maury.")

[9]Charles L. Lewis, *Matthew Fontaine Maury. The Pathfinder of the Seas* (Annapolis, 1927), pp. 202-204.

Thus it appears that Terry had embarked upon a colonization venture by early 1866. He and a group of persons had acted on their own initiative and without the direction but with the sanction of the office of immigration. It is possible that the group may have worked closely with the captain of the port of San Blas, who was an immigration agent.

Terry was not turning to unknown lands for his project. Having spent some time securing horses and supplies when going to Texas in 1863, he had become familiar with the west coast near Mazatlán. His wife had been even nearer the lands selected for she had disembarked at San Blas, not far from the region in which Terry was to settle. San Blas, which had been prominent as a port during the period of Spanish control of California, had been surpassed in importance by Mazatlán. One of the larger streams, the Rio Grande de Santiago, originates in the mountains and flows past Guadalajara, capital of Jalisco, from the uplands to the sea.

One hesitates to attempt to reconstruct Terry's life in Mexico, for the sources are meager and in some cases untrustworthy. It appears that after leaving Parras, Colonel Terry and a small group of men headed for the west coast of Mexico. Arriving at Mazatlán they paused to decide on a course of action. One account states that Terry's wife and sons were with him at this time.[10] If this is true, it is probable that they went by vessel to the Isthmus and then up the West Coast, since there is no evidence that the family was with Terry at Parras.

Terry's first venture is said to have been the raising of sheep. He and Major Beaumont rode south and then inland to Guadalajara and leased a sizable tract of land from a large landowner. The next step was to secure the livestock. Wagstaff states that since the judge did not wish to return to California at this time, his wife made the trip, bought sheep and horses, and had them shipped back to Mazatlán.

[10]Wagstaff, p. 232.

146

By the time the stock arrived the situation had changed. The Texans who had accompanied Terry to Mexico drove the sheep to Guadalajara only to find that the landowner had changed his mind and would not make land available to them. The disappointed group of men with Terry could only assume that the military authorities in the region had exerted pressure on the proprietor because of fear of foreign infiltration. After considerable effort Terry sold the sheep and with his horses and companions left Guadalajara.

As they neared the coast along the river, Terry and the others realized that they were in good bottom land. The judge made inquiries and this time was successful in leasing property. Instead of trying once again a venture with which he was unfamiliar, Terry turned to the production of cotton.

Unlike northern Mexico, Jalisco was moderately peaceful during the early stages of the Maximilian regime, and a strong military detachment maintained order. Terry evidently made no effort to align himself with the local officers of the empire and in fact was reported to have argued with a royalist officer over the arrest of one of the men in his party. This action may have counted in his favor when the republicans came to power.

Not only was Jalisco peaceful during the empire but it made the shift to republicanism with little difficulty. A republican force after little more than a skirmish effected the withdrawal of the royalist soldiers and entered Guadalajara without further opposition. Having gained control, the republican leader wisely exercised moderation. There is no evidence that Terry or the men with him participated in the struggle. The attacking force may have passed the cotton plantations on its way, but the fighting took place farther inland.[11]

Terry's family probably stayed in Mexico until early in 1867. It is likely that they remained much of the period in Mazatlán or Tepic. Part of the time there were no adequate facilities on the plantation, nor did the nearest town,

[11]H. H. Bancroft, *History of Mexico* (San Francisco, 1888), VI, 256-57.

Santiago, have accommodations. The desire to provide educational opportunities for the children prompted Mrs. Terry to return to California. She moved with her youngest son, Clinton, to the Stockton area, probably on the old family ranch between Linden and Clements, and placed Sam and Dave in a private school in Vacaville.

In the fall of 1867 Mrs. Terry received a long letter from her husband, who after months of thought had reached a decision regarding his future course of action. Were he alone in the world, he wrote, there would be no question. "I would stick it out and bear any fate the future might bring rather than return to the U. S." But there were others "whose future welfare" he was "bound by the most sacred obligations to consider," and he would be derelict to his "duty as a husband & father if I allowed any personal considerations to make me forget these obligations." Seeing no prospects for Mexico but "anarchy, bloodshed, oppression & outrage," and no hope of a stable government "able & willing to protect personal rights," he reluctantly concluded "to return to Cal and to work hard to educate my boys and try to save enough to give them a start in life." He could not act on the decision immediately, for he would have to wait until the cotton was ready for picking and dispose of the equipment that he could not ship profitably to California. If he could not secure within $600 or $1,000 of the value of his horses and mules he would drive them through by land. The trip would take a couple of months longer than by sea, but the judge wrote, "400 or 500 a month is good wages for a man as poor as I am and besides I could see a great deal of strange country & you know how fond I am of traveling by land."[12]

Ignoring her husband's request that she remain in California, Mrs. Terry returned to Mexico with her youngest son. Terry found it unnecessary to make the long drive from his Mexican plantation. Instead he and his family took passage on the steamer *Sierra Nevada*, which arrived in San Fran-

[12]Oct. 11, Terry MSS.

148

cisco, July 2, 1868. He brought some of his goods and possibly stock with him.[13]

The bands did not play for Colonel Terry when he returned to California after the war. Not only had he fought on the losing side, but to many Californians the shadow of the Broderick duel and the Vigilante affair still hung over him. Consequently times were so difficult that Mrs. Terry was reduced to sending bills to persons who in past years had become indebted to the Terrys, bills that in normal times probably never would have been sent. Terry found that the prejudices against him made it difficult to rebuild his practice, although he continued the effort for six months or so. Then he determined to strike out in another region. Once before he had attempted to regain success in Nevada but the Civil War had intervened, and the trial had not been fair or adequate. But now there was a new rush and opportunity again presented itself for quick wealth. Early in 1869 Terry left for the White Pine country.[14]

[13]*The Morning Call* (San Francisco), July 3, 1868. For an unenthusiastic response to Terry's return, see *Stockton Daily Independent*, July 6, 1868.

[14]In July Terry joined L. T. Carr and P. Wilkes in a law partnership. *Stockton Daily Independent*, July 22, 1868. The firm's card continued to appear in the Stockton papers after Terry went to White Pine until Aug. 9, 1869.

Chapter IX

The White Pine County Speculator

THE WASHOE COUNTRY in which Terry had tried his
luck in the early sixties lies near the California border.
The White Pine region toward which he headed late
in the decade is about halfway up the state near the eastern
boundary. The White Pine Mountains constitute a small spur
running north and south, and to the east is a lower elevation
known as the Base Range, about three miles in length. Beyond
this range is another mountain known as Treasure Hill, about
9,000 feet high, in which the richest strikes were made.[1]

Almost every mining strike has an account of its discovery
that quickly becomes shrouded in rumor and legend. The
miner, A. J. Leathers, had made some discoveries on the
slopes of the White Pines in 1865. He had organized the
Monte Cristo Mining Company, but the workings had not
lived up to the company's fabulous namesake. Then one
evening Leathers caught an Indian pilfering food and chased
the marauder from the shack. Apparently as a peace offering
the Indian, Jim, took the miner a piece of silver chloride. The
gift was so rich in quality that Leathers persuaded the Indian
to take him to its source. Thus, according to the story, was discovered the Hidden Treasure mine, one of the most valuable
in the area.

Taking a few men into his confidence Leathers began

(*Letters cited in this chapter are in Terry MSS, Huntington Library.*)

[1]Charles Drayton Gibbes, *Map of the White Pine Silver District, Nevada, with
the Surrounding Country* (San Francisco, 1869).

---

operation in January, 1868.[2] The news could not be kept secret; T. E. Eberhardt soon laid claim to rich deposits nearby, and even winter weather hardly checked the rush that followed. Some of the early finds were amazing. Two men who arrived on the scene erected a barricade of stones to shelter them from the bitter blast of the wind. The walls they had thrown up held ore to the value of $75,000.

While there was something of a rush early in 1868, the real boom did not commence until late in the year. A town developed; originally called Cave City, it was soon renamed Hamilton in honor of one of its chief promoters. By November its population was about six hundred and the real rush was beginning to get under way. One visitor estimated that about fifty new residents were arriving daily. The miners started another settlement, Treasure City, two and a half miles away from Hamilton and connected by a toll road.

By the time Terry moved to the White Pine country the boom was definitely on. The trip was still tiring, although a new road had been opened. He left San Francisco, waited overnight at Sacramento, and boarded the train the next morning at 6 o'clock, paying $46 for his ticket. Forty-eight hours later, having crossed California and half of Nevada, he reached Elko. He then paid approximately $40 for a stage trip about 110 miles south to Hamilton.[3] When he arrived in Hamilton late in February or early in March, 1869, he found it similar to the Nevada mining towns of the early sixties. There were about 150 "houses, tents and huts," to quote a contemporary observer, made of "every conceivable material—rough lumber, planed lumber, slabs, pine logs, cedar posts, cotton cloth, woolen blankets, willows, tin, raw hides, hay, mud and stone." Into these structures there were crowded nightly "1,500 human beings and any number of horses, mules, Indians, dogs, and whiskey-bloated, blear

[2]*History of Nevada*, ed. Myron Angel (Oakland, 1881), pp. 660-661.
[3]Albert S. Evans, *White Pine: Its Geographical Location, Topography* (San Francisco, 1869), pp. 21-22.

eyed bummers."[4] A local news item indicated what was perhaps the ultimate in congested conditions:

Crowded—The cell of the county jail 7 x 10 is at present over-crowded, there being seventeen inmates of that hospitable institution. It does seem that this county ought to be able to afford a building which would be more creditable, and better answer the purpose of a county jail.[5]

As in Washoe there was frenzied buying and selling of stock. There was also heavy speculation in town real estate; lots which first sold for $25 were selling in February for prices ranging from $1,000 to $10,000. Some of the mines gave evidence of being fantastically rich. Albert S. Evans visited the Eberhardt mine in February, 1869, and in amazement wrote:

Descending the shaft on a rope, we found ourselves among men engaged in breaking down silver by the ton. The light of our candles disclosed great black sparkling masses of silver on every side. The walls were silver, the roof over our heads silver, the very dust which filled our lungs and covered our boots and clothing with a gray coating was fine silver. We are told that in this chamber a million dollars' worth of silver lies exposed to the eye, and our observation confirms the statement. . . .[6]

Another factor drawing Terry to the region was great confusion over mining claims. By the first day of February, 1869, almost 2,200 mining claims had been entered for the White Pine mining district, and four-fifths were located within a circle two miles in diameter. Each person could claim 200 feet along a ledge or vein, 200 feet wide. The following statement normally accompanied the claims, "We claim the same with all its dips, spurs, angles and variations."[7] A contemporary visitor wrote, "These claims, located as sep-

[4]Ibid., p. 23. For another description of crowded conditions see *White Pine News* (Treasure City, Nevada), Apr. 5, 1869.

[5]*White Pine Evening Telegram* (Shermantown, Nevada), Aug. 6, 1869.

[6]Evans, p. 14.

[7]Ibid., p. 24.

arate ledges, run into and across each other in every direction, and in the most inextricable confusion"; and he predicted, "the crop of fights and ruinous lawsuits which will result from this confusion will yield a rich harvest for the legal fraternity, and beggar many a man now holding really rich and valuable claims."[8] Meanwhile until the courts got in their work, possession was more than 99 per cent of the law. Men claimed lots by the dozen and crudely "fenced" them with a single half-inch strip of rawhide fastened to stakes thirty feet apart. "Personal possession and a good revolver constitute a clear title, whatever the records at Austin may say." Twenty or thirty a night was considered a low average for "jumping" lots, and on a single night in February, 1869, sixty lots were jumped.

Almost immediately on his arrival in the White Pine country, Terry became involved in the two major speculations of the region, city lots and mines. He took most of his cases on a contingent basis and his fees largely consisted of an interest in the concern whose cause he was pleading. He found it easy to secure business, but the return in hard cash was slight and slow. Shortly after reaching Hamilton, the judge became counsel for a mining company and by February 19 he reported to his wife that the company owed him $1,800. There was, however, little chance of immediate collection. Times were "very dull" and it was "exceedingly hard for anyone to get money on any terms; collecting is very hard work." Optimistically he looked forward to the spring and summer.

In addition to aligning himself with a mining company in the hope of a bonanza, Terry became the attorney for Dan Whelpley who laid claim to many of the city lots in Hamilton. Terry won two cases for his client; one was for an entire tract of lots and the other was for a lot and a house that an alleged "jumper" had constructed on it.

Terry was not as enthusiastic over Hamilton's prospects as

[8]Ibid., p. 25.

was Whelpley and he told his wife, "I have felt rather low spirited over the future of this place but others and those who have the best means of knowing are very sanguine that in the Spring business of all kinds will revive." If the prediction proved correct Terry had a chance to profit heavily, for he held a third interest in a tract of 83 blocks, each with 28 lots. He wrote home, "who knows that I will not get 30 or 40000 dollars out of this land if the mines last a year longer." More realistically, he continued, "My chance is not bad but if some one were now to offer me $5000 for my 800 lots I think I should sell out & quit."[9]

Actually the Terrys were still hard pressed for funds and they had to meet the bills for the two boys in boarding school. Terry rented his ranch near Stockton and was relieved that the rent money was going to Mrs. Terry for he found it "almost impossible" to get money in Hamilton. Terry's loyalty to friends and relatives produced added financial strain. He mortgaged the ranch to raise funds for Dr. Richard P. Ashe, and after the death of Aurelius Terry in Texas, Judge Terry took his brother's son to raise. Approximately the age of Clint, young "Reel" Terry remained in Terry's household until he reached manhood.

Meanwhile Terry continued his work in Nevada. There was little money, but at least he could hope for "pay in the future." Hamilton had a serious water problem and in winter virtually the only source was snow water. Terry wrote, "I use no water except that which I get by melting snow every morning before going to breakfast I put a few shovels of snow in the water bucket & thus keep a constant supply."[10] In using snow the judge seems to have been in the minority. Evans reported with tongue in cheek that snow water if used too frequently caused "irritation of the bowels" and was considered dangerous. "Whiskey is recommended in its place. In justice to the people of the district," he continued, "we must say that they generally show a disposition to manfully

[9]Mar. 3.   [10]Mar. 11.

154

conquer their prejudices, and, restraining the temptation to indulge in water, swallow whiskey with as much grace as if they liked it from the start."[11] The situation was not much better in the summer, and on June 21 the *White Pine Evening Telegram* noted that the supply of water daily was becoming more limited.

By July 25, 1869, Terry was thinking of returning to Stockton. He told his wife, "I am beginning to be afraid that this country will not be so prosperous as all persons anticipate." Although the mines were rich, the necessary capital for development was slow in coming. Yet Terry was still hopeful; Easterners were looking at the mines with a view to investment and he stated that as far as legal practice was concerned, "There is beginning to be a good deal of litigation about the mines and will be a great deal more when money is not so hard to get hold of."

During the summer Mrs. Terry went to Hamilton, partly to be with her husband and partly to see if the climate would benefit her health. She improved and the summer was an enjoyable one for the couple. In the fall Terry insisted that his wife return to a more moderate climate. After her arrival in Stockton he wrote that he hoped to finish his cases by the middle of December and join her.

Terry's departure from Hamilton was delayed, for his practice improved. To a considerable degree his prosperity depended on the success of his clients. One of these, a man named Henderson, was reported to be clearing at least $2,000 a week from mining operations. Terry wrote, "I presume Henderson will be able to settle with me before I start to Cal." Another client named Brown had succeeded in some mining negotiations in which Terry had an interest. As a result the judge had the choice of $750 in cash or a fourth interest in $15,000 in stock in the mill and in eight mining claims. Terry asked his wife, "Don't you think I'd better take the money?"[12]

[11]Evans, p. 40.   [12]Nov. 11.

As the winter continued Terry entered other business schemes. As has been seen the water problem was acute in Hamilton, for melted snow water was not adequate for a population of nearly ten thousand. A group of men had formed a company and secured a virtual monopoly by controlling the nearby Illipah Springs and hauling water. Terry and some associates became interested in breaking this monopoly. Through manipulation and a show of force they secured access to another spring and made fair profits from the sale of the water.

Despite the modest profits he had been making, Terry was anxious to return to California. By April he was convinced that he could secure as much business in Stockton as in Hamilton, and he felt that an agent could handle the sale of his lots. "I do not think this country is at all likely to prove a good place for making rapid fortunes at the law. There is too much dread of the expense of litigation and very few people here have the means if they had the will to carry on mining suits which are greatly more expensive than any other class of cases." The usual practice, he explained, was to compromise cases. Litigation not involving mining matters, he believed, would "always be better in Stockton than here."[13]

Eager as Terry was to return to California, he did not propose jeopardizing his professional ethics. He heard of a case in California involving the railroad. It was an important matter that undoubtedly would produce a very satisfactory fee. The judge wrote his wife that "of course" he would like to have such a case but that he would "underbid nobody to get it."[14] Shortly before leaving Nevada, Terry received a tempting offer. His friend, Dan Whelpley, and an associate named Boyle had rented the White Pine mill at a low figure and had the contract to crush ores from the Hidden Treasure mine. They strongly urged the judge to join them in the venture. Terry did not have time to consult his wife, and

[13]May 12, 1870.
[14]May 22.

156

since he had determined to go to California he rejected the offer. He did so with some regrets, for he thought that with proper management the mill would clear $1,500 a month. Toward the end of May or early in June, 1870, having concluded his cases, Terry left Nevada once again to live in California.[15]

It was probably just as well that he left Hamilton, for the White Pine mineral deposits although extremely rich in quality were relatively shallow. From the Eberhardt mine on Treasure Hill for example ore worth $3,000,000 was taken from a hole only 70 feet across and at no place deeper than 28 feet. Terry left some time before it was known that Hamilton was no Comstock Lode, and production and hopes were still high. By 1873, however, it was clear that production was declining, and in that year the town suffered a disastrous fire. Some mining continued until the mid-eighties, but it was obvious that Hamilton's day was past. In 1886 the dying city was gutted by another fire, started by a cigar store owner who in the face of diminishing sales thought of the insurance on his building. Another fire in the same year provided the pretext for a shift of the county seat to Ely. From this event Hamilton moved inexorably toward complete abandonment, and it stands today as one of Nevada's ghost towns.

Far more important to David Terry than the modest share of these riches that he gained was the fact that Nevada offered him a place of post-war readjustment. Neither Terry himself nor the people of California were in the proper frame of mind to permit his quick return to the state after the war.[16] The Mexican interlude was of some importance as a temporary stopgap, but in Mexico Terry was not only in a

[15]A White Pine paper noted one of Terry's trips as follows: "Gone to California. Judge David S. Terry left by Beachy, Wines & Co.'s stage yesterday for California. He goes on professional business and will be absent about ten days." *Daily Inland Empire* (Hamilton), Apr. 7, 1870.

[16]J. W. Terry insisted that Judge Terry and his family "did not suffer any more than numerous other ex-Confederates and their families." Notes for Klette, p. 16.

strange land but in addition he was forsaking his profession. Nevada on the other hand permitted Terry to regain his feet professionally. He showed himself and others that he could still win cases. He became involved in no "incidents," and one hears not a word of a bowie knife during his stay in Hamilton. His main interest in acquiring money arose not from a wish for personal fortune but from a desire to bring security and if possible wealth to his wife and boys.

Hamilton also was sufficiently near California for Terry to re-establish his practice gradually in California. On occasional trips home he renewed professional contacts and may have handled some cases in Stockton before closing his office in Nevada. At the same time the reputation he made at Hamilton may well have been reflected in increased business after his return home.

Terry's second Nevada interlude was important, although in comparison with the more spectacular episodes of Terry's life it has attracted little public notice. The man who emerges from the rather extensive family correspondence of these months appears in sharp contrast to the usual stereotypes of him. Throughout the extant letters Terry clearly shows his deep love for his wife. On November 27, 1869, he wrote:

You ask me if I would think of you on the 25th. You should know my darling that no day passes over my head without thought of you and a longing for the sight of the dearest and loveliest the most loved and loving face that ever blessed my sight. It would be passing strange if we did not long for each others presence. For seventeen long years you have been to me my conscience, my other & better self. You have multiplied one hundred fold all my pleasures by sharing them and have been my comfort and consolation in all times of trial grief and misfortune.

You are dearer to me now than when I first held you in my arms for then I did not know the full value of the priceless jewel that I had found. I knew that in my eyes you were "the fairest among ten thousand & altogether lovely."

I knew that you loved me with your whole heart but I could not know that under all trials I should never find your eyes turned on me but with a look of affection, that you should never oppose even my whims and in all your actions seek to gratify my tastes even if you did not approve them. It would indeed be strange if a day should pass that I did not think of you and long to have you by my side, that my heart did not overflow with gratitude to the benificent Ruler of the world for the priceless blessing he had given me in you. This might seem strange language from a man of forty six to a woman of forty to those who have not loved as we have, but you my darling will feel their truth and will know that after seventeen more years shall have passed if we live so long they will still be true.

Mrs. Terry was ill during much of the period from 1869 to her death. Terry was concerned and in various ways sought to alleviate her condition. After her return from Hamilton he even sent her some patent medicine that his friend, Dan Whelpley, had prepared. The judge was lonely in Nevada and once impatiently wrote, "I did not receive my expected letter yesterday or today and am at a loss to know why you have not written as usual."[17]

In general the tone of Terry's letters was calm, but with pleasing good humor. These were not letters written for publication. The boys and Mrs. Terry featured prominently. The judge discussed minor points with major problems, sometimes even in the same sentence. On arriving in Hamilton he wrote, "To answer your questions I did not form a partnership and I did bring off the key of the corn popper. Did not discover it until I reached here and did not send it back because I thought the freight would cost more than a new key and beside the clock key would wind the machine."[18]

Terry enjoyed using colloquialisms. "I am glad the rain has come at last but fear it is too late for many of the farmers. At any rate it will prevent a *skacity*."[19] Reporting on the trip to Hamilton, he stated that he had had a pleasant ride on the train but had been "shook most Tremenjous" in the stage over twenty-five miles of corduroy road. In the same letter

[17]Mar. 11 [1869].
[18]Mar. 3 [1869].
[19]Ibid.

he denounced the "Hel's peppered cuss" of a baggageman who had stolen a silver whistle from his hunting jacket.[20] There was good-natured banter in the letters, and Terry occasionally gave his wife items of gossip about some of the people she had met.

Terry was a devoted parent. During most of his stay in Nevada, Dave and Sam attended boarding school, the grammar school of St. Augustine's College, an Episcopal school in Benicia. Mrs. Terry urged the boys to write to their father, since he had "but few pleasures in that rough cold country, and you should therefore add your mite."[21] Unfortunately the letters more often than not were designed to please the teacher rather than the parent. In fact Dr. Lloyd Breck, the head of the school, customarily delivered a sermon that was to be the basis for letters written. As a result parents opening a letter in the hope of learning of their child's activities during the past week received such information as the following: "I will begin this trial letter by telling you about Dr. Breck's missionary life among the Indians in Minnesota. The party if I remember rightly consisted of a clergyman and a divinity student. . . ."[22] "I write you this letter to inform you that I am well. We had a lecture by a bishop from Scandinavia upon the ancient scandinavians. The ancient scandinavians were unsurpassed. . . ."[23]

In addition to his insistence on scholastic excellence Judge Terry wanted his sons to lead an active life. He often took them hunting. While in Nevada he wrote in anticipation of a camping trip in the Sierras, "We can make a hut of bark which will be a sufficient shelter for the Summer and can have plenty of hunting & fishing. I think such a trip would be the very thing for Mama."

Toward the end of the school term at Benicia, Terry became

[20]Feb. 7, 1870.
[21]C. Terry to S. L. Terry, Feb. 20, 1870.
[22]S. L. Terry to C. Terry, Oct. 2, 1869.
[23]D. S. Terry, Jr. to D. S. Terry, Nov. 25 [1869].

critical of one phase of school life. Young Dave had written of a schoolmate who had been severely beaten for dropping a book on the parade grounds. The judge reacted as follows to his wife:

I think Dave's indignation at the cruel punishment of the boys in his school is just. No teacher should be allowed to administer severe punishment even for a grave offense. I quite agree with you that it would not do to treat one of our boys in the way Dave says the boy Earl was treated for in such a case if I did not treat the community to a funeral I would at least cut a clerical hide into ribbons with the heaviest mule whip I could find in the state.

If when I go down I find the case is as bad as stated I shall not send the boys back as I do not wish to take the chances of having to murder a preacher.[24]

[24]May 12, 1870.

Chapter X
The Respected Citizen

IN SOME WAYS the decade of the seventies constitutes one of the most satisfactory periods in David S. Terry's life. During these years he lived down to a considerable degree the reputation he had gained from the stabbing of Hopkins, the duel with Broderick, and service with the Confederacy —all acts regarded by many as ill-advised or worse. During the seventies also Terry gradually regained his eminence as a lawyer of marked ability and in the process he amassed once more a sizable family fortune. Throughout the first half of the decade he remained rather consistently aloof from politics and returned to it only when he had re-established his legal and financial position. On the personal side, apart from a single blinding tragedy, Terry's life was that of a fond parent watching his children grow to manhood.

At the same time, the very factors that made the seventies a pleasant phase in his life have caused the period to be underemphasized in accounts of Terry's career, for little that was spectacular occurred. Although his post-war adjustment was probably fairly well completed by the time he left the White Pine country, Terry found times still hard. Cases were not as numerous nor were the fees as lucrative as they had been in the early fifties or as they would become later in the seventies. The boys did not return to private school but continued their education in the public schools in Stockton.

The judge never limited himself to his practice when he needed more income. He had bought ranch land in California, acquired town lots and mining property in Nevada, and

162

tried cotton culture in Mexico. In the early seventies, partly for financial reasons and partly no doubt because of his interest in horses, he owned a stable. He did not advertise in the papers, but his horses were for hire. Early in 1871 one of his animals was stolen, and the thief and horse were captured at Angel's Camp.[1]

By the summer of 1871 Terry had formed a partnership with another attorney, L. T. Carr.[2] Whatever the cause, the partnership was brief, and the last professional card of the two men appeared in the papers on September 30, 1871. Terry evidently carried on his practice alone until February, 1873. Carr remained in Stockton for a time and then moved to San Francisco, although he still attempted to secure legal business in Stockton.[3]

As an attorney Terry was not a specialist and engaged in both civil and criminal practice. One of his cases aroused considerable local interest. Numerous suits developed in California from the expansion of the railroads. The city of Stockton and San Joaquin County in enthusiasm had subscribed heavily to bonds for the support of railroad construction. By 1871, however, the local railroad company had sold out to Leland Stanford and his associates who were putting together the network of rail lines that was to give them both wealth and political power. It had been agreed that municipal and county bonds would be turned over to the company upon the construction of a road from Stockton to Visalia. Instead the company referred to a short road acquired from another independent company as the satisfaction of its side of the bargain, and demanded the bonds. City and county officials disagreed with this point of view and contested the case.[4] Oddly enough Terry seems to have started as an attorney for the railroad and shifted sides. At first he was retained as local

[1]*Daily Evening Herald* (Stockton), Feb. 11.

[2]*Stockton Daily Independent*, Aug. 1.

[3]Ibid., May 8, 1874.

[4]Bancroft, *History of California*, VII, 588.

counsel by the company whose principal lawyers were from San Francisco.[5]

Starting in 1871 the Stockton and Visalia Railroad case wound its weary way through the courts for half a dozen years and then was settled out of court. By the summer of 1872 Terry had become one of the attorneys for the people. Associated with him was another former member of the state supreme court, Silas W. Sanderson. The district court's decision favored the city and county, but in 1875 the supreme court reversed the decision and held that the bonds should be delivered to the railroad company. Terry and his associates in the case managed to delay matters until May, 1877, and finally effected a compromise. City and county bonds to the value of $200,000 were to go to the railroad's representative, and in return $300,000 worth of bonds and their coupons were to be canceled. The total cancellations amounted to $530,000.[6] Terry and those who had worked with him on the case had saved Stockton and San Joaquin County a very substantial sum of money.

In another case Terry's clients won a legal contest with the Central Pacific Company. In 1869 and 1870 numerous settlers had entered contracts with the railroad company for the purchase of land to which the company expected to receive title from the government. Then the settlers discovered that the land was actually a part of a prior grant, known as the Moquelemos Grant, and, as reserved land, could not be ceded by the government to the railroad. The settlers consequently felt no obligation to pay the company. The matter went to court, and Terry handled the defense for the settlers and won the case in the district court.[7] Since valuable lands near the town of Lodi were involved, the company appealed. Some four years later the supreme court upheld the decision of the lower court.

[5]*Stockton Daily Independent*, Dec. 8, 1871.
[6]Ibid., May 14.
[7]Ibid., Mar. 19, 1872.

164

As in the fifties Terry traveled from one courthouse to another in the practice of his profession. He went frequently to Sacramento to plead cases before the supreme court and as a former member of that body was thoroughly at home when appearing before it. In the spring of 1872 he was in the Sierra foothill town of San Andreas defending an alleged murderer.[8] He was quite successful in criminal suits and was an attorney in several other murder cases.[9]

It will be recalled that in the fifties Terry and his partner had sought to bring to task a corrupt judge. In 1874 Terry attacked another example of malfeasance in office. He and his partner, Barna McKinne, on behalf of their client, B. Triplett, charged August Munter, justice of the peace, with accepting illegal fees. The amount involved was not great, but Munter was found guilty, discharged from his post, and ordered to pay $500 to the informant.[10]

Meanwhile as this legal practice was developing, the Terrys were leading the life of an average, moderately prosperous family in a California valley town. In 1872 by a show of great physical strength Terry halted a span of frightened horses he was driving and prevented a crash with another carriage containing a woman and several children.[11]

In their growing years the four boys tended to split into pairs. Sam and Dave advanced into high school, while Clint and his cousin, Reel, were still in grammar school. One account is related of Sam and the "gang" to which he belonged. Told years later by Theodore Steiny, one of the boys in the group, the story perhaps gained in the telling. One day when the boys were about twelve they made a dummy by stuffing a suit of clothing with straw. For a time they amused themselves by conducting lynching parties. Then the idea occurred to them of suspending the dummy by a rope from the limb

8Ibid., Apr. 29, 1873.
9Ibid., Aug. 15, 1873; July 25, 1877; Feb. 18, 1878.
10Ibid., Mar. 2, 1874.
11Ibid., Sept. 6.

of an oak that stood at the end of the bridge over the slough near El Dorado Street. As an unsuspecting passerby neared the spot, the dummy dropped immediately in front of him. The plan worked successfully for a time and the boys got the "laugh on one prominent citizen after another."

Then in the distance the boys saw the burly figure of Judge Terry headed for the bridge. Here was "big game" indeed. One hunter, however, was appalled at the prospect. Sam Terry, who even then spoke with a long, slow drawl, pleaded, "Gee, don't do it to Pa! Pa'll raise h——l."

The answer was prompt, "Your Pa ain't any different from anybody else's Pa." Despite this brave pronouncement Steiny admitted that the boys were nervous as they waited for the victim to approach.

The judge drew near, reached the target, and the boys let the dummy drop. Steiny later recalled, "Well, sir, I'll never forget what followed. Judge Terry's hand flashed back to his hip pocket, and before you could wink he had pulled a revolver and put two bullets into that straw dummy." The shots came close together, but according to the narrator, "By the time the second shot was fired there wasn't a kid in sight." Steiny concluded, "The Judge strode on, looking neither to right nor to left. If the joke was on him he certainly didn't show it."[12]

As they grew a little older Sam and Dave developed some studious tendencies. Fairly early Sam appeared headed for his father's profession.[13] In addition to schoolwork he participated actively in the local debating society and read law in his father's office. Although Dave also took part in high school debating and was a good student, he did not decide as quickly on a profession. In the fall of 1873, for reasons that are obscure, Dave was sent to the Tejon ranch near Bakersfield. It may be that he had shown an interest in ranching and that his parents wanted him to serve a period of apprenticeship.

[12]Told to Ernest J. Hopkins, *The San Francisco Examiner*, May 13, 1921, p. 12.
[13]*Stockton Daily Independent*, Oct. 17, 1873.

However, Dave did not work out satisfactorily as a ranch hand. In desperation B. F. Lee, the ranch manager, wrote to Terry that the boy should be sent for. All Dave was interested in was hunting, he was insubordinate, and he refused to try to learn the sheep business.[14]

The judge had no chance to reach his son. On Saturday evening, December 13, while Dave was cleaning his revolver it was accidentally discharged and the bullet struck the boy in the chest. Mr. and Mrs. Lee did all they could, but the wound was fatal. The nearest doctor was thirty miles away and Dave died almost eight hours before the physician arrived.

Later writers, notably those hostile to Judge Terry, have contended that Dave Terry committed suicide.[15] This writer has been unable to find that the death was anything but an accident. The newspapers of the region all speak of the shooting as accidental.[16] A few days after the tragedy Mrs. Lee wrote a letter to Dave's mother describing his last hours. Nothing in this letter indicates that the revolver was intentionally fired.

The parents were greatly shocked. Three sons already had been lost in infancy. Sam Terry's growth in stature and ability must have been a partial counterbalance to these losses. In April, 1875, as soon as he could meet the age requirement, he was admitted to the bar. David S. Terry had entered partnership with a young and popular attorney, Major Barna McKinne, and Sam went into the office first as an assistant and then in January, 1876, as a co-partner.[17]

In 1875 Terry's name began to appear again in the records of the Democratic party in Stockton. Rallying around New-

[14]Dec. 9, Terry MSS.

[15]E.g., *Themis* (Sacramento), Aug. 17, 1889.

[16]*Kern County Weekly Courier* (Bakersfield), Dec. 20; *Stockton Daily Independent*, Dec. 15; *Daily Evening Herald*, Dec. 15; Jennie Lee to Cornelia Terry, Dec. 18, Terry MSS.

[17]*Stockton Daily Independent*, Apr. 15, 1875; Jan. 11, 1876.

ton Booth, a faction of the Democrats became known as "Dolly Vardens."[18] Terry remained with the other element, which called itself the "Straight" Democracy. When the county Democratic convention met in Stockton toward the end of May, 1875, there was a struggle for the election of delegates to the state convention. Seeking to pave the way to victory, the "Dolly Varden" element had printed a slate and advocated a vote by ballot. The "Straight" faction demanded the customary viva-voce method, and a deadlock occurred when the time came to select ten of the twenty-two men who had been nominated. Finally, as though the idea had just occurred to him, Terry suggested that the secretary be instructed to call the list of candidates so that the delegates were forced to vote openly for one delegate at a time until ten were selected. Both sides agreed and the convention voted. On May 31 the jubilant editor of the *Stockton Daily Independent* wrote of Terry's proposal:

This looked smooth—it sounded smooth—it *was* smooth, but it struck the rotten Dolly Varden slate right in the center and shivered it into fragments, and the slate makers did not discover how it was done until about sixty minutes after the motion had been carried. . . .

The result was that a "Straight" ticket was elected to represent San Joaquin County at the state convention.

David Terry's activity in politics as the decade continued was that of a supporting role. He sought no public office and concerned himself with issues rather than personalities. In the election of 1877 he spoke several times for his party. Early in September for example he was the main speaker at a gathering in Hunter Square in Stockton. The ardently Republican editor of the *Stockton Daily Independent* commented on Terry's address, "The speech was the best one of the evening, because the speaker is greatly the superior intellectually of his colleagues on the stump."[19]

[18]Davis, *Political Conventions*, pp. 323-24.
[19]Sept. 4.

Terry had made his comeback. The man who had stabbed Hopkins, shot Broderick, and been feared as a public enemy in the early months of the Civil War had become a highly respected citizen of a California city. His family was well regarded, he was a lawyer of ability, his income was substantial, and his political astuteness was recognized. He was ready to assume an active role once again in state affairs. This time the part was not that of interpreter of the law but of constitution-maker in the second constitutional convention.

Chapter XI
The Constitution-Maker

IN A rapidly increasing society institutions may easily become outgrown or outmoded. Such was the case with California's first constitution, which had been drawn under unusual circumstances in 1849 for a projected state that was still sparsely settled. By the later seventies the population had jumped to well over 700,000 from about 100,000 in 1849, and life had become more complex. Although mining was still important, agriculture was becoming increasingly significant. San Francisco's growth had brought with it urban problems, not the least of which was the relationship between capital and labor. Throughout the state the power of corporations, especially railroads, had reached monopolistic stages. To complicate the situation still more, Chinese had immigrated in sufficient numbers to create a political and economic issue.[1]

In the midst of these problems came the call for a new constitution. Some people felt that the document of 1849 was inadequate to serve the more populous and wealthy state. Others believed that a new constitution might provide a panacea for the ills of the day. The issues ran across regular party lines, and in addition a new party had arisen. Dennis Kearney and other members of this Workingmen's party found convenient scapegoats at both extremes of social and economic life in the state. On the one side they breathed fire and venge-

[1] For the background of the convention, see Carl B. Swisher, *Motivation and Political Technique in the California Constitutional Convention, 1878-1879* (Claremont, California, 1930), pp. 5-16.

ance on the huge corporations, and on the other, maledictions upon the Chinese. As the movement spread, its ideas appealed to workers in the cities and towns and to many miners who by this time had been reduced to the economic level of laborers. When the time came to elect delegates to the constitutional convention, many Republicans and Democrats in fear of the Workingmen presented a Non-Partisan ticket, which more accurately should have been termed bi-partisan.

Late in May, 1878, a Non-Partisan county convention met in Stockton's Mozart Hall. T. K. Hook placed the name of David S. Terry in nomination and, according to a local reporter, "eulogized his nominee as a man of the highest sense of honor; a man of ability equal to any in the State; of the highest integrity; one whom no interest can purchase; and a lawyer of large experience in the affairs of the State." Terry won the nomination over his opponent by a substantial majority, and the vote was then made unanimous.[2]

During the campaign, Terry spoke at a Non-Partisan meeting held in National Hall, Stockton, on June 15, and outlined his views. The journalist reporting the meeting was impressed by the speech which crystallized "the issues pending into the fewest words possible." The reporter wrote of Terry, "He has the faculty of divesting an intricate subject of all unnecessary matters, and presenting the main proposition with wonderful force and brilliancy." Terry told his audience that the old constitution was a good one and that all it needed was to be changed in a few places. The main problem was that of taxation. For some time taxation had worked well, until the supreme court decided that the "taxation of a solvent debt was double taxation." Terry proposed to "make that matter so plain that the 'wayfaring man though a fool' would not have any difficulty interpreting it." The speaker believed that all property should be taxed and that it should be taxed equally.

As far as the Chinese were concerned Terry showed that he had matured. The state could do little about the Chinese

[2]*Daily Evening Herald*, May 25.

171

for the national government would protect them. Terry noted with candor that once he had been a vigorous defender of states' rights but he had lost and he saw the folly of trying again to beat down federal power. The speaker indicated that he was still against Chinese immigration and that much could be done by "unfriendly legislation." Terry then concluded with a criticism of the Workingmen's party. His attack was without invective and emphasized the view that in reality Kearney had nothing new to offer.[3]

In August General Volney E. Howard of Los Angeles was the main speaker at a political gathering. Terry presided and with pleasure introduced his old friend of Vigilante days. By this time the elections were over and both Terry and Howard were among the men selected to frame the new constitution. The Workingmen's party had carried San Francisco but had lost in the rest of the state. The result was that the Non-Partisans together with a few delegates who had run as Democrats or Republicans had a clear majority.[4]

The convention had its initial session in Sacramento on September 28, 1878, and got off to a stormy start.[5] The Workingmen delegates were bruised from the beating the press had been giving them. Most of them were unfamiliar with the processes of a body such as that they were joining. They looked with scorn on some of the delegates as mere tools of a despised monopoly. They suspected the lawyers with which the convention was heavily weighted, for they feared that these men through parliamentary procedure would seek to outmaneuver and outwit them. Bitter feeling became evident almost immediately. On the first day, Saturday, there was a brief quarrel over adjournment. William Irwin, governor of the state, presided until the convention could elect its own

[3]Ibid., June 17.

[4]Swisher, op.cit. (above, note 1), p. 24.

[5]*Debates and Proceedings of the Constitutional Convention of the State of California*, E. B. Willis and P. K. Stockton, official stenographers, I (Sacramento, 1880), 13. Hereafter cited as *Debates*.

172

officials. A Workingmen's delegate, one of the few lawyers of that party, challenged the governor's right to call him to order and declared, "I deny your right to silence me, sir. I want to know your authority. I am elected here by the sovereign people of the State of California, and you are not."[6] After lecturing the convention for applauding, the governor put the appeal from the decision of the chair to a vote and was sustained in his action.

David Terry was one of three men who missed the first meeting and arrived on the following Monday. A senior member of the body, William Van Voorhies, moved that the three men be sworn in as delegates, as the rest had been the preceding Saturday. Probably because of his spectacular background and well-known ability as a lawyer, Terry was viewed with distrust by members of the Workingmen's party. They sought to take advantage of the existing constitution to prevent the judge from helping to draft the new document. The constitution of 1849 provided that anyone who had participated in a duel should "not be allowed to hold any office of profit, or to enjoy the right of suffrage under this Constitution." The provision was a dead letter; both Broderick and Gwin had fought duels for example yet no one had questioned on this account their right to hold office.

That Governor Irwin was not disposed to listen to the Workingmen's effort to exclude Terry is indicated by the following excerpt from the minutes of the convention:

Governor IRWIN. The members who have not yet been sworn in will now please come forward and take the oath.

Mr. BEERSTECHER. Mr. President: I object to David S. Terry being sworn in, and base my objections upon this——

Governor IRWIN. The gentleman is out of order.

Mr. BEERSTECHER. Section seven of article eleven declares——

Governor IRWIN. The gentleman will take his seat—he is out of order. The law makes it my duty to swear in the persons elected to

[6]Ibid., 16.

the Convention. Then any objection to the eligibility of members can be raised. The power to determine who are members rests in the Convention, and not in the Governor, who presides temporarily.

Mr. O'CONNELL. Mr. President: I think we have a right to enter our objections.

Governor IRWIN. The gentleman will please take his seat, he is out of order.

Mr. O'SULLIVAN. Mr. President: I think so also, and I protest against the gentleman taking his seat.

Governor IRWIN. The gentleman will take his seat; the gentleman is out of order.

(D. S. Terry, of San Joaquin, Alexander Campbell, Jr., of Alameda, and Daniel Inman, of Alameda, were sworn in and subscribed to the oath of office.)[7]

The matter was not yet ended and continued in the heated election of convention officials. Unable to elect their own candidate, Henry Larkin, the Workingmen threw their support to W. J. Tinning, a member of the state legislature, a Non-Partisan who was normally a Democrat. The Workingmen preferred him because of a belief that his opponent, Joseph P. Hoge, a prominent San Francisco attorney, represented corporation interests. The vote was close, 74 for Hoge and 73 for Tinning.

Before the vote was announced Clitus Barbour protested the vote of Judge Eugene Fawcett on the ground that as judge he could hold no other office. James O'Sullivan also objected to Judge Fawcett's vote. C. J. Beerstecher who had already attacked Terry's presence in the convention then protested Terry's vote. Governor Irwin chose to ignore all three protestants and the minutes blandly note, "The Chair then announced the result of the vote which was received with applause."[8] Mr. Hoge, having been escorted to the chair, made a conciliatory speech and the convention continued its course.

The Workingmen apparently gave up their struggle to

[7]Ibid., 15.
[8]Ibid., 22.

unseat Terry. Later, whether they would admit it or not, most of them would be glad of his presence. The attempt to remove Judge Fawcett on the other hand led to long and at times acrimonious dispute. The judiciary committee to which the matter was referred reported in favor of Judge Fawcett on the grounds that his own constituents had not protested and that a seat in the convention was not an "office" in the sense of the constitution. The Workingmen could have found little comfort in the fact that one member of this committee was the other man they had failed to exclude, David S. Terry.

Although he voted in favor of Judge Fawcett and obviously felt that he was rightfully a member of the convention, Terry did not hesitate to oppose seating a man whom he thought unfit for the position. Former governor H. H. Haight had been elected a delegate to the convention but had died before that body convened. The contest for his replacement was lively, and one of the men first mentioned was A. C. Peachy of San Francisco. Terry strongly opposed the selection of Peachy and commented vigorously on some elements of Peachy's earlier career. The result was that the San Francisco politician challenged Terry to a duel. The details are not clear. Nothing about the matter appears in the *Debates* of the convention, but the story leaked out to the newspapers and one report stated, "The dullness of Sacramento life was somewhat enlivened last week by a rumor of an approaching duel between two prominent attorneys and politicians." The men, the account alleged, had quarreled "in connection with some domestic matters," and during the altercation Terry had "offered Mr. Peachy an affront, which Mr. Peachy was quick to resent." The customary "friend" waited on the judge and "although not submitting a challenge, invited him to meet Mr. Peachy in Nevada for purposes of settlement." According to the newspaper report Terry "refused to have anything to do with the matter, professing to have had sufficient experience of that character before."[9] Writing some years later of

[9] *The Morning Call*, quoted in *Daily Evening Herald*, Oct. 8.

this affair, the Los Angeles *Times* editor stated that Terry refused to fight a duel "because his courage needed no vindication and his challenger was not his equal on the duelling field."[10] Peachy was extremely nearsighted. A few days after the dispute mutual friends brought the two men together and an amicable solution was reached. Terry must have had cause for criticism, for Peachy evidently paid blackmail to prevent having the entire problem aired in the press.[11] Peachy's name was mentioned on the floor of the convention, but it was not placed in nomination.

The selection of standing committees was one of the first important actions of the convention, and on October 8 Terry became a member of the committee on judiciary and judicial department. Although he proved to be a valuable member of this committee, far more important was his selection as chairman of the committee on legislative department. Terry's major contribution to the convention was in his direction of this committee which drafted the part of the new constitution dealing with the legislative branch of the government.

The judge was not one of the garrulous members of the body and made no long speeches. When he had an interest in the discussion he entered it, but in general his comments were succinct and pointed. Considering his reputation for bellicosity, it is interesting to see Terry acting as a mediator on one or two occasions. Some delegates were highly critical of the regular branches of the state government but at the same time made demands on them. On October 19 the convention made a request to the secretary of state for all the information he had on corporations, including number and classification, place of business, amount of capital stock, and amount of capital stock actually paid up. Secretary Thomas Beck threw up his hands at the request and either in irritation or in jest sent back as his answer fifty-two volumes of material

[10]Quoted in *The Mail*, Aug. 20, 1889.
[11]*The Morning Call*, quoted in *Daily Evening Herald*, Oct. 8, 1878.

from his office. Some of the delegates did not appreciate the joke, if such it was, and criticized the state official both on and off the floor of the convention. Evidently Beck asked Terry to placate the delegates, for on October 22 he rose to make an explanation on behalf of the secretary who, Terry explained, intended no disrespect "but simply desired to demonstrate the utter impossibility of complying with the request."[12] The explanation did not soothe the delegates. They lashed back at him, and even criticized the mediator. When one of the offended delegates referred to Terry as the "representative of Mr. Beck," the judge quickly responded, "I beg to correct the gentleman, I am not the representative of Mr. Beck. I represent the people of San Joaquin."[13]

The convention was slow to get to its real business. The heated contest for presiding officer was followed by the appointment of standing committees, and then as has been noted, the convention became involved in a debate over Judge Fawcett's eligibility for membership. Much of the real work was done in the standing committees. The constitution then, piece by piece, was to be examined by the committee of the whole, and finally by the convention itself.

Resolutions to guide the standing committees began to pour in as the convention got under way. One of the rules of the convention was that a resolution must deal with only one subject. The number of resolutions consequently mounted rapidly. On October 10 Terry sought to cut through some of the red tape that was stifling the body, and moved to suspend the rules to permit Thomas H. Laine of Santa Clara to introduce the draft of a whole constitution that he had prepared. Laine was a lawyer of ability who had worked hard on the preparation of his document. Terry's effort failed, for some of the delegates became so concerned with the possible dangers of suspending the rules that they voted down the motion. The seed apparently took root, however, for a few days later when

[12]*Debates*, I, 167.
[13]Ibid., 171.

another entire constitution was introduced, the rules were waived without question, and the draft of the constitution was received, broken up, and referred to the appropriate committees.

Terry was naturally interested in the provisions of the constitution dealing with the judiciary and on November 7 he took issue with the man whose right to sit in the convention he had advocated. Judge Fawcett introduced an amendment dealing with the functions of the jury in criminal cases involving libel. His amendment stated that instead of having "the right to determine the law and the fact" it should have "the right to find a general verdict as in other criminal cases." Terry's main point emphasized his general concept of the duty of the convention to leave alone what was good in the old constitution. There had been no complaints against the old provision and the new one might increase the power of the judge at the expense of the jury. Terry's comments touched off a sharp debate. Terry lost his point, and Fawcett's amendment was accepted by a vote of 74 to 67.[14]

From time to time Terry entered the discussion on other legal problems. Eli T. Blackmer, a music teacher and county superintendent of schools, was a delegate from San Diego on the Workingmen's ticket.[15] Like others, he felt that the gubernatorial pardoning power had been abused, and on November 9 he introduced an amendment limiting the pardoning power to cases involving the introduction of new evidence establishing either the innocence of the convicted party or the injustice of the penalty. Terry rose in quick protest and in view of his later difficulties some of his comments are of interest. In case of a sentence of from one to four years for example the governor should have a right after a reasonable time

[14]Ibid., 338.

[15]The most convenient sketches of the members of the convention are to be found in D. G. Waldron and T. J. Vivian, *Biographical Sketches of the Delegates to the Convention* (San Francisco, 1878). The accounts are laudatory and in places inaccurate, but they contain material not easily found elsewhere. See p. 121 for sketch of Blackmer.

and under certain circumstances to pardon the prisoner. Then Terry spoke of the possibility of a sentence by a biased court, and declared, "I say every man who is consigned to prison by a prejudiced Judge should have a right to have his application for executive clemency heard." Terry also gave evidence of his continued belief in "personal justice," for, he stated, "A man may commit murder under the influence of a knowledge of an outrage upon wife or sister, and be technically guilty, to be sure, but in such cases why should not the Governor be allowed to pardon him?"[16] After a good deal of debate, Blackmer's amendment was defeated.

By this time the committee on legislative department was ready to present a part of its work. On November 11 Terry offered a substitute for Article IV of the constitution. A minority report was introduced at the same time, and both were ordered printed.

Some delegates were becoming annoyed at the delays in the work of the convention. Terry spoke in favor of using the "previous question" to speed up the functioning of the committee of the whole. Speaking bluntly, he said there was an additional reason for the rule. A great many speeches had been made that were "no doubt very edifying," but because of the poor acoustics of the building could only be heard by those in the vicinity of the speaker. The other members, said Terry, could "hear the racket but not the words." The judge also stated that in his opinion the delegates had been in convention a sufficient time and the reports had been printed and considered long enough for the members to have made up their minds. Therefore, he concluded, "I do not think that we want any more long speeches by members of the convention."[17] Terry's plea was in vain; he made it in November, and the convention was not to grind to a halt until the following March.

Terry held strong convictions regarding corporations, and

[16]*Debates*, I, 357.
[17]Ibid., 365-66.

his beliefs more nearly coincided with those of the Working-men than with conservatives. On November 13 he introduced an amendment to the report of the committee on corporations, which was being considered by the committee of the whole. It was short but pointed:

The directors or trustees of corporations and joint stock associations shall be jointly and severally liable to the creditors and stockholders for all moneys embezzled or misappropriated by the officers of such corporation or joint stock association during the term of office of such director or trustee.[18]

Recently there had been a number of bank failures and similar losses resulting from the actions of corrupt officials. Terry hoped by making all directors jointly responsible to check such occurrences, and he spoke directly of one case, that of the French Bank in San Francisco. The directors left everything in the hands of the president, and the result was, said Terry, "that after a series of disastrous speculations in stocks he left the world by means of suicide." The example was apt, for there were those in the convention hall who had lost money in the French Bank.[19] The proposed amendment occasioned extended debate. O'Donnell of San Francisco provided comic relief by reading the proposed amendment as "Directors and trustees of corporations and joint stock associations shall be jointly and severely liable." Another Workingman, Patrick Dowling, denounced monopolies as "barnacles clinging to the body of the people." They were, he asserted, "as big a nuisance as Chinatown, and render the poor man a slave."[20]

After listening for some time to the debate, Terry entered the discussion. Saying that he had not expected "that such a clamor would be raised," he rejected a suggestion that the provision be left to the statutes and not placed in the constitution. He declared that he proposed to put it into the constitution,

[18]Ibid., 396.
[19]See comments of J. F. Lindow, ibid., 399.
[20]Ibid., 402.

where it could not be "amended or repealed, and let it stand for all time as a protection to the people of this State against the robberies which are committed by the officers of these corporations."[21] The judge was applauded for his remarks, and it is to be suspected that the Workingmen delegates were beginning to revise their opinion of the man they had sought to exclude from the convention.

Shrewd Eugene Casserly of San Francisco attempted to embarrass Terry by asking him if his amendment included "charitable, benevolent, and religious associations." Terry, undisturbed, answered in the affirmative, "I do not think a charitable or religious corporation has any better right to steal money than a lay corporation."[22] When the amendment passed, its supporters cheered loudly. Morris M. Estee, who had opposed the amendment, said, "Mr. Chairman: I see gentlemen in the lobby who are applauding, and the next time it occurs I shall move that the lobby be cleared." Tyler Davis Heiskell, a farmer from Stanislaus County, responded, "I hope the gentleman will not be particular. This is the first victory for the people that has occurred in four years."[23]

A few days later Terry introduced another amendment designed to curb corporations. This was a detailed provision preventing any agency of the state, from legislature to township, from investing funds in a private corporation. There was some debate, but it was decided to postpone a vote until later.

The corporations most delegates had in mind were those dominated by the so-called "Big Four," Mark Hopkins, C. P. Huntington, Leland Stanford, and Charles Crocker. One proposal coming before the convention was to establish a railroad commission that would check the power of the railroad. At first Terry opposed this solution, and on November 21 he stated:

[21] Ibid., 403-404.
[22] Ibid., 418.
[23] Ibid.

I say here and now, that I do not propose to give, by my vote, to any triumvirate the power that is proposed to be given to three Commissioners in the State of California. If they would give me the appointment of the Commission, I do not know where I would find three men that I would be willing to trust so far. It is against the principle of the Lord's Prayer. These men are being led into temptations which they would be more than men if they could withstand.[24]

Later when it became apparent that a railroad commission would be established, Terry rose again. Restating his earlier objections to the creation of such a body, he said that he was submitting to "the will of the majority." Further, he declared, "I now desire that the means to secure the end shall be made effectual." Opposing a proposal to weaken the commission's power to regulate rates, he successfully sponsored an amendment to give the commissioners power to punish contempt of their orders "in the same manner and to the same extent as Courts of record."[25]

Many persons felt that an excess of stock speculation, which had been an attribute of quartz mining in California and Nevada, had been partly responsible for the depressions of the period. Terry sought to check this excess by an amendment voiding any contracts made for the sale of capital stock on margin. Saying that he was told that the amendment would drive the stock market to Virginia City, the judge remarked, and he thought the people of California were of the same opinion, that he "would be willing to see the whole business in —— a climate much farther south than Virginia City." It would be "good riddance to bad rubbish," and "The country would be prosperous now but for that."[26]

In the discussion that followed Samuel Wilson of San Francisco apparently became annoyed at Terry's persistence in making his points and characterized him as follows:

[24]Ibid., 472.
[25]Ibid., 609.
[26]Ibid., II, 807-808.

No gentleman more thoroughly understands the art of presenting the worse as the better reason. He has the capacity, as shown in his argument, beyond any man that I know of on the floor. It is with the greatest difficulty, at times, that I resist him, for he rises with that earnest, honest expression of his, and can almost make us believe that wrong is right. But he evades the question. . . .[27]

Terry paid no attention and continued making his points until Wilson gave up in disgust. The judge then summarized by stating that what he wanted to do was to protect the "honest people outside the stock board." He was not interested in the gamblers themselves. "Let the dogs eat the dogs. Let the thieves rob the thieves." The laws, he asserted, were "not to protect the gamblers against each other, but to protect other men against gamblers."[28] Ultimately Terry's proposal found its way into the constitution.

As Terry had indicated in his campaign for election as a delegate, he felt that there should be some changes in the system of taxation. The convention reached the problem toward the end of December. It was, as one speaker remarked, a "moot" question, and tempers became more than a little frayed during the course of the discussion. The following brief extract from the debates will illustrate the point:

Mr. HOWARD. My friend cannot befog that decision.

Mr. EDGERTON. Nor you either.

Mr. HOWARD. I am not in a befogging state.

Mr. EDGERTON. You are always in a fog.

Mr. HOWARD. I always find you there, if I am.

Mr. MORELAND. I hope this side show will come to an end, and that I will be able to proceed with my remarks.

The CHAIRMAN. The gentleman must not give up the floor, then.[29]

During the more constructive part of the discussion, W. W. Moreland of Sonoma County introduced an amendment to the

[27]Ibid., 808.
[28]Ibid., 809.   [29]Ibid., 864.

effect that all property in the state was to be taxed in proportion to its value. His definition of what constituted property was the debatable part of the amendment. For the purposes of taxation, urged Moreland:

. . . bonds, notes, mortgages, evidences of indebtedness, solvent debts, franchises, and everything of value capable of transfer or ownership, shall be considered property.[30]

Opponents of the amendment charged double and even triple taxation. Terry favored the amendment, basing his argument for taxation, even though it be double, upon protection. "People go into society," he said, "for the purpose of protection. Upon what other principle do we pay taxation except that we have a protection for our persons and property."[31] He further supported the principle of taxing solvent debts. In defending his position he also explained what he considered to be his duty as a member of the convention. When another delegate said that he did not believe the amendment proposed would satisfy the people, Terry stated:

Now, what the opinion of a majority of the people may be I do not know. What the people demand I do not know. I have never received any instructions in regard to what the opinion of the people of this State may be on this subject. But I proposed to them before I came here, and I propose now to do, as far as my actions and words can have any influence, what, in my opinion, will be for the best interest of the people of the whole State.

The judge was not too much concerned about the outcome and continued:

When I have done that I shall have done my duty. Whether the people shall approve of the Constitution when we get through with it is their business and not mine. I do not propose to stop to inquire whether it is popular or not popular. I propose to exercise my best judgment as to what is right, and I do not care whether it is popular or not.[32]

[30]Ibid.
[31]Ibid., 867.   [32]Ibid., 873.

184

It was inevitable that anti-Chinese provisions be proposed for the constitution. The most rabid opponent of the Chinese among the delegates was Dr. C. C. O'Donnell of San Francisco. He had been one of the first men in San Francisco to start an "anti-Coolie" crusade and he continued his attacks on the floor of the convention. He was so extreme in his utterances that he found few supporters. One of his obsessions was a fear that the Chinese constituted a menace to the health of other persons in California. Once after he had digressed on the highly communicable nature of leprosy, one of a number of delegates who took delight in heckling him introduced a resolution stating that since Dr. O'Donnell had been in contact with the disease he be "quarantined and isolated, and that a portion of the gallery be set apart for his use and benefit."[33]

Unfortunately for O'Donnell, he was not only extreme in his replies to hecklers in the convention but he made the error of criticizing the *San Francisco Chronicle*. The newspaper immediately replied with countercharges, including "quack, imposter, and abortionist," to which O'Donnell responded with a suit for criminal libel. A special committee of the convention reported early in January that the *Chronicle's* charges were true and, therefore, not libelous. The committee consequently moved that O'Donnell be expelled from the convention. The so-called doctor, however, apparently had provided so much comic relief that the delegates could not bring themselves to expel him. Instead they procrastinated for a time and then moved to postpone the case indefinitely. Terry was among those who favored this course of action.

O'Donnell represented the extreme anti-Chinese point of view. Terry and other delegates objected to the continuance of Chinese immigration but were more practical in their attitude. An amendment that Terry presented on December 13 showed that he was thinking perhaps as much of monopoly as of the Chinese:

[33]Ibid., 671.

No corporation now existing or hereafter formed under the laws of this State shall, after the adoption of this Constitution, employ, in any way, any Chinese or Mongolians. The Legislature shall pass such laws as may be necessary to enforce this provision.[34]

In his accompanying remarks Terry showed that he felt the Burlingame Treaty between the United States and China to be an almost insuperable obstacle to Chinese exclusion. The state, he said, did not have the power to abrogate a treaty made by the United States, and the convention could not prevent the Chinese from immigrating nor private individuals from hiring them. On the other hand the convention could prevent corporations from employing Chinese, for corporations existed "by the will of the State." Terry made it clear that he would work by all legal means to discourage Chinese immigration but, he declared, "I do not propose, so far as any vote of mine is concerned, to bring the State of California into conflict with the power of the government." In a good-natured way, he explained:

I tried that on once when I had a great deal better backing than now, and I proved my faith by my works. I went to where the fighting was going on, and felt some of the missiles. I was whipped, and I had sense enough to know it after it was done. I do not propose to provoke any more conflicts of that kind. (Laughter) I propose to exercise all the power we have got, and no more.[35]

Terry found support for his amendment, and it was incorporated into the constitution.

As the convention progressed the attitude of the Workingmen changed markedly toward Terry. Those who had sought to exclude him came to listen with respect to his comments. His ideas on such questions as corporations, Chinese, and taxation made sense. Terry showed no resentment of the early attitude toward him and in fact on at least one occasion attempted to perform a service for a member of the Work-

[34]Ibid., 699.
[35]Ibid.

186

ingmen's party. A San Francisco delegate died and the convention moved to the election of a successor. Terry obligingly replied to a request by John C. Stedman of the Workingmen's party, and placed the name of R. A. Leonard in nomination. Unfortunately the Workingmen had not caucused and they nominated other candidates as well. When a Workingman, Patrick M. Wellin, stated that Leonard was not the choice of the San Francisco delegation, Terry washed his hands of the matter by asking, "Don't you know I was requested to place him in nomination by one of your colleagues, Mr. Stedman." Apparently Stedman had not secured the support of the delegation; in embarrassment he acknowledged that he had asked Terry to make the nomination and he withdrew his candidate's name in favor of the man being supported by the bulk of the San Francisco delegation.[36]

There were some persons who felt that Terry became more than a friend of the Workingmen in the convention. An editorial in the Oakland *Enquirer* expressed this view not long after Terry's death. The editorial reviewed the early effort of the Workingmen to exclude Terry:

And thereupon followed a singular transformation. In opinions and temper Terry was a good deal like the Workingmen delegates, and having about ten times as much brains as the smartest among them, he soon became their actual though not their acknowledged leader. The man they had so recently execrated and called by all the vile names they could invent, really directed the movements of the Workingmen during that long and eventful session.[37]

As he indicated during the course of the convention, Terry's main interest was in the drafting of the constitution. Throughout the constructive period of the convention he was present and always ready to explain or defend a point. Once the document had been framed and had gone past the

[36]Ibid., 766.

[37]Quoted in *The Mail*, Aug. 19, 1889. Wagstaff (p. 255) asserts that Terry gained "the support of the workingmen," and could work "with an almost absolute certainty of carrying every point he desired."

committee of the whole, he lost interest. He was not concerned with making last-minute speeches nor, it is suspected, with the routine of securing final approval by the convention. His business needed attention, and he began to absent himself for days at a time, as did other delegates.

Although he had said his work would be finished when the constitution was drafted, Terry found it impossible to remain aloof from the campaign to secure ratification of the document by the people. He addressed a large meeting in Stockton's National Hall on April 10. As usual he avoided extravagant rhetoric and won interest and applause by considering piece by piece the changes that were proposed. He stressed the theme that this was an important election and that upon it depended "whether this state" had "in the future, as, unfortunately, it has for many years in the past, to be ruled by corporations, rings and monopolies." The alternative, if the constitution should be ratified, would be "a government for the people, of the people and in the interest of the people." He brought out such points as the item veto of appropriations bills, and the requirement that a majority of the members elected to the legislature was necessary to pass a bill, not merely a majority of those present. This requirement, he observed, would prevent lobbyists from watching "for a thin house to get their bills through." The speaker was roundly applauded when he stated later that the new constitution proposed to "treat those stock gamblers the same as bunko sharps, so that the cheated can get their money back." As on the floor of the convention Terry showed his belief in control of railroads and other corporations. In his conclusion the judge not only gave evidence that he could turn a neat phrase but in so doing he anticipated in one sentence both Theodore Roosevelt and Franklin D. Roosevelt. Urging his hearers to vote for the new constitution, Terry exhorted, "Let us have a new deal and a square one."[38] Early in May when the election was held the constitution carried San Joaquin County

[38] *Daily Evening Herald*, Apr. 10.

188

and the state. In a celebration at Stockton's Hunter Street Square there were "speeches, music, bonfires and liberal hurrahing." Terry appeared as one of the speakers.[39]

Many supporters of the new constitution believed that it needed friends in office and as a result they formed a New Constitution party. Its aim was to cut across party lines and elect men who would prevent the enemies of the document from destroying its effectiveness. The *San Francisco Chronicle*, virtually the only important California newspaper to support the constitution, may be said to have launched the movement. Leading in its organization were prominent men from the Republican, Democratic, and Workingmen's parties. Terry was one of them, and he aided the local formation of the party in San Joaquin County and became one of the key men in the state organization. When the state convention met in San Francisco on May 22, 1879, Terry became a member of the committee on resolutions. His name was placed in nomination for chief justice, but he declined the nomination.[40]

As matters developed Terry became a candidate, but not for the supreme court. Charles W. Cross, the convention's nominee for attorney general, declined the nomination on August 19, and the state committee of the party then nominated Terry.[41] It is not clear whether he wanted the position or simply yielded to the importunings of the committee. He does not appear to have campaigned on his own behalf.

Although the new party was designed to draw votes from all parties, it did not supersede any party. The Republicans, Democrats, and Workingmen met and nominated their own candidates. The New Constitution party added zest to the campaign, but the Republican party won the election. David S. Terry ran fourth.[42]

[39] Ibid., May 10.
[40] Davis, *Political Conventions*, pp. 410, 413.
[41] Ibid., 413.
[42] Ibid., 421.

Participation in the constitutional convention was a high point in Terry's career. His work in that body did much to counterbalance the ill will directed toward him as a result of the Vigilance affair, the duel with Broderick, and his pro-Southern proclivities. Men who had been prejudiced against him came grudgingly to admit that Terry was a man of integrity and ability. On the other hand to representatives of entrenched wealth Terry may well have appeared as a menace. His forcible words against monopoly and his shrewd suggestions regarding control, coupled with the fact that he could not be bought, made him a strong foe.

Chapter XII

The Divorce Attorney

THE PERIOD FROM 1880 to 1885 was for David S. Terry one of political disappointment, professional and financial success, and personal sorrow. Toward the end of that time, as a result of his widening reputation as a lawyer, he became associated with a case that was to have a significant influence on his life.

On the political scene in 1880 Terry found that animosities are long lived. In that year the Democrats in their state convention in Oakland nominated him without opposition to be an elector at large for the presidential campaign. Normally voters pay little attention to electors and are interested only in the candidate himself. In the November, 1880, elections, however, enough voters scratched Terry's name from the ballot to defeat him. Although the nation went for the Republican James A. Garfield, in California all the Democratic electors except Terry were elected.[1] Terry's past had been too great a handicap. Feeling justified in his earlier actions, the judge was hurt by the outcome, but according to his nephew, John Wharton Terry, then living in the Terry household, "In a few days he got over that and was in his usual good spirits."[2]

Terry continued his interest in political matters. In March, 1882, he addressed an anti-Chinese mass meeting in Stockton. His remarks were consistent with his earlier position on the subject, but he was temperate in his utterances. In May the

[1]Davis, *Political Conventions*, p. 431.
[2]Notes for Klette, p. 26.

Democrats held a typical "whoop-up" attended by about 2,000 persons in Hunter Street Square. A brass band "appealed to the patriotism of the multitude by playing national and irreligious airs." At eight o'clock men poured oil on two huge bonfires and lighted them. Speeches were then in order from a stand improvised from a grain wagon. After the announced orator had finished, according to the contemporary press, "David S. Terry then made his appearance in response to repeated calls." In his usual direct style the judge extolled the principles of Democracy and exposed the weaknesses of Republicanism.[3] In the following month, when the Democratic state convention met in San Jose, Terry as chairman of the committee on platform was in an excellent position to make certain that the principles of the party were placed on record. In addition he seconded Stephen M. White's nomination of George Stoneman for governor.[4] Stoneman won the election. Terry wanted no favors for himself but sought patronage for a friend. He came to feel that Stoneman had not lived up to his promise and broke with the governor. As a result Terry refrained from open participation in the convention of 1884.[5]

With one minor exception Terry's professional life during this period was highly creditable. The exception was an incident ignored by the local press but noted by a San Francisco paper. The *Call* on December 21, 1882, reported that Terry and an opposing attorney, S. J. Hinds, had had a "set-to with fists" in which Terry had used his boot as well as his fist. Both lawyers paid a fine of $25. If the incident was accurately reported, it constituted one of the few losses of self-control by Terry since the fifties.

In the early eighties in addition to prospering in his profession Terry could derive pleasure from the fact that the

[3]*The Stockton Daily Evening Mail*, May 10.

[4]Ibid., June 23. For details of the convention, see Edith Dobie, *The Political Career of Stephen Mallory White* (Stanford, 1927), pp. 32-37.

[5]*The Morning Call*, June 13, 1884.

---

young men reading law in his office were reaching maturity and beginning to show their ability. Reel Terry, who had been with the judge's family since childhood, persevered in his aim to enter the legal profession and was admitted to the bar in February, 1881. Aided by his uncle in launching his practice, Reel soon became locally prominent as both an attorney and a politician. After serving as district attorney in Fresno he sought and won the Democratic nomination for congress from the sixth district but lost the election to his Republican opponent. For reasons that are not clear, Judge Terry opposed his nephew's election.[6]

Another nephew, John Wharton Terry, spent several years in Judge Terry's home, reading law in his uncle's office. After admission to the bar, in 1881 he returned to Texas and made a distinguished record in his own state.

Terry was naturally most concerned with his son's progress. Sam had moved easily into the legal profession and as early as 1880 was being mentioned for public office. In 1882 he became city attorney of Stockton and later in the year he ran successfully for the state assembly. The San Francisco *Call* made him the subject of a feature article on January 25, 1883. Calling him the "smiling legislator," the writer noted:

There is nothing in his appearance or mannerism suggestive of his father's impulsiveness and big black-bearded face. During a debate in which he is especially interested, he generally appears to be half asleep, or day-dreaming of the duck-hunting glories of his native tule lands.

The youngest son, Clint, was interested in things mechanical rather than academic. He moved into various types of engineering, and his father's influence may have helped him secure such posts as chief engineer of the United States mint at San Francisco and superintending engineer of the state prison at San Quentin.[7]

[6]*Fresno Daily Evening Expositor*, May 16, 1888.
[7]The only long-lived member of his family, Clinton Terry, after retirement lived with his daughter, Cornelia Terry McClure, in Ukiah until his death in April, 1931. *Ukiah Republican Press*, May 6, 1931.

Although father and sons traveled frequently for political or business reasons, they felt the pull of the large family home facing McLeod Lake in Stockton. The drawing force was Mrs. Terry, whose balance had much to do with the judge's return to a position of prominence. Unfortunately she spent years in illness. Her last months were cheered somewhat by the arrival in the Clint Terry family of a baby, named Cornelia in honor of the grandmother. Late in 1884 David S. Terry wrote to his daughter-in-law of his wife's disappointment at his failure to take the baby to Stockton for a visit. He explained, "My whole time was occupied in San Francisco so that I could not go over to see you without being another day from home, and in the condition of Neal's health I wish to be home as much as possible."[8]

By the middle of November it was apparent that Mrs. Terry's illness had become serious. On the fifteenth Sam Terry notified his father and brother that she was "very much worse."[9] The invalid lingered for about a month, and when it was apparent that the end was near, Reel Terry joined the family group. On December 16, 1884, Cornelia Terry died.[10]

Only the judge and Sam remained in the Stockton home, as the Clinton Terrys lived at San Quentin. David Terry's sorrow was not yet complete. Within four months after his mother's death, young Sam was stricken. Complications developed from an operation performed the previous year, and after a brief illness, he died on April 1, 1885.[11]

The Stockton house had indeed become a "mere shelter from the elements."[12] The fateful course of action upon which the judge was to embark may be explained in part by the inexpressible loneliness that came upon him in the winter and early spring of 1884-1885.

[8]Oct. 24, Terry MSS.

[9]Terry MSS.

[10]*Stockton Daily Evening Herald*, Dec. 17.

[11]Ibid., Mar. 20, 27; *The Mail*, Apr. 1.

[12]The Terry home is described in *The San Francisco Chronicle*, Dec. 17, 1939.

On March 12, 1884, Terry openly became an associate counsel in a case that already had attracted wide attention. In the preceding September charges of adultery had been brought in behalf of Sarah Althea Hill against William Sharon, multimillionaire and former senator from Nevada. What aroused public interest was not the allegation of the senator's moral aberration but the implication that he was married. His wife had died in 1883 and it was generally believed that he had remained a widower. William Nielson, a newspaperman acting for Miss Hill, announced that he had a contract proving that a second marriage had taken place.[13]

The adultery charge was evidently a device to center attention on the alleged marriage and it dropped into the background. Efforts to reach a settlement failed mainly because of the obduracy of both parties. Early in October, therefore, legal action began in earnest. On the third William Sharon launched a suit to have the alleged marriage contract declared a forgery and surrendered to the court for cancellation. Sharon sought a decision from the federal court on the ground that he was a resident of Nevada and that since the issue was between residents of two states it fell under federal jurisdiction. The opposition soon contested this view and, contending that Sharon was a resident of California, Sarah Althea Hill began a suit for divorce in the state courts. Actually the purpose of the suit was a triple one, to establish the fact of the marriage, to obtain the divorce, and to share in the community property acquired after the marriage took place.

After the institution of the suits there was a period of legal maneuvering. General W. H. L. Barnes, a prominent San Francisco attorney, at first led the fight for Sharon. A delegate to the constitutional convention of 1878-1879, as a

[13]George C. Gorham, *The Story of the Attempted Assassination of Justice Field by a Former Associate on the Supreme Bench of California* ([n.p., n.d.]), p. 9. Hereafter cited as Gorham, *Story*.

conservative he had clashed with Judge Terry. George W. Tyler was the principal attorney for Sarah Althea Hill. Known for his rough courtroom tactics, Tyler confirmed his reputation as the trial progressed. On March 11, 1884, the trial in the state court got under way, and it was on the following day that Tyler announced that Terry was joining him as associate counsel.[14] The judge still remained largely in the background as Tyler handled the case almost exclusively in the court. The issues began to emerge as the case proceeded. The Sarah Althea Hill version was briefly along the following lines.[15]

Sarah was a native of Missouri whose parents had died when she was young and left her a substantial income. In the early 1870's she had come to California with an uncle and her younger brother, Morgan Hill, and for a time lived with elder relatives, including a grandmother. The arrangements had not proved satisfactory and the young woman moved into her own hotel room. When she met William Sharon in 1880, the senator was about sixty years old, a banker who had made millions in the Comstock through mine manipulation and speculation. The marriage of one daughter to Lord Fermor-Hesketh indicated the social aspirations of the family. Another daughter married Francis G. Newlands and died in 1883. A son, Frederick W. Sharon, with his brother-in-law, Newlands, was to carry on the legal battle after his father's death.

Sharon had noticed Sarah Althea Hill, who had been moderately successful in stock speculation. He met her in his bank one day and complimented her on her success in stocks. The acquaintance ripened rather rapidly after this chance meeting. Soon, according to Sarah, Sharon suggested a strictly extramarital arrangement in which he would pay her $1,000 monthly. Sarah merely "told him he had made a

[14]*The Morning Call*, Mar. 12.

[15]For a convenient summary of Sarah Althea's story, see Oscar Lewis and Carroll D. Hall, *Bonanza Inn* (New York, 1939), pp. 121-32 and passim.

mistake in the lady." The millionaire protested that he had made the suggestion only "to tease her" and that his real desire was to marry her. "That was a different matter," Sarah answered, and the discussion continued. Sharon wished the marriage to be kept secret, and the young woman agreed. As a result the two, according to Sarah, signed a marriage contract on August 25, 1880.[16] In the same document Sarah agreed not to divulge its contents for two years.

After signing the contract Sarah was persuaded to move to the Grand Hotel, which was connected by a covered passageway to the Palace Hotel, where Sharon lived. Thereafter in fancied secrecy the couple lived as man and wife until 1881. Sharon tired of the arrangement and tried to terminate it. Sarah objected and the result was a series of quarrels, temporary reconciliations, and then a complete break. At one time Sharon sought to have Sarah evicted from the Grand Hotel. She refused to co-operate and stubbornly remained in possession until Sharon had the carpets ripped from the floor and the doors removed from their hinges.

The Sharon side of the controversy denied the authenticity of the alleged marriage contract. The evidence was too strong for the senator to deny a very intimate relationship with the plaintiff. A primary aim of the defense, therefore, was to attempt to establish Sarah as an adventuress who by means of forged documents, the marriage contract and the so-called "Dear Wife" letters, sought to share the millionaire's vast estate. Early in the trial Sharon created a sensation by having his attorneys announce that he had had "illicit intercourse" with a number of women other than the plaintiff, had paid them money, and had not introduced them to his family.[17]

The press naturally reported the case with all the details that the period permitted. Judge Terry was occasionally pulled

[16]Sharon v. Sharon, 16 Pacific Reporter, 346-47.
[17]*The Morning Call*, May 29.

into the arguments, one of which was a sharp exchange with General Barnes. Sarah Althea Hill was a delight to the spectators and a problem to the court and no doubt at times to her attorneys. She was a spectacular woman in her early thirties, a person of theatrical mannerisms and no known inhibitions. After watching her on the witness stand one reporter wrote, "She had acquired a manner of owning the courtroom, and could not be repressed by the combined efforts of counsel and court." One of the numerous emotional peaks of the trial was reached when one of the attorneys, Tyler's son, appeared armed in court, as was a hostile witness on the stand. When a suggestion was made that attorneys be unarmed, David S. Terry said, "I have carried no weapon since the war. I carry no weapon now, nor have I for many years."[18] Judge Sullivan, trying the case, refused to leave his chambers the following morning until everyone entering the courtroom was searched for arms.

During the trial questions began to arise concerning the plaintiff's source of funds. Toward the end of May the San Francisco *Call* speculated on the matter. It was apparent from the well-fed appearance of the plaintiff's attorneys that "someone's money" was satisfying the existing demand for legal fees. Tyler, it was rumored, had a contract of a contingent sort with Sarah Althea Hill, and it was further rumored that a wealthy lady was advancing the bulk of the money. As later disclosed, the "wealthy lady" was an almost legendary octoroon. Mammy Pleasant was one of the most debatable figures in San Francisco history. Coming to San Francisco during the gold rush, she was financially successful in the operation of boardinghouses of an unsavory reputation. Later she became housekeeper for Thomas Bell, one of San Francisco's millionaires, and virtually controlled the household. At an earlier time Mammy Pleasant and Sarah Althea Hill had become friends, possibly as a result of a common interest in the occult. The Negro woman became Sarah's almost constant

18Ibid., Supplement, Apr. 10, 1884.

companion in court. Mammy Pleasant's biographer asserts that it was she who conceived the idea of the marriage contract.[19]

The first phase of the trial ended with the adjournment of the court in May, 1884. The break conveniently enabled the attorneys to turn their attention to politics. Although the state Democratic convention met in Stockton, Terry took little open part in it. Discouraged by his defeat for presidential elector in 1880, he sought no post himself, and having broken with Governor Stoneman, he deliberately stayed away from the convention halls.

Despite his failure to attend the convention, Terry was in Stockton part of the time and was visited by various members of the party.[20] One of the most heated controversies centered about a justice of the United States Supreme Court. Stephen J. Field had succeeded Terry as chief justice of the California supreme court. In 1863 an act of congress created a tenth justice of the supreme court of the United States and reorganized the judicial circuit on the West Coast. Field was appointed to this post and was to serve on the bench for thirty-four years.[21] Early in the campaign of 1884 some politicians began to push Field as the Democratic candidate for president. There was strong opposition, for both on and off the bench Field had demonstrated that his interests lay with the conservative class and that he was especially friendly toward the railroads. Since men of opposite beliefs controlled the state Democratic convention, they attempted to block the presidential aspirations of the justice. The last resolution presented to the convention specifically repudiated his claims by pledging the convention not to vote for any delegate who was for Field. Two points concerning this resolution might be noted in connection with the Sharon affair. One was that the strongest speech made in support of Field in the convention was that of Francis

[19]Helen Holdredge, *Mammy Pleasant* (New York, 1953), p. 185.
[20]*The Morning Call*, June 13.
[21]Swisher, *Field*, passim.

G. Newlands, Sharon's son-in-law.[22] The other was that some persons considered that despite his nonattendance David S. Terry was the power behind the convention, which by a vote of 453 to 19 adopted the resolution repudiating Field.[23]

The Sharon case resumed about the middle of July as the superior court began its second term. Tyler and Barnes still dominated the proceedings, but when the case came to a close in September, Terry made the final argument for the plaintiff.[24] As far as can be determined he took no further part in the case until the decision was made, although he was undoubtedly conferring with other counsel on the case that was to start in the federal court.

It is to be assumed that Terry spent a good deal of time at home toward the end of the year, for it was at this period that his wife entered her last illness. While the Sharon case was in court the judge spent most of his days in San Francisco. According to J. Wharton Terry who was in Stockton during the summer of 1884, Terry customarily visited Clint and his wife in San Quentin one weekend and went home on the other.[25]

On the day before Christmas Judge Sullivan gave his decision in the Sharon case. Spectators crowded the courtroom, and all the attorneys but one, Terry, were present. It was Sarah Althea Hill's day in court, for Judge Sullivan held that the contract was valid and that the marriage was legal. Sarah was magnanimous in her victory. Clothed in a "shrimp wrapper of a very elegant pattern," she said to the press, "I am so happy, I feel just like a young kitten that has been brought into the house and set before the fire." Of the former senator who had implied that she was nothing more than a

[22]Ibid., pp. 305-306.

[23]*The Morning Call*, June 12. Terry was convinced that one of the reasons for Field's later animosity toward him was his refusal to support Field for the presidency.

[24]Ibid., Sept. 11, 16.

[25]Notes for Klette, pp. 18-19.

discarded mistress, and one of a number at that, she commented, "The poor, dear old 'Sen.' I'm sorry I beat the old man, for I love him still; he's a dear, sweet fellow." Sarah continued that she would have compromised long ago, but that it was the senator's name she wanted and not his money.[26]

If Sarah did not want Sharon's money there were those who did. Soon after the judge had made his decision it became known publicly that the plaintiff and her attorney had signed a written agreement a year earlier in which the lawyer was to advance certain funds and in return receive fifty per cent of anything secured from Sharon. It was his privilege to obtain additional counsel, and as we have seen he had secured the services of Terry and others.[27] The overhead expenses were heavy, and Tyler and his associates made their next move in January, 1885. According to Section 137 of the California civil code while a divorce case was pending the judge at his discretion could require the husband to pay alimony and provide funds for attorneys' fees for the wife to maintain her side of the court action. On January 8 Sarah's counsel recommended such a procedure to Judge Sullivan. Modesty did not characterize their suggestion; they asked for alimony and fees totaling half a million dollars. The judge gave his answer on February 16. He was not as generous as the lawyers had proposed, but the allowance was adequate. The plaintiff was to receive alimony of $2,500 monthly, and the sum of $60,000 was to go to the attorneys. Tyler and Tyler were to receive $25,000, and Terry and two other attorneys were to be paid $10,000 each.[28]

A few days later, on February 19, Judge Sullivan made his last contribution, the decree of divorce. So far the victory was complete for the plaintiff. Sharon, however, was by no means defeated. There remained the case in the federal court and

[26]*The Morning Call*, Dec. 25.
[27]Ibid.
[28]Gorham, *Story*, pp. 20-23.

of course the opportunity of appeal from the superior court. In fact two appeals were made, one from the grant of alimony and one from the divorce decree.

Meanwhile a new development was taking place. It is not known exactly when Sarah Althea began to view David S. Terry as other than a legal adviser. There is little doubt as to who was the hunter and who was the quarry, and it also seems clear that the chase was on by February, 1885. Terry's critics have made insinuations and charges that the relation had begun before his wife's death.[29] The only evidence found in the newspapers for 1884 was a comment made on May 1 that "Mr. Terry, as gallant as ever, was unceasing in his attentions to the plaintiff."[30] On the other side is the strongly phrased denial by John Wharton Terry that his uncle took any untoward action.[31] One is inclined to dismiss the charges for lack of evidence.

In February, 1885, Terry helped secrete his client as a maneuver to avoid summons to court. Not long after this Sarah began to make trips to Stockton and by May rumors were beginning to circulate about the couple. These rumors were few in number, and as the summer progressed it was the course of the trial in the federal court rather than any growing romance between Terry and Sarah Althea that occupied attention.

A new facet of Sarah Althea's character began to emerge as the case in the federal court progressed. In addition to her sparkling ways and quick tongue it became evident that at times she had a violent temper and a lack of balanced judgment. She made extreme accusations and at one time brandished a revolver in court. On the following day both judges, Field and Sawyer, lectured her on her conduct, and Field issued an order that she be kept disarmed while in court and that a deputy be detailed for this purpose.

[29]George H. Tinkham, *California Men and Events* (Stockton, 1915), p. 316n.
[30]*The Morning Call.*
[31]Notes for Klette, pp. 18-19.

The trial moved ahead slowly and Terry found himself confronted by an old adversary as William M. Stewart of Nevada days joined the battery of Sharon's attorneys. Once again Stewart was a difficult foe, and he drew heavily on a volume that was published attempting to show by handwriting analysis that the crucial documents were forgeries. He also endeavored to prove that Sarah Althea had not conducted herself like a married woman during the period in which she and Sharon were friendly and, according to her, married.[32]

The case closed August 12, 1885. William Sharon did not live to hear the verdict. If he had ever been fond of Sarah, not a vestige of that affection remained. On November 5, 1885, the former senator dictated a statement that read in part:

> I am exceedingly weak in body and suffer great physical pain, but my mind is perfectly clear. In this condition I declare that I never proposed or offered marriage to Sarah Althea Hill at any time or in any form. . . .

The document specifically stated that the marriage contract and letters were forgeries and as a parting shot declared that the representatives of the Sharon estate had been instructed to continue the legal battle. A little over a week later William Sharon died.[33]

In 1884 Sarah's Christmas gift from Judge Sullivan had arrived a day early and been gratefully received. The 1885 yuletide offering of Judges Deady and Sawyer of the circuit court was a day late and of a different sort. The circuit court, in direct contrast to the state superior court, declared the marriage contract and the "Dear Wife" letters to be forgeries.

Although Sarah had suffered this defeat in the federal court, shortly after the first of the year rumors spread that she was about to make another type of conquest. She had been

---

[32]R. U. Piper, *An Examination of the "Marriage Contract" and the "Dear Wife Letters" and other documents* (San Francisco, 188-?), passim; Wm. M. Stewart, *The Sharon Case. . . . Argument of Wm. M. Stewart* (San Francisco, [n.d.]), passim.

[33]Lewis and Hall, op. cit., p. 181.

enjoying herself in San Francisco shops but had parried most questions regarding a possible marriage. Later she was reported to have told one of her legal advisers, "Yes it is true. We are to be married in a few weeks. Judge Terry is now fitting up his house in Stockton as a home for me."[34] Sarah, who to this date had been anything but publicity shy, refused to allow reporters to witness the wedding.[35] Terry's law partner, P. W. Bennett, had already obtained the marriage license for the judge. The ceremony was performed by the Reverend Father O'Connor in the parish house of the Catholic church at Stockton. There were only two witnesses, State Treasurer Oullahan and Bennett. Terry had forgotten an important detail and as the ceremony got under way it was discovered that there was no ring. Oullahan rushed to the nearest jewelry store and soon returned with the needed article.

The marriage naturally created widespread interest. One uninhibited reporter wrote:

After many months of severe struggling, unaided and alone, with the numerous minions of Mammon, Sarah Althea at last decided to let her head rest upon the bosom of her stalwart legal friend and defender and to be henceforth protected by him. Judge Terry has stood by her nobly in all her troubles since he became acquainted with her and the lady should be well satisfied with the kind fate that has landed her in such a safe harbor.[36]

The reaction to the wedding was not altogether favorable. A Stockton editor, instead of wishing the couple happiness, headed his editorial "May He Be Happy." The writer commented that the "peculiar prominence of the bride" made her a subject of public interest and that the life of Terry was "really a part of the history of California. . . . He is a man universally liked and respected, and we hope that he will be happy in his choice of a matrimonial partner."[37]

[34]*The Daily Democrat* (Stockton), Jan. 7, 1886.
[35]*Daily Alta California* (San Francisco), Jan. 8.
[36]*The Daily Democrat*, Jan. 7.
[37]Ibid. (editorial), Jan. 7.

Clint and his family had been living in the judge's home and the son's disapproval of his father's second marriage soon became a matter of public knowledge. The Clint Terrys not only did not attend the wedding but left for Fresno the day before it took place. It was reported that Judge Terry bought a ranch in that area for $12,000 and gave it to his son to ease the shift. Clint did not attempt to hide his dislike of the marriage and reportedly said that his father should have had more respect for the memory of Cornelia Terry.[38]

It is quite likely that Clint's views were rather widely shared. Old friends of David and Cornelia Terry were shocked to see the judge succumb to the wiles of one who was in their eyes a notorious woman. Whether this disapproval went to the point of social ostracism is a debatable point, vigorously denied by J. Wharton Terry who visited the Terrys in 1888. It seems likely that some of the judge's former friends made him aware of the fact that they would have preferred to see him remain a widower, or at least unmarried to Sarah Althea.

Strange though the alliance was between the elderly Terry and the youthful Sarah, there is no evidence that for the first two years at least it was anything but a happy marriage. The judge apparently had no misgivings concerning his wife's background. Even one of his sharpest critics wrote of Terry, "He had decided that Sarah Althea had been the lawful wife of Sharon, and that therefore he had married a virtuous widow."[39] The new wife accompanied her husband on his business trips, and at first the couple managed to keep rather well out of the public eye.

In the summer of 1886 Terry took a step that in retrospect appears either quixotic or ill-advised. He made charges against two members of the supreme court and asked that they be removed from office. Terry alleged that Chief Justice R. F. Morrison, "since his election to the office of Justice of said Court . . . has by reason of disease, become, now is, and for all

[38]*Daily Alta California*, Jan. 8.
[39]Gorham, *Story*, p. 35.

205

time hereafter will be totally incompetent, by reason of physical and mental infirmity to discharge the duties of his said office."[40] Terry raised the same charge of incompetency as a result of disease against Judge John R. Sharpstein.

Judge Terry addressed his petitions to the senate and assembly on July 29, 1886.[41] Thomas C. Morris, assemblyman from Alameda, who introduced the petitions for Terry in the lower chamber, immediately moved that a committee of seven be appointed to investigate the charges and that a copy of them be furnished Morrison and Sharpstein. Delaying efforts failed and the assembly adopted the resolution. Terry had won his first move.

Next the special committee examined the charges. The justices under fire declined to appear before the committee. In their reply they recognized the power of the legislature to remove justices for cause, but alleged that this right rested with the houses as a whole and not with a special committee. Failing in its effort to question the justices directly, the committee examined other witnesses. Terry was not only present, but was given the right to examine the witnesses. By interrogating a deputy clerk of the supreme court, he attempted to show that neither Morrison nor Sharpstein had written any decisions since the preceding May. However, as the committee continued its work it became clear that Terry was losing his case. He could get men to agree that the court was weak and that the two men in question were in poor health, but he could not persuade any significant number of attorneys to admit that the mental powers of either judge had been impaired.

On August 9 the committee ended its examination of witnesses and on the following day submitted its report to the assembly, "That the said charges are groundless, the evidence taken and herewith submitted to the House showing neither

[40]California. *Legislature. Assembly. Journal* . . . 26th (Extra) Sess. . . . 1886 (Sacramento, 1887), p. 22.

[41]Ibid.; California. *Legislature. Senate. Journal* . . . 26th (Extra) Sess., p. 32.

mental nor physical incapacity on the part of either Justice to perform the duties of his office." The committee recommended, therefore, the adoption of a resolution that the charges be dismissed, "being wholly unsupported by evidence."[42] That afternoon over some opposition the assembly adopted the resolution of the special committee. The senate, which had been procrastinating to hear the assembly's decision, after some parliamentary skirmishing, moved to postpone the matter indefinitely.

The motives that prompted Terry to this attack are obscure. It seems to have been largely a one-man venture. Several interpretations of his actions are possible. Terry had a high regard for the law and did not like to see it in corrupt or incompetent hands. Earlier in his career he had attempted to remove lesser officials for corruption, and he may have had the same motive against Morrison and Sharpstein. The *Argonaut*, certainly no friend of Terry, on July 31, 1886, wrote:

This court must be reorganized in the interest of common justice and for the practical administration of the law. Morrison is mentally incompetent longer to perform the duties of Chief-Justice. Assistant-Justice Sharpstein is an invalid, and, as we are informed, has for two years been incapacitated for the performance of his judicial duties.

Yet after Terry's petitions had failed, the same editor wrote, "We are delighted to know that Chief-Justice Morrison and Mr. Justice Sharpstein have been fully vindicated from the attack made on them by Mr. ex-Justice Terry." Having issued these congratulations, the writer proceeded to repeat his assertion that the court was a weak one.[43]

[42]California. *Legislature. Assembly. Special Committee of Investigation.* . . . Appendix to Journals of Senate and Assembly. . . . 27th Sess. (1887), VIII, 66.

[43]Aug. 14. Stephen M. White wrote to Barclay Henley, ". . . a great many things concurred to create a sentiment antagonistic to the Supreme Court. In the first place there is no doubt that some of the members of the tribunal are pretty well 'played out.' In the next place, the decision in the Sharon case rendered the court obnoxious to those who were interested in the plaintiff's behalf." White also cited another court decision and did not mention Terry. Aug. 6, 1886, White MSS in the Stanford Library.

It is possible then that Terry was right in his assessment of the mental abilities of the two justices. The cure, however, was a drastic one on the body of the supreme court, and it appears that others shrank from performing the surgery. Another possible interpretation of Terry's action was that it was related to the Sharon matter. If he sought to remove two justices who might be hostile to Sarah Althea's interests, he was of course open to sharp criticism. No such charge was made at the time, and furthermore such a motive as this does not accord with Terry's customary concept of legal standards.

Meanwhile the suits connected with the Sharon affair were moving slowly through the courts. In one important instance Terry appears to have made a blunder. The United States Circuit Court, it will be remembered, had declared the marriage contract void. Terry thought that he had appealed the case and turned to the matters pending in the state courts. Actually he had failed to follow the proper procedure in the federal court. The case in the district court had been abated by the death of Sharon and an appeal had to be made within two years. The Sharon heirs remained quiet until this period had elapsed and then brought action of revivor so that the decree of the court which had now become final could be enforced.

The cases began to reappear in the press early in 1888. Frederick Sharon and Francis G. Newlands had replaced Senator Sharon in the controversy. The two appeals from Judge Sullivan's decisions finally reached the state supreme court, which on January 31, 1888, handed down its decision. The result was a modification of the original findings. If Sarah truly had wanted the "Sen's" name and not his money, she was still the victor, for the court reaffirmed the decision regarding the marriage and divorce. On the other hand it reversed the lower court's order granting legal fees and alimony, eliminated the fees, and cut the alimony from $2,500 to $500.[44] In March the Sharon heirs filed their bill of revivor.

[44]Sharon v. Sharon, 16 Pacific Reporter, 345.

The defendant countered with a demurrer to this action, and the battle was on again in the federal court. The case was also revived in the state supreme court by an appeal from Judge Sullivan's denial of a new trial.

One suspects that the judge's living expenses rose sharply after his second marriage. The couple apparently did not entertain frequently, but when they did the guests remembered the event. In June, 1888, Judge and Mrs. Terry entertained five newspapermen at dinner. One of the guests reported the evening in superlatives both as far as the food and the hosts were concerned. Entertaining was an art in which Mrs. Terry had "reached the pinnacle of perfection. Through her natural grace of manner she makes every person feel at home, and unconstrained by conventionality." The dinner was "enlivened by anecdotes, of which Judge Terry has a full share, and better still knows how to tell them, and the grace and wit of his charming wife." The food, "From the delicious soup to dessert," was "of the highest order of culinary art, and served in a manner that would put a Delmonico to envy."[45]

Late in July Judge Terry moved his law office in Fresno to a building in the Donahoo block. It was an unfortunate move, for in the following month the entire block was razed by fire. Terry lost his complete library, uninsured and valued at $8,000.[46] Destroyed also, it was later asserted, was the famous marriage contract.

Toward the end of the summer Sarah Althea gave minor evidence of the emotional storm that was to come in September. The Terrys had moved from Stockton to Fresno, either as a result of social ostracism in the former city or increased business in Fresno. On the fourteenth of August Judge and Mrs. Terry boarded the train for San Francisco. As it happened, another passenger on this train was Judge Sawyer, one of the members of the district court which had handed down the decision favorable to Sharon. The versions of the incident

[45]*Fresno Daily Evening Expositor*, June 28, 1888.
[46]Ibid., July 25, Aug. 13.

differ considerably, but all agree that Mrs. Terry made a fairly successful attempt to ruffle the judge's dignity by pulling or "wooling" his hair as she passed him.[47] Terry later told his nephew that she merely raked the back of the judge's head with a hairbrush.[48] Hostile authorities insist that she gave the judge an "ugly glare," "hissed out in a spiteful and contemptuous tone" at him, and later gave his hair a "spiteful twitch." One critical source claimed Terry made no effort to check his wife but instead commented of Sawyer that "The best thing to do with him would be to take him down to the bay and drown him."[49]

Far more serious were the events of early September. The rumor had spread that Justice Field was going to rule on the demurrer in the Sharon case, and a large crowd filled the courtroom as the circuit court began its proceedings on the third of the month. The court consisted of Stephen J. Field, Lorenzo Sawyer, and George M. Sabin. Both Terry and his wife were present to hear the ruling. With them was Porter Ashe, son of Terry's old companion, Dr. R. P. Ashe, who had become a close friend of the judge and his second wife.

As Justice Field read the unanimous report of the court, Mrs. Terry listened and became increasingly disturbed. By the time the judge was about a fourth of the way through the document it became clear that the decision would be adverse to the Terrys. Losing her meager amount of self-control, Sarah rose and interrupting Field asked, "Judge, are you going to take the responsibility of ordering me to deliver up that marriage contract?"

Field paused in his reading and said, "Take your seat, madam."

Others might have been intimidated by this order, but not

[47]Ibid., Sept. 7. This episode received little publicity at the time but was recalled after the Sept. court scene took place.

[48]J. W. Terry notes for Klette, p. 20.

[49]Gorham, *Story*, pp. 42-43.

Sarah Terry. "How much did you get for your decision?" she asked.

Justice Field was not one to converse in court with a disappointed litigant. Turning to Marshal J. C. Franks, he ordered, "Marshal, remove that woman from the courtroom, and the Court will deal with her hereafter."

"I won't go out and you can't put me out," declared Sarah.

Marshal Franks had to move past Terry to reach Mrs. Terry. The judge stood and said, "Don't touch my wife; get a written order." He then attempted to place himself between the officer and Sarah, and when Franks started to seize the woman's arm, Terry struck him a blow in the face.

From that point on matters quickly developed into a serious brawl. The judge put up a violent struggle to protect his wife but was pinned down in the courtroom. Sarah fought lustily in her own behalf and was unsparing in her vocal disapproval of Marshal Franks and those who came to his aid. Affidavits sprinkle the judge's remarks with epithets, and according to the contemporary press, Sarah "broke out with a horrible string of oaths" and "cursed" the opposition "in the vulgarest fashion." Her efforts were unavailing and she was hauled, screaming and struggling, to Marshal Franks's office.

The scene was not over. Released after his wife's removal, Terry went into the hall in which a crowd was milling. Then he heard his wife calling and made the worst blunder of the affair. Unfortunately after his second marriage Terry had forgotten his vow not to bear arms. On this day he had a knife, a sheath knife rather than a bowie knife. Hearing his wife, he pulled out the weapon and headed in her direction. Several deputies saw him and there was a second scuffle. Terry apparently made no effort to use his knife, but according to some accounts struggled vigorously before being forced to release his weapon. As he fought, he shouted such threats as "Let go . . . I will cut you to pieces, I will go to my wife."

There was one further act in the affair. Mrs. Terry had dropped her satchel and lost her bracelets, which had been broken in the struggle. Bitterly she accused Franks of stealing her jewels, and she demanded that her satchel be returned to her. Porter Ashe found the satchel and attempted to return it to her but it was appropriated by a deputy marshal who took the precaution of searching it before giving it to the owner. His discovery was damaging to Mrs. Terry, for the satchel contained a 41-caliber Colt pistol, with five of the six chambers loaded.

While they waited under arrest, both Terry and Sarah said things that would have been far better unspoken. Sworn affidavits asserted that the latter threatened on several occasions to kill both Field and Sawyer. Terry was not quite as definite in his statements but he was reported to have said, "Field thinks that when I get out, he will be away, but I will meet him when he comes back next year, and it will not be a very pleasant meeting for him."[50] The court wasted little time in disposing of the Terrys, and sentenced them to imprisonment in the Alameda County jail for contempt of court, David Terry for six months and Sarah for thirty days.

By their ill-considered actions the Terrys had laid themselves wide open to attack. The explanation of the reasons for these actions is not quite as simple as the enemies of Terry would have one believe. Their version was that Mrs. Terry was an uncontrollable and dangerous woman, and that the judge was a murderous, violent-tempered menace to society. On the surface the conduct of the two gave evidence that this interpretation was correct. There is, however, another side that in fairness must be mentioned. On January 4, 1889, Mrs. Terry brought suit against the marshal who had ejected her from the courtroom in September. In the papers that were filed, she stated that at the time of the episode she was

---

[50]The most detailed source is the Transcript of Record, *In Re* Neagle, 135 U. S., 1, in Law Division of the Library of Congress (Microfilm in possession of writer). Important extracts are in Swisher, *Field*, pp. 332-43. *The Terry Contempt* ([n.p., n.d.]) is a pamphlet containing most of the documents in the case, including affidavits. Terry charged that Field distributed this pamphlet in Washington. *The Daily Examiner*, Oct. 23, 1888.

"gravid," to use the wording of the charge. In this condition the excitement and somewhat rough handling she received could not fail to have serious results. She became dangerously ill after her removal to the jail and underwent a miscarriage. In the charge Mrs. Terry asserted that when Marshal Franks pushed her against the table she realized her danger and called for her husband. The judge knew her condition and that fact explained the use of the knife in the effort to reach her. For her own suffering and the loss of the child, Sarah had launched the suit to recover $50,000 damages against Marshal Franks.[51] There is no record that the Terrys pressed this suit, but the existence of the pregnancy might well cast a different light on the motives and actions of the couple. It is not for a layman to judge whether or not her condition had any bearing on Mrs. Terry's loss of self-control, but even a layman might be justified in making the conjecture that his wife's condition and call for aid might go far to explain Terry's violent action.

The stay in the Alameda County jail was an embittering experience for Terry. Physically the imprisonment was no hardship, and the couple received better than average attention, despite their later criticism of the sheriff and the jailer. They made copy for the press, which detailed their daily statements and actions. At first the two were in good spirits, but the mood was short-lived. Sarah became ill and apparently recovered toward the end of September, but early in October the newspapers reported again that she was ill. It is possible that at this time she had her miscarriage. The press spoke only of her illness, but that was probably a customary euphemism, for on one occasion a newspaper account referred to Mrs. Terry's "misadventure." She was too ill to leave when the end of her sentence was reached, and when she recovered she decided to remain with her husband until he was released.

Judge Terry spent much of the time reading, writing letters, and making legal efforts to secure his freedom. On Sep-

[51]*Oakland Daily Tribune*, Jan. 4, 1889.

tember 12 he addressed a petition to the circuit court asking for revocation of the six months' sentence. He based his case mainly on the assertion that he had not produced a weapon in the sight of the court and that he had attempted to quiet his wife. On September 17 Justice Field ruthlessly turned the petition down.[52] Terry then tried a legal maneuver to force Field to be a witness and swear that he had seen Terry with a weapon. This and another effort with the same aim in mind proved unsuccessful. Porter Ashe and the judge's nephew, J. Wharton Terry, went to Washington to try to obtain a presidential pardon. President Cleveland had little love for Justice Field, but since he was engaged in a presidential campaign a pardon could have been viewed only in a political light and was not given.[53]

Without any doubt the six months' jail sentence had a serious effect on Terry. His was a temperament that chafed under restraint, and the irritation was intensified by a belief that the lengthy sentence was unwarranted. The change in the judge was one of attitude rather than actions. Although he had always been quick to resent an insult, he had also prided himself on not speaking ill of other men. When he did criticize anyone he was willing to back up his statement with his life if necessary. As his jail sentence progressed, however, Terry exercised less restraint in his criticism of others. Two factors helped produce this change in Terry. One was his belief that he was receiving unfair treatment. Field's biographer stated, "A fair analysis of the situation can not but lead to the conclusion that the judges involved, in spite of their protestations that their sole desire was to enforce the law, were partisans in opposition to Terry."[54] It was the second factor that led Terry to act as he did. No longer was the

[52]For some of Terry's legal maneuvers, see ibid., Sept. 11, 12, 22, 1888; *In Re Terry*, 9 Supreme Court Reports, 77.

[53]*Oakland Daily Tribune*, Oct. 3, 11, 12, 23, 1888; J. W. Terry notes for Klette, p. 20.

[54]Swisher, *Field*, p. 340.

judge under the restraining influence of Cornelia Terry; beside him now was Sarah Althea, whose sharp tongue and unrestrained ways had become a byword among the people of her day. Thus Judge and Mrs. Terry who had begun their stay in the Alameda jail "as happy as a lark" became critical and querulous as the months passed. During Terry's life and while he was still in jail he was not reported to have threatened anyone's life, although after his death there were charges and denials on this point.[55] Undeniably while he was in jail and after his release he was highly critical of Field.

Terry's conviction that he was being mistreated increased when his efforts to secure thirty days off for good behavior failed. Instead he was obliged to serve his six months' term almost to the minute. By this time the press had become hostile and an Oakland paper headed its story with the line, "The Cantankerous Prisoner Will Be Released To-night."[56]

The jail sentence of the couple had not ended their punishment for the wild scene before the circuit court, and there remained indictments for such matters as obstructing the marshal in the performance of his duty and the use of dangerous weapons. The *Daily Alta California*, never friendly to Terry, helped to develop in the public mind a concept of the Terrys as a potential menace to society, in describing their appearance in court to receive warrants. Headed, "A Disappointed Crowd," the article reported that Marshal Franks "had made preparations for any emergency that might arise by distributing his full staff along the corridor" leading to the courtroom. In addition the marshal, after consultation with Judge Hoffman, "gave instructions to the United States Secret Service agent, who with several followers reinforced the Marshal's staff." To the disappointment of the crowd and, one suspects, of the reporter, the judge and his wife made no

[55]Gorham, *Story*, p. 53; statement of Mrs. E. O. Hill, *The Mail*, Aug. 22, 1889; *Stephen J. Field Arrested for Conspiracy and Murder of the Hon. David S. Terry* (Fresno, 1889), pp. 20-21. This pamphlet was "compiled and published by the friends of the late Judge David S. Terry" (p. 21).

[56]*Oakland Daily Tribune*, Mar. 2, 1889.

scene at all. They produced bondsmen for bail and received their warrants. Terry maintained a "composed demeanor" and accepted service with a comment that "it was all right."[57]

During the next months Terry and his wife shuttled back and forth between Fresno and San Francisco while the judge made several legal moves in relation to the indictments. Meanwhile the Sharon case had been appealed from Judge Sullivan's denial of a new trial; Terry gave the final argument, and the case went to the state supreme court on May 4, 1889.

Before this court acted the United States Supreme Court handed down its decision on the appeal taken by the Terrys on the adverse decision in the United States District Court. Terry had claimed that the federal court had no jurisdiction in the matter. On May 13 the supreme court crippled Sarah's cause by stating that the federal court did have jurisdiction and by affirming the decree of the lower court reviving the suit in the name of Frederick W. Sharon.[58]

A little over a month later the state supreme court issued its decision. William M. Stewart's argument in the lower court seems to have been the decisive factor in producing the opinion of the upper court, which reversed Judge Sullivan's decision. Instead of attempting to determine whether the alleged marriage contract was genuine or forged, the supreme court said that the question was beside the point. The deciding factor was that if there had been a marriage it had been kept secret, and, held the court, secret marriages were not recognized as valid under California law.[59] Disastrous as this decision was to Sarah's cause, it met with strong editorial support as a bulwark for the institution of marriage.

Terry was past the view that the opinion could be the result of honest belief. He charged prejudice and said that he had been expecting the decision since the election of the pre-

[57]*Daily Alta California*, Mar. 5.

[58]Terry *et ux v.* Sharon, 9 Supreme Court Reporter, 705.

[59]Stewart, *The Sharon Case*, passim; Sharon *v.* Sharon, 22 Pacific Reporter, 26.

216

ceding year. He asserted "Justice Beatty and Works were placed on the Supreme bench by the Sharon crowd," and he further claimed that Judge Niles Searls had been defeated for chief justice by "Newlands and the Sharon crowd." Sarah Terry was vocal but briefer than usual. "Ask these Judges," she suggested to a reporter, "what they would do if I were married by Father Burchard and the marriage was kept secret. My marriage with Mr. Sharon was just as binding as if I were married by a priest."[60]

Still the Terrys did not give up. Sarah asked for a delay in the appointment of a receiver for the Sharon estate and announced that she planned to ask the state supreme court for a rehearing. With victory in sight the Sharon attorneys made no objection, and Judge Sullivan agreed to postpone the appointment of a receiver for six weeks.

Early in August Judge and Mrs. Terry were again in a San Francisco court, this time before Judge Hoffman of the United States District Court in connection with the indictments against them. On August 7 the indictments charging the Terrys with obstructing Marshal Franks in the performance of his duty were sustained. The other indictments were taken under advisement.[61]

Judge and Mrs. Terry returned to Fresno. They were to reappear in court in San Francisco on the following Monday. Other factors intervened.

[60]*The Daily Examiner* (San Francisco), July 18, 1889. Shortly after the Nov., 1888, election, Stephen M. White, who had been campaigning in southern California wrote to Niles Searls, "I am in hopes from what I see tonight that you and Sullivan will pull through. The Sharon people certainly did what they could to knife you both. This, however, is private, as I would be unable to establish it as a judicial fact, though certain indications in this neighborhood satisfy me thoroughly regarding it." Nov. 9, White MSS in the Stanford Library. John D. Works, who defeated Sullivan, later wrote that the Sharon case was soon to be appealed to the supreme court. "This fact," he asserted, "arrayed all the influences of Sharon and his friends against Sullivan and for me in the campaign, not that they loved me more but that they loved him less." Works declared that he had "no part in the fight made" against Sullivan and that at the time he had no "convictions or predilection" regarding the Sharon case. "Some of My Experiences in Political and Official Life," MS in the Stanford Library.

[61]*Daily Alta California*, Aug. 6, 8.

Chapter XIII
The Victim

JUSTICE FIELD had returned to his circuit in California in June. Terry had not sought him out, nor had the two men met. After attending to official duties in Los Angeles, Field boarded the train for San Francisco at one-thirty in the afternoon of August 13. With him was a deputy marshal named David Neagle.

By coincidence the Terrys took the same train when it reached Fresno. There was nothing unusual about their act for they were to appear in court in San Francisco the following day. Train connections in Fresno were awkward, and the Terrys ordered a carriage for two o'clock in the morning. The hack driver, Frank Wilson, arrived promptly but had to wait until almost departure time before the couple emerged from the house with their bags. He drove them to the station, and they boarded the train at three o'clock.[1]

At Lathrop not far from Stockton the train as usual stopped long enough between seven and eight for passengers to eat breakfast. Justice Field and Neagle walked into the restaurant, which was furnished with long tables. They seated themselves at the first of these and ordered their food. Shortly thereafter Judge Terry and his wife entered. Apparently not seeing Field Terry walked past him and took a seat at the second table, facing Field. Mrs. Terry on the other hand saw Field and according to the justice's later testimony "wheeled around suddenly, and went out in great haste."[2]

[1]*The San Francisco Chronicle*, Aug. 15, 1889.

[2]*In re* Neagle, 39 Federal Reporter, 838. T. W. Stackpole stated, "Mrs. Terry passed and looked at Judge Field who partly rose from his chair. He looked disturbed." From testimony at inquest, *The Daily Examiner*, Aug. 15.

One of the Stackpole brothers, proprietors of the restaurant, learned that Mrs. Terry had left the room. Fearing difficulty, he reportedly approached Terry and said that he hoped Mrs. Terry would not be "so indiscreet as to get a pistol and create a disturbance." Terry is then said to have asked, "Why? Who is here?" When Stackpole informed the judge that Field was present, he "looked disturbed" and told the proprietor to keep Mrs. Terry from re-entering the room.[3]

The fullest accounts of the next minute or so unfortunately come from strongly biased witnesses, Justice Field and David Neagle. The others in the room probably were paying little attention and did not notice Terry get up. When he reached the table Terry suddenly struck Field two blows on the face and head. According to Field it was "a violent blow in the face, followed instantaneously by another blow."[4]

Neagle, a small man, jumped to his feet and shouted, "Stop, stop."[5] Field states that Terry then raised his hand for another blow; Neagle says he thought Terry was reaching for a knife. The deputy marshal wasted no time. Left-handed, he quickly drew his gun and fired twice. One bullet found a fatal mark paralyzing the spine; the other cut the lobe of an ear and resulted in a flow of blood that for a time caused people to think that there had been a direct shot in the head. It made little difference; by the time the body hit the floor, David S. Terry was at the point of death.[6]

[3]Ibid.

[4]*In re* Neagle, 39 Federal Reporter, 838. The courts apparently made no use of the testimony at the inquest.

[5]Field and Neagle agree on this point. Ibid., pp. 838, 840. On the other hand the hotel man, F. J. Lincoln, standing a few feet away from the scene, stated that no words were uttered at all, so rapidly did Neagle fire after Terry bent over Field. Interview with Lincoln, *The Mail*, Aug. 15.

[6]Autopsy report, *The Daily Examiner*, Aug. 15. Field stated that Terry had his hand raised for a blow; Neagle agreed but added that Terry started to reach as if for a knife. The autopsy showed that the bullet took a downward course. If Terry had his hand raised, one wonders how Neagle, who was short, fired a bullet at Terry, who was well over six feet in height, so that it went downward from Terry's heart. Years later Neagle told Harry M. Gorham, "As he [Terry] fell I fired again and under my breath as he sank slowly to the floor, I muttered to myself,

219

The shot created a commotion in the restaurant as people jumped up to see what had happened. Justice Field explained to one of the spectators, "I am a justice of the supreme court of the United States. My name is Judge Field." He continued, "Judge Terry threatened my life and attacked me, and the deputy marshal has shot him." Neagle, "perfectly cool and collected," according to Field, next said, "I am a deputy marshal, and I have shot him to protect the life of Judge Field." Shortly thereafter the two men left the scene of the killing and returned to the car.[7]

In the meantime Mrs. Terry had gone to the car, and when she heard the shot returned with the satchel in her possession. As she sought to enter the building, the satchel was taken from her, some say by force. Unquestionably the discovery of her husband's death was a terrific blow to her. All contemporary accounts agree that her actions were extreme, as the following news account indicates:

All, however, agree in stating that Mrs. Terry's grief was something pitiable to see. She called upon her husband, and caressed his inanimate form; then, receiving no response, she would rise in a terrific passion of rage and grief, and in a voice made hoarse by agony of soul, call down the judgments of heaven upon her husband's slayer. Then she would make a wild, despairing outcry for revenge, calling upon all bystanders to hang the man whom she accused of being responsible for her husband's blood. When the train moved off she remained keeping guard over her husband's stiffening corpse, and uttering threats and curses against those whom she called his murderer.[8]

Field and Neagle were on the train as it left Lathrop. The sheriff of Stanislaus County had boarded the train as well.

'That one is for Broderick.'" Harry M. Gorham, *My Memories of the Comstock* (Los Angeles, 1939), p. 171. Neagle's reminiscences are not too reliable. On another occasion he said that Terry knocked Field to the floor. *The San Francisco Chronicle*, Mar. 2, 1949.

[7]*In re* Neagle, 39 Federal Reporter, 838.

[8]*The Morning Call*, Aug. 15.

Neagle had shot a man, and the sheriff was determined to hold him until the matter was cleared. Over the protests of Justice Field, who insisted that the sheriff did not have a warrant and had not witnessed the killing, the officer removed Neagle from the train at Tracy and took him to the Stockton jail.[9] The sheriff of San Joaquin County took it upon himself to wire to San Francisco ordering a detective to cross the bay and arrest Field when he arrived in Oakland. Field's friends were already working for him; Marshal Franks also crossed the bay and told the detective that if he attempted to hold Field he would be arrested himself. The detective weakened, and Field proceeded without further interruption to San Francisco.

In the evening Sarah Terry swore out a complaint charging both Field and Neagle with the murder of her husband. Neagle was already in custody. Field made a great show of abiding by the laws and accepting the warrant, and then had little difficulty avoiding a return under arrest to Stockton. He was released on his own recognizance with a modest bond of $5,000.

Terry's funeral was unusually depressing. Clinton Terry won his point but aroused the ire of Sarah Terry by arranging for the judge's burial between Sam and Cornelia Terry in the family plot in the Rural Cemetery. The funeral services took place in the Episcopal church, but the judge went to his grave without the services of an ordained minister. The local clergyman was ill, no other was available, and a layman read the service. The ceremony was marred not only by the excessive heat and the crowd of morbid onlookers but by the extravagant behavior of the widow, who on several occasions gave way completely to her grief.

There are numerous theories concerning Terry's motives for striking Field, some more logical than others. On the one extreme is the charge that Terry planned to murder Field. The theory does not stand up under the evidence, although

[9]R. B. Purvis statement, *The Daily Examiner*, Aug. 15.

the courts accepted this view.[10] Terry was unarmed.[11] His enemies claim that Sarah secretly extracted the knife from Terry's clothing as she wept over his body. A knife is worn in a sheath, and if Mrs. Terry could have withdrawn a knife without being seen—and even this performance seems unlikely—she could not have unstrapped a sheath and secreted it unnoticed. It is worth noting further that Terry's threats to kill Field all appear in post-mortem statements.

Probably the most logical of the explanations of Terry's act is that he was attempting to humiliate Field. Terry felt that he had great cause for grievance at the hands of Justice Field. In support of this theory one finds the statement of W. T. Baggett, Judge Terry's attorney. Shortly after his client's death Baggett said:

I have had frequent conversations with Terry about Field, and he has often told me that Field used his court and his power as a Judge to humiliate him, and that he intended to humiliate Field in return to the extent of his power.

"I will slap his face," said Terry to me, "if I run across him, but I shall not put myself out to meet him. I do not intend to kill him, but I shall insult him by slapping his face, knowing that he will not resent it as he is a coward."[12]

In support of this thesis is the fact that although Field had been in California since June, Terry had made no move to run him down. It seems quite clear that the meeting at Lathrop was fortuitous.

Another theory, which has no documentary support, is that Terry's temper simply exploded when he saw Field in the restaurant, and that without pausing for reflection he made an assault on the justice. This interpretation fits in well with a public concept of Terry that had been created to a considerable degree by a hostile press. If Terry had a violent temper,

[10]Cunningham v. Neagle, 10 Supreme Court Reporter, 664.

[11]John Barrett, deputy coroner, testified that he examined Terry's body at Lathrop, and found "$190 in gold, $5.75 in silver, some papers and keys and a small pocket knife, but no weapon." *The Daily Examiner*, Aug. 15.

[12]Ibid., Aug. 16.

he kept fairly good control of it in later years.[13] Aside from the episode leading to the contempt sentence, which is susceptible of different interpretations, and of one minor courtroom scuffle with another attorney, Terry's record for keeping his temper is clear after the late 1850's.

There is another interpretation of Terry's actions, rather curiously overlooked or ignored by the supreme court justices who later passed on Neagle's zeal as a bodyguard. This is that Terry struck no heavy blows at all, but merely tapped Field lightly on the side of the face to attract his attention. There were three close witnesses to the affair who lived to testify. Of these, neither Field nor Neagle could be looked upon as a disinterested spectator. The third person was F. J. Lincoln, hotelkeeper at Lathrop. At the inquest, Lincoln gave testimony as follows:

I went for a cup of tea for Field, then showed two gentlemen to a table and as I turned around I saw Judge Terry bending over Judge Field. This was probably five or six minutes after Judge Terry sat down to the table. Mrs. Terry was not in the room then. As I turned about Judge Terry was bending over Judge Field and looked as if he was going to speak to him. Then he raised his hand as if to call his attention, not to hit him a blow, but just a sort of a tap (illustrating on the right side of the face). Terry apparently just brushed him with his open hand and did not strike him any place. I did not know whether he touched him or not.

When Terry did this he was right behind Field and a little to his right. He used his right hand in making this motion toward Field, but I could see where his left hand was. He was bending over him when he did this and just as he rose up Neagle shot him. I was about four feet from Terry at the time this occurred. I think Terry was standing about twelve or fourteen inches from the chair of Judge Field. He was facing Neagle. Immediately on the shot being fired he fell to the floor on his back with one foot under him. There was a second shot fired instantly after the other one. After the second shot Neagle said he was a United States officer. When the second shot was fired Terry was in the act of falling.

[13]J. W. Terry to Dumas Malone, Sept. 17, 1934, MS in the Bancroft Library. J. W. Terry admitted that on "very rare occasions" his uncle had failed to control his temper but that he personally had never seen the judge lose it.

I saw Terry give Field but one tap of that kind with his open hand, and I was looking at them all the time. His hand was not closed at all; he just brushed the face, if he touched Field at all.

It couldn't have been more than two seconds from the time Judge Terry raised his hand until the first shot was fired. I didn't have time to take a move or step forward. I don't think there was any perceptible lapse of time from when Judge Terry brushed his hand across Field's face to the time of the first shot. A man would have to have his hand on his pistol to draw it between the time I saw Judge Terry's hand brush Field's face and the shooting. . . .[14]

Coupled with this version of the shooting is the statement of R. B. Purvis, sheriff of Stanislaus County, who arrested Neagle. He did not witness the shooting but went to the railroad car to which Field and Neagle had retired. Purvis stated, "When I entered the car Field stated to me that Terry had come up and slapped his face and then struck him a fierce and heavy blow in the face." The sheriff continued, "This could not have been true, as I examined his face carefully, and there was not even a red mark on it."[15] If the statements of Lincoln and Purvis are true, it would appear that there is a black mark upon the cloak of justice.

Still another interpretation of Terry's act remains, one that must be classed as conjecture for lack of evidence. This is that Terry planned to create a scene to forestall more serious action by his wife. It must be remembered that he told Stackpole to prevent Mrs. Terry from returning to the dining room. His nephew, J. Wharton Terry, is convinced that Judge Terry knew that his wife was showing definite

[14]*The Daily Examiner*, Aug. 15. From the Transcript of Record, *In re* Neagle, it does not appear that the courts considered Lincoln's testimony.

[15]Ibid. The Terrys had been "shadowed" for a month by a detective, Henry Fenton of Finegass' Detective Service. It was reported that as early as June 17 this individual had told Marshal Barker of Fresno that he had been hired by Justice Field and Marshal Franks to watch Judge and Mrs. Terry. Other persons were also trailing the couple, and Fenton allegedly said, "All of us were fixed for him. And if he ever makes a break we will take no chances." Fenton had been drinking rather heavily the night of Aug. 13 and missed Terry's departure on the train although he was at the station. *Fresno Daily Evening Expositor*, Aug. 14, 16. See also Wagstaff, pp. 401-403.

signs of insanity.[16] He also knew that there was a pistol in her satchel. When the couple left Fresno, according to Wagstaff, Terry's partner, W. B. Grady, had forced the weapon on the judge against his wishes, and the latter had slipped it in Mrs. Terry's satchel after boarding the train.[17]

Life might no longer have held any particular attraction for Terry. All but one of the members of his first family were dead, Cornelia and five boys. The one remaining was virtually lost in spirit because of the father's second marriage. The marriage to Sarah Althea had brought the judge notoriety, heavy financial burdens, indignities, and loss of prestige in his profession. The worst was not over; there were still indictments to be faced, and Terry knew that Field was no man to stop hitting when his opponent was down. Then there was the final blow, the realization that his wife was going insane. Probably Judge Terry did not anticipate the result of his striking Field, but no doubt he did not care greatly what the result might be.

The story of David S. Terry was ended in the Lathrop restaurant, but two or three phases of the aftermath should be included in this account. One was the matter of public reaction. In general the first responses were to refrain from comment or to be sharply critical of Terry in both editorials and news accounts. The hastily compiled obituaries featured the sensational aspects of Terry's career. Some journals went quickly to Neagle's defense. The *Argonaut* charged that since Terry and his wife plotted to kill Field there was "in the action . . . nothing to criticize. . . ."[18] *Themis* diagnosed the affair as a tragedy resulting from the second marriage. Harshly the eastern *Nation* wrote, "Somebody ought to have killed Terry a quarter of a century ago," and denounced the judge as a "desperado of thirty years' standing, who during all that period carried his life in his hand, and lived among

16Notes for Klette, p. 26.
17P. 408.
18Aug. 19.

other desperadoes as bad as himself." The Sacramento *Daily Record-Union* not only censured Terry editorially but interjected such items as the following as news from New York:

In the clubs, on the elevated trains, in the downtown exchanges and business centers everybody is talking about the fate of fire-eating, blood-drinking Terry.[19]

There was a reaction as some journalists who probably had not been happy at Terry's actions became tired of the continual flogging of the dead judge. As an antidote the editor of *The Mail* (Stockton) introduced a satirical theory concerning the killing:

Terry had a bowie knife all the way from a foot to eighteen inches long, with the blood of his last victim still upon the blade. He stood picking his teeth with it when the Rev. Mr. Nagle, a distinguished prelate from Arizona entered the room upon the arm of Stephen J. Field, a sacred personage descended from Heaven to execute the will of God upon earth. (It is unusual for a person to pick his teeth before eating, but any person hesitating upon this point will be in contempt of the Federal Circuit Court and may be shot at any time convenient to the shooter. . . .[20]

The Mail also began to collect editorials and comments from other papers to show that public opinion was not unanimously behind Terry's killing, and announced that "Newspapers that Haven't Been 'Fixed' Invariably Condemn It as Cowardly and Brutal." The Mountain *Echo* went so far as to say, "A Judge who is under the necessity of hiring a bodyguard to protect him in his judicial rounds is a coward, and very likely to be corrupt."[21]

There never was much doubt but that Field would go free of the murder charge against him. Governor R. W. Waterman rushed to his aid with a letter to the attorney general stating that the arrest of Justice Field on the "unsupported oath of

[19]Aug. 17.
[20]Aug. 22.
[21]Quoted in ibid., Aug. 19, 20.

226

a woman who, on the very day the oath was taken, and often before, threatened his life," would be unless disavowed "a burning disgrace to the State." One suspects that the governor had been reading Justice Field's petition for a writ of habeas corpus presented at the time of his arrest, in which he denounced the "abandoned character of Sarah Althea Terry."[22] The attorney general responded quickly by bringing pressure on the young district attorney of San Joaquin. On August 20, 1889, the justice of the peace who had issued the warrant against Field dismissed it.[23] The reputation of California was saved.

The case against David Neagle was a little more difficult. In the district court, Judges Sabin and Sawyer apparently wanted to make certain that Easterners knew what a really bad man Terry was, for they wrote:

But it is not for scholarly gentlemen of humane and peaceful instincts—gentlemen, who, in all probability, never in their lives saw a desperate man of stalwart frame and great strength in murderous action—it is not for them, sitting securely in their libraries, 3,000 miles away, looking backward over the scene, to determine the exact point of time when a man in Neagle's situation should fire at his assailant in order to be justified by the law. It is not for them to say that the proper time had not yet come.

Neagle on the other hand did know, and the judges continued:

Neagle, on the scene of action, facing the party making a murderous assault, knowing, by personal experience, his physical powers and his desperate character, and, by general reputation, his lifelong habit of carrying arms, his readiness to use them, and his angry, murderous threats, and seeing his demoniac looks, his

[22]Gorham, *Story*, pp. 116-19.

[23]Years later District Attorney Avery C. White of San Joaquin County retold the story. Judge Field had charged White with conspiring against him with the justice of the peace and Mrs. Terry. White commented, "It was weirdly false, but we had no chance to reply. The writ was granted." In 1921 White bitterly remarked, "I learned within three days that laws are what men want them to be; that men are bought and sold; that judges are men. I should have known it in advance. But even today, as I look back, I cannot see that I acted wrongly—for a boy." *San Francisco Examiner*, May 12, 1921.

227

stealthy assault upon Justice Field from behind, and remembering the sacred trust committed to his charge, Neagle, in these trying circumstances was the party to determine when the supreme moment for action had come. . . .[24]

It soon became clear that Neagle had been especially commissioned as a deputy by Marshal Franks to protect Justice Field as he went from one court to another. The appointment had been prompted by a letter to the marshal from United States Attorney General W. H. H. Miller dated April 27, 1889. Because of the episode in the circuit court, Miller advised Franks to take steps to protect Field and wrote, "Of course I do not know what may be the feelings or purpose of Mr. and Mrs. Terry in the premises, but many things which have happened indicate that violence on their part is not impossible."[25] The United States District Attorney, John T. Carey, wrote to the attorney general commending the course of action that he had advised. He was highly critical of the Terrys and suggested "That publicity may not be given to the matter. It is important that the deputies whom he [Franks] may select be not known as such; and that efficient services may be assured for the purpose indicated, it seems to me that they should be strangers to the Terrys." Acting on the authorization of the attorney general and with the strong

[24]*In re* Neagle, 39 Federal Reporter, 864-65. Stephen M. White felt that the case against Field should have been dismissed, but of Neagle he wrote, "He certainly ought to be tried and fully prosecuted. He has committed a homicide & if he can show he acted in self defense, all right, but he should be made to show it. . . ." White to Attorney General G. A. Johnson, Aug. 26, 1889, White MSS in the Stanford Library. White still had no love for Field and wrote to George R. B. Hayes, Aug. 16, 1889, "To be candid, it makes me tired to listen to the flunkey talk that is going on at this time about a man, who, in my judgment, is one of the most dishonest characters that ever discharged the function of a judicial office. This is strictly personal." White was asked to act as counsel against Neagle, but declined because of the known ill feeling between him and Field. See W. D. Grady, J. C. Hays to S. M. White, Aug. 17, 1889. In his reply to Grady, Aug. 21, White stated that if he entered the case, "Field would use his very great influence on Sawyer whom he controls and upon Deady or Brewer or whoever might sit in the matter to prejudice them against me. . . ."

[25]Cunningham *v.* Neagle, 10 Supreme Court Reporter, 662-63.

228

support of the district attorney, Franks deputized Neagle on June 17.[26]

The courts showed little sympathy for Terry and ignored the argument that since Terry was unarmed the shooting was hardly justified. The only stumbling blocks were finding any legal authorization for Neagle's action and deciding whether the jurisdiction lay with the state or federal government. On the latter point Stephen M. White wrote:

That Terry-Field episode was a most unfortunate affair. I think it is a grave mistake to assert federal control of the case. The United States judges are *personally bitterly* hostile to the Terry side and I believe they will take jurisdiction and discharge Neagle without a trial. The case is practically being tried by Field, though he is behind the scenes. When Field "hates" he hates "for keeps" and will do anything to win.[27]

After the district court decided in Neagle's favor, he was released from custody. Judge Field presented his bodyguard with a watch and chain. On the watch was the inscription, "Stephen J. Field to David Neagle, as a token of appreciation of his courage and fidelity to duty under circumstances of great peril at Lathrop, Cal., on the fourteenth day of August, 1889."[28]

Sheriff Cunningham appealed the case to the supreme court. The attorney general, who had some interest in the matter, was among those who appeared for Neagle. The court, in an opinion written by Justice Miller, upheld the lower court. Two justices, Chief Justice Fuller and Associate Justice L. Q. C. Lamar, dissented. The latter wrote a vigorous dissent-

[26]Ibid., pp. 663-64.

[27]White to James McCreery, Sept. 11, 1889, White MSS in the Stanford Library, quoted in Swisher, *Field*, p. 356. John D. Works wrote of the shooting of Terry, "There has [sic] always been grave doubts whether this homicide was justified or not, but the perpetrator of it was acquitted of the charge of murder made against him . . . ," "Some of My Experiences . . . ," p. 13.

[28]Wagstaff, pp. 525-26. For a bitter attack on Field, see *Character and Career of Stephen J. Field, As It Is Known in California* ([n.p., n.d.]), passim.

ing opinion, in which his main concern was the authorization for Neagle's action. Lamar held that Neagle should not have been taken from the jurisdiction of the state court and discharged on habeas corpus by a court of the United States. The justification for granting the writ of habeas corpus had been the assertion that Neagle had killed Terry in accordance with a law of the United States. No such law was produced, wrote Lamar, hence Neagle should have been left in the jurisdiction of the state court.[29] Lamar's opinion was in the minority, but it is of some significance to note that Charles Warren in his *The Supreme Court in United States History* asserts that the sanction given to Neagle's act "was the broadest interpretation yet given to implied powers of the National Government under the Constitution."[30] Terry had lost his last battle for states' rights. Even in his death he had contributed to the growing power of the federal government.

The tragic end of David S. Terry was sudden; that of Sarah Althea Terry was protracted. Engaged in legal controversy with Clinton Terry over the estate, she spent her time in Fresno, Stockton, or San Francisco.[31] Improvident as ever, she exhausted her own funds and existed at times on the generosity of her friends. Early in 1892 while living in San Francisco she began to show more definite signs of mental instability. After harboring her for some time, her old acquaintance, Mammy Pleasant, swore to the complaint to the insanity commissioners. As she appeared in court on March 9, 1892, Sarah was a marked contrast to the striking figure that had impressed courtroom audiences in the early days of the Sharon case. One reporter wrote:

[29]Cunningham *v*. Neagle, 10 Supreme Court Reporter, 672. See also Willie D. Halsell, "L. Q. C. Lamar, Associate Justice of the Supreme Court," *The Journal of Mississippi History*, V (1943), 71-73. The fullest account of course is in Transcript of Record, *In re* Neagle, 135, U. S. 1.

[30](Boston, 1922), III, 419.

[31]Local and San Francisco newspapers followed the struggle over the estate. Mrs. Terry was listed in the Fresno directory for 1891. *Slater's Directory of Fresno County* (Fresno, 1891).

As she appeared in the courtroom she was a picture of woe. Her raiment was in a wretchedly dilapidated condition, her hair unkempt and her eyes glassy and staring. Even the curious spectators, hardened to such scenes, were touched with the sadness of this one.[32]

Found insane, Sarah Althea Terry was sent to the state hospital for the insane in Stockton, of which in the early fifties Terry had been a director. Except for an occasional writer who wanted a feature story, she was forgotten. Finally on February 15, 1937, some forty-five years after her arrival at the hospital, she died.

One person took note. Cornelia Terry McClure, Clint's daughter, decided that there was space in the Terry family plot in the Rural Cemetery, not far from the hospital. It seems obvious that the granddaughter performed the act out of respect for David S. Terry more than for any other motive, as did the local attorneys who provided for the burial services.[33] Terry's coffin was already flanked by those of Cornelia and Sam. On the other side of Sam, cramped against the Creanor plot, the second Mrs. Terry was laid to rest.

[32]For details of Mrs. Terry's commitment, see *The Morning Call*, Feb. 15-17, Mar. 9-12. Her case was first diagnosed as acute mania and later changed to dementia praecox. Copy of order of commitment furnished by California State Hospital, Stockton, California.

[33]*Stockton Daily Evening Record*, Feb. 15-20, 1937.

Index

233